Cracking the SAT II:
HISTORY
Subject Tests

THE PRINCETON REVIEW

Cracking the SAT II: HISTORY Subject Tests

GRACE ROEGNER FREEDMAN

1999–2000 EDITION

RANDOM HOUSE, INC.
NEW YORK

Princeton Review Publishing
2315 Broadway
New York, NY 10024
e-mail: comments@review.com

ISBN 0-375-75300-1
ISSN 1076-528X

SAT II is a registered trademark of the College Board.

Editor: Gretchen Feder
Production Editor: Kristen Azzara
Production Coordinators: Iam Williams and Scott Harris

Manufactured in the United States of America on partially recycled paper.

9 8 7 6 5 4 3 2

ACKNOWLEDGMENTS

This book would not have been possible without the help, advisement, proofreading, editing, creating, care, love, and support of Michael Freedman.

Additionally, I would like to thank my family, especially my mother, Judith Ruland and my grandmother-in-law, Florence Freedman. I would particularly like to thank my original inspiration in the field of history, my high school history teacher, Ms. Desta Horner.

For the folks at The Princeton Review, my thanks looms large. Shout out to Julian Ham, Cynthia Brantley, Leland Elliott, Chris Kensler, John Bergdahl, Adam Hurwitz, Sung (Peter) Jung, Sara Kane, Meher Khambata, Illeny Maaza, John Pak, Dinica Quesada, Christopher (Short-hair) Scott, Christopher (Long-hair) Thomas, Joe Cavallaro, Andrew Dunn, Scott Karp, Kris Berger, Ian VanTuyl, Julian Fleischer, Kamala Karmen, Marcia Lerner, Ann Moses, Amy Bryant, Bruno Blumenfeld, Maria Russo, James Petrozzello, and, of course, Alicia Ernst.

Thanks also to Nathan Weber, Andy Dunn, and Scott Karp for their expert reviews.

CONTENTS

PART I

Test Taking

1

Orientation

HEY THERE!

In case you haven't heard, the College Board is running a three-for-one special, the best bargain in the pre-college, test-taking racket. Word has it that you get three fabulous, eye-straining, brain-draining, 60-minute, 95-question test-taking experiences for one low price! You're probably asking, "Where do I sign up?!"

How Ready Are You?

Maybe you already knew about the three-for-one deal, and now you're checking this book out to find out even more. You're prepped, you're psyched, and you're ready to take an SAT II (this stands for Scholastic Assessment Test, formerly known as the College Board Achievement Test (CBAT)). Maybe you're ready for the Math IC or IIC, or the Writing, or the Biology, or perhaps the foreign language you've chosen to fulfill your course requirements. But you might not be ready to take a test on American History and Social Studies or the World History and World Cultures SAT II (we will refer to these as the American History SAT II and World History SAT II, respectively). Odds are that neither one of these history tests is your first choice in your upcoming, triple-play SAT II experience. No, you're probably gunning for Math or Writing, or maybe you want to show your language or science prowess. A History SAT II might be your second choice, maybe even your third. And you figure, "No sweat, I've taken the course. All I need to do is to brush up a little."

It's Not What You Know, It's How You Know

Well, maybe you're right. And then again, maybe you're wrong. Today you could certainly take either of the two SAT II History tests and get some of the questions right. But you'd probably miss a good portion of the questions you *could have gotten right* if you understood *test taking* a little better.

Or you could study all your old history assignments, hoping they'd be less boring this time around. You could even try one of those gargantuan study guides crammed with tons of useless information. But you'd *still* miss a good portion of the questions you could have gotten right if you just understood how to take the test.

Face it: The only way to beat a standardized test is to develop a system or a strategy that allows you to answer the questions correctly and to get a higher score. Don't be haphazard in your approach to the test. Knowledge of history will, of course, help you out. But to answer the questions, it isn't so much *what* you know as *how you apply* your knowledge.

That's because the SAT II History Subject Tests are not just about knowing history. Nor are they just about testing you to find your "scholastic assessment," whatever that means. In other words, getting a good score on this test depends on more than just the depth of your history knowledge or your scholastic abilities. Scoring high on this test, and frankly any other standardized test, comes right down to the sharpness of your test-taking abilities. But don't be intimidated—this is actually a cause to rejoice. Why? Because the simple skills of test taking, which you can master quickly, will put you—not the College Board—in the driver's seat!

> The best way to improve your score is to learn HOW to take the SAT II History tests.

This is where The Princeton Review comes in. Our mission is to understand, analyze, and simulate standardized tests so we can help students beat these tests and make their scores soar. For over a decade we have been breathing down the necks of the College Board, studying their every move, and watching every alteration they make to their tests. Then we devise and deliver test-beating techniques to our students. Our easy style has proven effective in helping students raise their scores. Our proven techniques here at The Princeton Review have taken us far from our base in New York City to locations across the country and around the world.

A Word About Titles: SAT II Versus CBAT

Don't let the mere name SAT II make you nervous. If those letters cause your palms to sweat and your heart to miss a beat, you are playing right into the College Board's hands. By naming it the SAT II the College Board can associate the tests with the regular SAT; it's just a marketing ploy to make the tests seem harder, scarier, and more important than they sounded with the old name. "Scholastic Assessment" might sound meaner than "Achievement," but don't buy it. The new SAT II tests, especially the history tests, are not substantially different from what were formerly called the Achievement Tests; the biggest change is the name printed on the test booklet: SAT II. But if the tests ever do change, we'll be there. The Princeton Review revises and updates its books and manuals every year, responding to every change that the College Board makes. So don't worry; we're on your side.

Predictable—Just the Way We Like It

Furthermore, the history tests are very predictable, whether they're called achievements or the SAT II. Unlike history itself, these tests don't change very much from year to year. That's because the writers of these tests, unlike the writers of history, do not change, probably because they are not asked to change. The people at the College Board do not regularly release previously administered tests; that is, they don't make too many of their tests publicly available. Consequently, it is very easy for them to write the same test, with the same types of questions, every year. And this makes it easy for us to know and understand the test and to find ways to beat it. This book is the result of serious research specifically on the most recent American History and World History Achievement Tests and the new SAT II History tests. We've mastered all the changes that occurred in the tests when they switched from the achievements to the SAT II in 1994.

Stop Wasting Time Memorizing Factoids

To be sure, history, like all other subjects, consists of facts. But we at The Princeton Review will show you a new way of looking at history. Rather than wasting your precious time learning or memorizing a jumble of names and dates, we want you to think about history *as a long stretch of time*, punctuated by certain important markers. Each marker will signify an historical era that will be important for you to know on either the American History SAT II or the World

If you memorized all the facts in the average history review book, your head might explode. We have a better (and safer) way to prepare for the SAT II History tests.

History SAT II. Within each era, or time period, there might be events or important people that you'll need to know and remember. But this information won't stand alone, like disconnected facts, names, or dates. Rather, it will be connected to the era (the marker) along the long road of history.

BUT WHAT IF I AM A LITTLE SHAKY ON THE HISTORY STUFF?

No problem. You just have to approach your review the right way. There's more than one way to study, review, or learn history. Unfortunately, most test-taking study guides give you the *wrong* way. At this point, you don't need to cram tons of little factoids into your brain: "What was the Albany Congress of 1754?" "Who was Millard Fillmore's Secretary of State?" "Who was Millard Fillmore??" Even if this focus on minutiae is appropriate at times, it is certainly not appropriate for you now as you prepare for either the American History SAT II or World History SAT II.

Remember, no one is born a good test taker or a bad test taker. A good test taker realizes the importance of knowing both what to expect from a test and how to deal with the information. The fact is, the better you know and understand the SAT II History tests, not just history, the better you will score on these tests. We will show you the ins and outs of both SAT II History tests, so that when you take your exam, you'll know your "enemy" (the College Board) and know how to attack their tests.

TAKE A HIKE

Here's an analogy to explain The Princeton Review strategy. Suppose you and a friend are hiking in the woods. You want to take it easy for a while, but your friend wants to keep hiking. So he says he will leave you a trail, and you can follow him and catch up whenever you are ready. Sounds good to you, so he leaves and you take a nap. Now suppose, after you wake up, you go looking for his trail. Several things could happen at this point . . .

Imagine that your friend left a marker every few inches, dropping small and insignificant items to mark the trail: first, a penny, then a few inches later, a button, then a toothpick, later a small piece of string. It's as if he were just cleaning out his pockets, not really paying any attention to what he was doing. You'd probably get very frustrated trying to find your friend. Following this trail would be painstakingly slow and difficult; every few seconds you'd have to stop, pick up the tiny little something, and hope that you're still moving in the right direction. Meanwhile, your friend would be at the campsite having dinner.

Now imagine that your friend is a very organized and very together person. He knew that you'd wipe out after the first mile and be begging for some rest, so he came prepared. He brought along signs marked with large fluorescent arrows (made on 100% biodegradable paper, of course) and pinned them on trees, spacing them about twenty yards apart. So when you wake up, you hit the trail running. It's easy to see the signs, and you can move quickly through the forest guided by them. With the arrows, you always know you're going in the right direction. At this pace, you meet up with your friend in no time, and you crack open some franks and beans together.

This book is like your organized friend, whereas some other history review books are like the disorganized friend. The disorganized friend either doesn't know or doesn't care how to be a good guide. In studying for either of the SAT II History tests, it will not help you to learn every small and insignificant fact concerning the last 300 (American History) or 3,000 (World History) years. Just as in the first hiking scenario, learning all that would take a long time and you wouldn't get very far. Instead, you want to approach your history review like a well-marked trail. In the following chapters, we will present this history trail to you—the story of the last 300 (or 3,000) years clearly divided into its important time periods. If it's not marked, it won't be important.

You see, if this book were to present to you an unorganized and detail-laden series of facts, as many other guides do, you would have a slim chance of remembering any of the information, important or insignificant, on the day of the test. So you would have a slim chance of scoring high on your History SAT II. The history reviews (chapters 4 and 7) will describe the most important eras according to the test writers for each history test, what you need to know about each era and how you'll apply this knowledge with other test-taking techniques. Do not fear, we'll show you how to get right answers.

We hope you find The Princeton Review approach to be an easy and fun way to think about history. It is most definitely the way to "score more" on the SAT II History Subject Tests.

2

Test Techniques

HOW TO APPROACH THE SAT II HISTORY TESTS

To beat either of the SAT II History Subject Tests, it's important to understand the basics of taking them, and to understand era-based thinking, pacing, and guessing.

THINK "ERA" FOR ERROR-FREE THINKING

History is a long continuum of time that consists of many overlapping events and people, some of which are more important than others. And, as if all these names and dates were not confusing enough, history books often try to relay this information in a helter-skelter format. Books like that are useless; we might learn something about a president here or a war there. It is easy to be intimidated by all the stuff you have to know, or think you have to know, for the SAT II History tests. But you don't have to remember all this information as one historically jumbled mass.

The easiest way to think about the hundreds and thousands of years of history is to break the continuum into bite-sized chunks. This book will refer to each time period, each chunk of history, as an **era**. You can organize all the history facts you know into eras, or historical time slots. Just keep all the tidbits of important information in a particular time period under one heading in your mind. The heading should be some name—a person, an event, a war—that reminds you of the era. When you have the vast and varied amount of information organized into only a few important eras, you will find it easier to recall the material on the test.

The History Review chapters in this book are organized into eras and are designed to give you the information you need to know about each time period. From now on, whenever you learn anything about a certain time period, file it away in your brain under the title of its era. In fact, you probably do this already for some time periods.

THINK ABOUT THE 1960s

What comes to mind? Maybe it's the Beatles, dancing hippies, or Vietnam. Or perhaps civil rights demonstrations, the Space Race, the Cold War, Dr. Martin Luther King, Jr., or John F. Kennedy. Whatever you remember is helpful; the specifics don't really matter. The point is that when you think about the era of the 1960s, you should automatically recall some key events and people connected to that time.

True or False?

Q: During the Colonial Period, everyone believed in religious freedom.

Now answer this question:

1. The civil rights legislation signed by President Lyndon B. Johnson in 1965 mandated

   (A) a Constitutional amendment guaranteeing equal rights for women

   (B) that Latinos and Asians have the same employment rights as blacks

   (C) protection of the voting rights of southern blacks

   (D) that affirmative action programs be established in all state universities

   (E) that in light of national security, Vietnam War protesters be denied the right to demonstrate publicly

The era in this question is the 1960s and it concerns civil rights. You should immediately think that the answer must say something about the civil rights of blacks and racial discrimination. Answer choice (A) should be eliminated because the issue of women's rights reflects the feminist movement of the 1970s, not the civil rights movement of the 1960s. (Also, the Equal Rights Amendment has never been added to the Constitution.) Choice (E) should be eliminated because, although many people protested the Vietnam War and the police and the government didn't much like it, the protesters were not legally denied their freedom of speech.

So, of the remaining choices (B), (C), and (D), which one of these is *most closely* identified with the era of 1965? To some extent, all three choices reflect that era's concerns, but if you think about it, choice (B) is off the mark because the civil rights movement was largely about guaranteeing the rights of *black* people in the face of white injustice, even though there were other ethnic minority groups also protesting injustices that they experienced. Choice (D) misses, because affirmative action represents *moving beyond* basic rights to compensate for past injustices, but the civil rights era was more about *protecting* basic rights. Therefore, answer choice **(C)** is the best choice, because the movement's major aim—after desegregating public accommodations—was defending the basic right of Southern blacks to vote. The movement hoped that once Southern blacks were protected when they sought to vote—from police dogs, hoses, lynch mobs and poll taxes—they would gain the political power necessary to secure the respect and resources that had been previously denied them.

This example sounds like a specific question, but you really didn't have to know a great many details about civil rights legislation in order to answer it. You only had to think about the era of the 1960s, remember generally what was happening at that time, and then choose the *best* answer to fit the era.

True or False?

A: False! The Puritans came to America to seek religious freedom, but once they arrived, they didn't exactly welcome other religions with open arms.

PACING YOURSELF

Any SAT II is an endurance test, the academic equivalent of running a two-kilometer race over hurdles. Each SAT II History Subject Test consists of ninety-five multiple-choice questions to be completed in sixty minutes. That leaves you with only thirty-eight seconds per question. This means that you must be test-savvy in order to get your best possible score. The fact is, you may run out of time and you may not be able to finish all of the questions.

Don't worry. It's okay to run out of time, but you must pace yourself. Pacing means that you choose which questions to answer and which questions to skip for the time being—for example, skipping questions here and there throughout the test, answering only the very easy ones, and then returning later to those you missed. Or it may mean that you spend a few extra seconds on a question you think you can get right. Basically, it means choosing questions to answer according to your own strengths and weaknesses, not according to how the SAT II test writers happen to lay them out on your particular test.

ETS wants you to do 90–95 questions in an hour. (Aren't they cruel?) Give yourself a break—skip some questions along the way and answer the questions that you know first.

You certainly want to finish the test, but you want to do so on your own terms. To get you started, we've provided you with two Pacing Charts, one for American History, the other for World History. But be careful: when the Pacing Chart suggests you can leave up to ten blank, those ten should not be questions 86–95. That would mean that you ran out of time on the SAT II's terms, not your own. Of those hypothetical ten, you want to leave blank only those questions that have you completely stumped. For each of the other questions, if you can safely eliminate even one answer choice, you should guess; we'll explain why in the section on scoring below. Maybe you'll skip five questions in the first eighty-five, and then quickly decide which of the five or so out of the last ten questions to come back to if there is some time left. It is in your interest to at least "eyeball" every question in the test.

The Pacing Charts that follow can show you how many questions you need to get right and how many you can afford to miss in order to achieve your target score. Tailor these charts to your own test-taking style as much as possible. When you take the practice SAT IIs in this book and when you take the practice test released by the College Board, pay attention to your strengths and weaknesses. Do you start out great and then lag in the middle of the test? Do you rush through the beginning of the test and then make stupid mistakes? There will always be questions that you are going to miss, so don't worry about these. Concentrate on the ones you could have or should have gotten right. Did you get it down to two? Did you misread the question? Did you pick a choice that didn't make sense within the era of the question? After you take any practice test, be sure to spend some time analyzing what questions you missed and ask yourself, "Why?" This way you can concentrate on not making the same mistakes on the real SAT IIs.

The charts will help you target the score you want on the test you are taking. But remember that they are only guides. Even if they tell you that you can safely skip ten questions, it is to your advantage to guess smartly on as many questions as possible for the answers you do not really know.

Pacing Chart for the American History Subject Test										
		Questions 1–35			Questions 36–70			Questions 71–95		
Score on Practice Test	Shooting for	Time spent	Must answer	Guess or leave out	Time spent	Must answer	Guess or leave out	Time spent	Must answer	Guess or leave out
200–390	450	35 min	25	10	25 min	20	15	0 min	0	0
400–460	520	30 min	30	5	20 min	25	10	10 min	10	15
470–540	600	25 min	30	5	20 min	30	5	15 min	15	10
550–600	660	25 min	32	3	20 min	32	4	20 min	20	7
610–660	700	20 min	34	20	20 min	33	3	20 min	22	5
670 or above	740 or above	20 min	35	0–1	20 min	35	0–2	20 min	25	0–3

Pacing Chart for the World History Subject Test										
		Questions 1–35			Questions 36–70			Questions 71–95		
Score on Practice Test	Shooting for	Time spent	Must answer	Guess or leave out	Time spent	Must answer	Guess or leave out	Time spent	Must answer	Guess or leave out
200–340	450	35 min	25	10	25 min	20	15	0 min	0	0
350–440	520	30 min	25	10	20 min	20	15	10 min	10	20
450–540	600	25 min	30	5	20 min	28	7	15 min	15	15
550–600	660	25 min	32	3	20 min	30	5	15 min	18	7
610–700	750	20 min	34	1	20 min	33	2	20 min	22	5
710–800		20 min	35	0	20 min	35	0	20 min	25	0

TIME IS OF THE ESSENCE

In order to pace yourself correctly, you must be aware of the time and where you are in the test at any given point. It's easy to do. In your mind, separate the ninety-five questions of the test roughly into thirds. For the first third—questions 1–35—give yourself twenty to twenty-five minutes. The middle third, consisting of questions 36–70, should take you about twenty to twenty-five minutes. Finally, for questions 71–95, or the last third, target about fifteen minutes. A little more time per question is allowed in the first and second thirds of the test. This is because you are likely to be more alert at the start of the exam, so it pays to spend time on these questions. In the last third, you may be a little more tired, stressed, perhaps a tad panicky. So this third only gets twenty-five questions and fifteen minutes. Your goal in the last third is to "eyeball" the questions so that you can make a quick educated guess on them, even if you only have ten minutes left. If you have been pacing yourself well, and happen to have fifteen to twenty minutes left for the last third, you will be able to maintain your pace and answer the questions with the same relative speed you used in the previous sections.

To accurately keep track of the time, you may want to jot a time frame down at the top of your Scantron sheet near your name. For example, if the test starts at 11:20 A.M., jot down 11:40, 12:05, and 12:20. Then you can refer to these to quickly see that you must complete the first third by approximately 11:40, the middle third by 12:05, and that the exam will end at 12:20. (Be sure to either erase

If you don't know the answer to a question, don't get stuck. If you can eliminate any anti-era choices, GUESS and then move on! Time wasted = lost points.

your jots or write only in a designated area, like where you put your name. Stray marks elsewhere make the College Board computers crazy.)

Questions	Time per Section	Total time into Test	Time Frame
1–35	20–25	20–25 minutes	11:40
36–70	20–25	40–50 minutes	12:05
71–95	10–20	60 minutes (exam ends)	12:20

Use these time guidelines in conjunction with the Pacing Chart for your specific subject test.

You Win A Dollar!

Would you play this game? First, guess a number between 1 and 3. If you guess right, you win $1. If you guess wrong, you lose a quarter. Hmmmmm....

SCORING: WILD GUESSES VERSUS SMART GUESSES

The SAT IIs are scored on a scale of 200 to 800. This score, the one that is reported to you and to colleges, represents a translation of the raw score you actually acquire in taking the test. The raw score is tabulated by counting one point for each question you answer correctly and subtracting a quarter of a point for each question you answer incorrectly. Each blank gives you zero, no points either way. Think about this mathematically: one correct guess balances four incorrect guesses.

Now that you know about the guessing penalty, you can safely ignore it. Why? Using era-based thinking, you will always be able to make *educated* guesses, and every educated guess wipes out the negative effect of the penalty. In other words, by guessing smartly rather than wildly, you place the guessing odds in your favor. If you can safely eliminate 1 answer choice out of 5, and then guess on the remaining 4, you have a 1 in 4 chance of getting it right. At first sight, 1 in 4 odds may not sound so great, but over the whole test, these numbers are significant. If you pace yourself and follow the Era technique carefully and thoughtfully, you are likely to make many more "correct" guesses than "incorrect" guesses.

A TALE OF THREE STUDENTS

Let's look at how three hypothetical students approached their History SAT II. Scaredy Sam is a good history student, but a bad test taker; he took the test slowly and carefully, correctly answering most of the questions that he tried, but he ran out of time around question 80. Guessing Geena is an okay student, a great tester and an aggressive guesser; she finished the test by working carefully on the ones she knew and quickly guessing on the harder questions. And finally, Average Joe is an average student and an average test taker; he took the test as he would any other, without any real concern about pacing; he guessed on a handful, and he ran out of time at the end.

In looking at the following chart, remember that correct answers receive 1 raw score point and incorrect answers result in a loss of 1/4 raw score point. Blanks result in 0.

	Scaredy Sam		Guessing Geena		Average Joe	
Answered Correctly	60	(+60)	50	(+50)	50	(+50)
Answered Incorrectly	20	(-5)	15	(-3.75)	30	(-7.5)
Guessed Right	0	(0)	15	(+15)	1	(+1)
Guessed Wrong	0	(0)	15	(-3.75)	4	(-1)
Left Blank	15	(0)	0	(0)	10	(0)
Total Raw Score	55		57.5 = 58		42.5 = 43	
Final Score*	**590**		**600**		**520**	

On this chart, "Answered Correctly" means that they knew the answer with their own history knowledge and got the question right. "Answered Incorrectly" means that they thought they knew the answer but got the question wrong. "Guesses" mean that they didn't know the answer and they knew they were guessing. Scores are calculated for the American History SAT II; World History SAT II scores would be slightly higher but in the same proportion.

These scores are calculated from the genuine SAT II scoring system. Yet it doesn't seem quite fair that Geena got a better score than Sam even though he knew more. Too bad he didn't get to finish the test. And compare Geena to Joe; they both "knew" the right answer to fifty questions, and they both answered wrong on thirty questions—yet their scores differ by eighty points! Why? Because Geena was a better guesser—she guessed right fifteen times, while Joe guessed right only once.

The key, therefore, is in the guessing. Geena was simply a better guesser—more aggressive and better able to narrow down the choices when guessing.

TENTATIVE GUESSERS! LISTEN UP!

If all this talk about guessing makes you think about how you hate to guess, think about this. You've probably heard that boys tend to score higher than girls on these standardized tests. A lot of this score discrepancy can be accounted for by studying the difference between how boys and girls guess. Boys, as a general group, are more aggressive test takers. They guess when they haven't even read the question. They guess when they have no idea what the question is about. They guess, they guess, and they guess again. And they score more. So, girls, and any not-so-guess-oriented boys, account for this unfair discrepancy. Guess more—do it smartly—and score more.

You Win A Dollar!

If someone had a million dollars, would you keep playing this game? Of course you would! Odds are you'd end up rich. Guessing on the SAT II is the same thing, only you win a point. Guess and your score will go up!

REVIEW: ERA-BASED THINKING AND GUESSING

1. Think of history not as a collection of a billion tiny facts (or "factoids") like exact dates and names, but as a series of eras, like the Colonial Era, the Reconstruction Era, the Post-World War II Era, and so on, all of which are in a continuum.

2. For any question you do not absolutely know the correct answer to, define in your own mind what era that question refers to. Sometimes the wording of the question will actually state the era, although often it will not.

3. Read all of the answer choices and see which of them clearly, definitely do *not* relate to the era. Eliminate those choices.

4. Of the remaining choices, try to decide which one *most closely* relates to the Era. That is the right choice.

5. But if you cannot figure out the right choice, guess anyway. In the long run, you'll win.

PART **II**

The American History
Subject Test

3

Cracking the American History Subject Test

THE TEST

The American History SAT II focuses primarily on the history of America from just after the American Revolution to the present day (eighty percent of the test). Within this broad period, about half the questions refer to the pre-Civil War period (late eighteenth century and the nineteenth century) and the other half refer to the period after the Civil War and through the twentieth century. The remaining twenty percent of the questions are based on pre-Revolution colonization, with a smattering of questions regarding indigenous Native American peoples and pre-colonial history.

True or false?

Q: Before the Revolutionary War, American colonists were allowed to trade freely with all European nations.

90–95 Questions	
1 hour	
200 to 800 scoring scale, with guessing penalty	
The Post-Civil War to present (1865–present)	40%
American Revolution to the Civil War (1776–1865)	40%
American colonization and earlier	20%

THE SYSTEM

HISTORY AS ERAS, NOT ISOLATED FACTS

The American History SAT II, at first glance, seems like a test of facts. After all, there are 95 specific questions which cover all the important people and events of all of American History. In fact, however, it is a test of major historical trends or eras. The Princeton Review system of Era-based thinking described in chapter 2 will help you effortlessly to turn these fact-like questions into general questions that you can answer with your basic knowledge of American History.

Look at the big picture. The questions on the American History SAT II usually require that you know about some major topic or event in American History. But these questions are often written in a way that make them seem harder than they really are. To avoid being confused by any of these questions, we suggest Era-based thinking as a foolproof way to wade though the SAT II questions.

PACING

Pacing is the most important aspect of taking the American History SAT II, since it is a long test and you are under strict time pressure to finish it. As we noted in chapter 2, pacing simply means spending your limited time where it is best used. This may entail skipping questions throughout the test so that you can reach the questions near the end. You may pace yourself by spending a few extra seconds on a question that you feel you can get right, or by bailing out and guessing on a question that has you boggled. Overall, pacing yourself means taking control of the testing experience so that you can get your best score possible.

AMERICAN HISTORY SAT II QUESTION ARRANGEMENT

Unlike some other standardized tests, the American History SAT II is not really arranged in order of difficulty or chronologically. Questions on the American History SAT II are arranged in sets according to a particular time period. Within these sets of questions, which vary in number, there is a rough order of difficulty, with the last question in a set being the hardest. For instance, questions 1–5 might concern the 1930s, with question 5 being the hardest in the set. Then questions 6–9 might deal with the American Revolution, with question 9 being the hardest in *this* set and question 6 being the easiest. On questions 10–14, the focus may become the 1880s, and so on. Time periods will appear again throughout the test. For instance, questions 50–53 might also be about the American Revolution.

This format actually works perfectly with the Era-based approach. If one question gets you thinking about the Civil War, it's likely that you will get to answer a few questions about this same Era. Just be sure to switch out of that thinking as soon as you are presented with a new Era. This could also help you with Factoid questions, since these would probably be the hardest, or the last, in a question set. If a question gives you no clue about the Era in which it is set, quickly look to the Era of the questions you just answered, the ones just preceding this question. It may help to place the Era of the Factoid and help you eliminate Anti-Era choices.

Your best tactic when dealing with this strange question set-up is to have no tactic at all. Because this format is not standard (sometimes there are two questions per set, sometimes five, sometimes one), it will cost you more effort to worry about it than to just go with the flow. Bear in mind that the Eras will keep flip-flopping and use their pattern to help you if you can. Otherwise, don't sweat it.

A question

Let's take a close look at a question.

> Many Americans viewed the War of 1812 as a "second war of independence." Which of the following best explains this sentiment?

This question seems pretty specific when you look at it standing alone, but the trick to answering it is to figure out what you are really being asked. You are not being asked anything specific about the War of 1812. You are being asked something very sweeping about it: "Why would people compare this war to the War of Independence, that is, the American Revolution?" Now, the question seems pretty general. You want to find the answer choice that has something to do with the American Revolution.

True or False?

A: False! During the Colonial Era, England wanted exclusive rights to all the goods and services produced by the American colonies. To this end, they placed heavy taxes, called duties, on just about everything, which made it very expensive for the colonists to trade with any country other than England.

So let's look at the question with its answer choices.

Many Americans viewed the War of 1812 as a "second war of independence." Which of the following best explains this sentiment?

(A) The war forced Europe to accept the Monroe Doctrine.
(B) The national anthem, "The Star-Spangled Banner," was written during this war.
(C) The independence of Latin American republics from the colonial powers of Europe was established.
(D) Despite some military successes by the British forces, the United States showed itself willing and able to protect itself against a dominant power.
(E) The war was a contributing factor in the defeat of Napoleon at Waterloo.

Common Sense POE

Q: Which group of voters were a deciding factor in the 1860 Presidential election? What do you think of this answer choice? (C) Women who held abolitionist views

Answer choices (A), (C), and (E) might seem logical if you weren't thinking about the question, or if you were thinking about other American wars. But these answer choices have nothing in common with the American Revolution and so they can't be the link between it and the War of 1812. Choice (B) may seem like the answer as well, because an anthem reflects and glorifies a nation as an independent entity. Still, an anthem is merely symbolic; it is not a major issue or development of war. Therefore the only correct answer is **(D)** and the only thing you had to know to get this question right was that America fought Great Britain in both the American Revolution and the War of 1812.

Era-based thinking will help you on most of the American History SAT II questions. Your primary strategy of attack is to:

1. READ THE QUESTION—CONNECT THE ERA

Once you read the question and connect it to a particular Era, you can:

2. ELIMINATE ANTI-ERA OR NON-ERA ANSWER CHOICES

Even if the correct answer doesn't immediately jump out at you, you will be able to eliminate two or three answer choices that are "Non-Era" or "Anti-Era."

Use era-based common sense

Common sense is a powerful tool on the SAT IIs, but you must always be thinking about the Era of the question. Would it make sense for Andrew Jackson to support the Indians? Would it make sense for Lyndon B. Johnson to support Native American groups? Did Thomas Jefferson own slaves? Did Abraham Lincoln own slaves? [The corresponding answers would be No, Yes, Yes, and, No.]

The SAT II writers commonly use wrong answer choices that make sense within current thinking, but are ludicrous statements if you are thinking within the Era of the question. For example, if someone said,

"Person X believes that women should have the right to vote,"

you'd say, "Sounds reasonable." But if a SAT II answer choice read,

"George Washington was an advocate of women's rights..."

you would want to say, "No way." George was probably a great guy in many respects, but always think about the Era (not the E.R.A. in this case). Women's rights were not in vogue back then. What might be reasonable today could be ridiculous when placed in a different historical Era.

The "politically correct" answer will only be applicable to questions concerning the last twenty years. The political response to the "Indian problem" in Andrew Jackson's days was a federally legislated policy supporting the decimation of Native American tribes. But Lyndon B. Johnson favored improvements in the education of Native American youth and increased tribal self-reliance through the reservation system. Though some bits of history may not jibe with our modern sense of morality, always consider the Era when answering these test questions. Your own contemporary perspective can lead you to incorrect answer choices.

The SAT II never criticizes our forebears
Using Era-based common sense, you can eliminate unlikely answer choices, but you will almost never find questions that put our country's past leaders in a wholly negative light. You will not find the following question:

> Which of the following U.S. Presidents was responsible for the Indian Termination Policy of 1830?

It will never happen. But you may find a question like this:

> Andrew Jackson's presidential administrations were known for all of the following EXCEPT
>
> (A) its rejection of the institution of the Second Bank of the United States
> (B) the humanitarian aid given to the Cherokee Indians following the tribe's dispute with the state of Georgia
> (C) a veto of legislation from Congress which proposed the building of roads and other infrastructure in the western states
> (D) the maintenance of the spoils system which allocated federal jobs on the basis of personal and political loyalties
> (E) the willingness to use federal troops to defend federal laws and their precedence over states' laws

The trick to answering this type of question is not knowing whether each of the five answer choices is or isn't true. It's knowing which one is definitely,

Common Sense POE

A: No way! Get rid of (C)! Women couldn't vote in the nineteenth century. They didn't win the right to vote until 1920.

positively, WRONG. Maybe you are saying, "I dunno" to answer choices (A), (C), (D), and (E), but you should be saying "Not at all!" to answer choice (B). Back in the time that the "West was being won," you wouldn't find too many presidents in support of the rights of Native Americans whose lands were being taken. Answer choices (D) and (E) surely don't make Mr. Jackson seem like a great guy, but they are far more likely, given the historical Era, than answer choice (B). So, **(B)** is the correct answer.

Notice how the question is phrased. It is not stating anything blatantly negative about Andrew Jackson, and the SAT II never would. It is your job to decipher what cannot be true about a person (i.e., that Andrew Jackson liked Native Americans). If you're thinking about the Era of a question and using Era-based common sense, this isn't too difficult. You must be on your toes in order to translate the knowledge you have into the power to eliminate wrong answer choices.

Translate The Answer Choice

(D) conflicts between labor and management resulted in strikes and boycotts. Translation: workers got angry with their bosses and walked out.

3. ASSESS THE REMAINING ANSWER CHOICES

The answer choices themselves are usually long, complicated sentences. In order to understand them, you have to pare them down. Translate the *test* language into *your own* language. Often when you try to swallow the whole answer choice, they all end up sounding the same. By reading the remaining choices slowly and then translating them into your own words, you get a better idea about what is going on. This may sound time-consuming or complex, but it really isn't.

Here's why: First, you will only be using this process with the two or three choices you have remaining; second, you do all the translating in your head. And finally, with practice, this type of thinking will become quicker and more natural to you. Let's look at an example.

Which of the following statements best describes the opinion of the majority of Americans regarding the onset of World War II in Europe?

Answer Choices:
(A) They were not concerned with international politics and they were indifferent to who would be the victor.
(B) They did not agree with the use of U.S. military force or intervention at the time.
(C) They were enraged by the policies of Hitler and were anxious to declare war on the Nazi forces.
(D) In order to end the economic strife of the Great Depression, they hoped the U.S. could sell supplies and equipment to both sides of the conflict.
(E) They wanted to remain out of the war so that the participants in the war would each be weakened and the U.S. could rise as a world power.

Translations:

     (A) Didn't care at all!?
     (B) Wanted to stay out.
     (C) Raring to go!
     (D) Sounds pretty slimy!
     (E) Sounds way slimy!

Quick translations should get (A), (D), and (E) out of there. Then you have to decide between (B) and (C). But before you do that...

4. STOP, REREAD THE QUESTION

Once you have eliminated the anti-Era answer choices and assessed the remaining choices, you may have two or three choices remaining. This is the crucial moment because, most likely, one of these answer choices is right. A common mistake is to be very careful up to this point and then carelessly choose the wrong answer. You've spent some time on this question and it's foolish to let the right answer elude you when you are so close to it. Rereading the question should take a few seconds, at most.

Back to our example question.

> Which of the following statements best describes the opinion of the majority of Americans regarding the **ONSET** of World War II in Europe?

Ah, now you see the word in bold, capital letters. Sure, you know that the U.S. was in World War II, but this question asks us about the *beginning* of war. And you should know that the U.S. didn't enter the war right away. Remember the Pearl Harbor bombing? That's what dragged us into the fray. If you were lazy and tried to answer this question quickly, you might have gone for (C), since you know that eventually the U.S. went over to Europe belatedly to fight Hitler's forces. But the U.S. did *not* enter at the onset of the war and that's what this question is all about. So, the correct answer must be **(B)**.

Maybe this last example was easy for you and you're complaining about this last step, saying, *"But I already read the question. Won't it be a waste of time?"* No; rereading the question will get you the right answer, especially when you can't decide between two or three choices.

You see, by the time you get to choosing between the right answer and a couple of straggling wrong answers, you've probably forgotten about the question entirely. You're thinking about that crazy answer choice (D) (*"Should I have gotten rid of it?"*) and about the next question (*"How much time do I have left?"*). You're not thinking about the question, and that, of course, is the whole point. Usually, after rereading the question, it's easy to choose between the two or three "translated" answer choices you have left. Reminding yourself of the question makes the answer much more clear. Don't short-change yourself at this critical moment.

5. LAST RESORT: GUESS AND MOVE ON!

"What if I still don't get it?" Going through the above process makes it highly unlikely that this will happen very often, but on a handful of questions you may not be able to pin down the correct answer. Don't worry, just guess and move on. Reread pages 13–14 if you are not convinced of the joy of guessing.

Pop Quiz

Q: If you don't know the answer to a question, and you can eliminate at least one answer choice, you should:

    (A) Look for the answer on the ceiling
    (B) Look under your desk
    (C) Stare at the question for ten more minutes
    (D) Guess and move on!

REVIEW: THE SYSTEM

1. Read the Questions—Connect the Era

2. Eliminate Anti-Era or Non-Era Choices

3. Assess the Remaining Choices: Translate

4. Stop, Reread the Question

5. Last Resort: Guess and Move On!

SPECIAL TYPES OF QUESTIONS

Pop Quiz

A: Choices (A), (B), and (C) might be tempting, but if you can eliminate at least one answer choice, always guess.

For almost all of the questions on the American History SAT II, you can use the Era-based approach. But watch out for the following special types of questions on this test.

EXCEPT QUESTIONS

EXCEPT Questions strike fear in the hearts of most students. Now is the time to overcome this fear! There may be up to twenty-five questions in this format on the American History Test. Variations include questions that use NOT and LEAST in the wording of the question. For example:

All of the following are true EXCEPT:

Which of the following is LEAST likely to be the cause?

Which of the following was NOT a ratified amendment?

When you approach these questions in the right way, they can be easy. (If you've dealt with SAT *Verbal* EXCEPT Questions, forget about them for now. Because of the subject matter, SAT II EXCEPT Questions are not as hard.)

These questions are highly susceptible to the technique of elimination, but you have to remember to eliminate the right ones! It's usually the word EXCEPT that's confusing, not the question itself. So, eliminate the cause of your troubles. To answer EXCEPT Questions, get rid of the EXCEPT, LEAST, or NOT word in the question and look at each answer choice as if it were a true or false question.

Except questions are true or false questions in disguise

Literally cross out the word EXCEPT, LEAST, or NOT and answer "Yes" or "No" to each answer choice. The "Yes" answers should be eliminated; true answer choices would not be the exceptions. And the "No" answer is the correct answer; the false answer is the exception. Let's look at an example.

All of the following were presidents of the United States EXCEPT

(A) George Washington   YES! Eliminate.
(B) Thomas Jefferson   YES! Eliminate.
(C) Fred Smith   Who? NO! (C's the answer.)
(D) Ronald Reagan   YES! Eliminate.
(E) Abraham Lincoln   YES! Eliminate.

Answer choice **(C)** "Fred Smith" is a resounding NO! It's the exception and the right answer.

These questions are not tricky if you just look at the subject matter. Usually students get confused by the "Looking for the Opposite" aspect of answering this type of question. You can avoid this entirely by forgetting about the words EXCEPT, LEAST, NOT, and just thinking Yes or No.

There's another trick to answering EXCEPT Questions on the American History SAT II. A trick that stems from way back in your own history—back to kindergarten.

"One of These Things is Not Like the Others"

Pop Quiz
Q: Which one of these is not like
   the others?
   (A) judicial review
   (B) presidential veto
   (C) preferential choice
   (D) congressional override

Just like the game from your youth, many of the EXCEPT Questions have one answer choice that really sticks out from the others. On these questions, you want to find the triangle among the squares. Since you're looking for the exception, the one that's different from the others is the right answer. Let's look at these answer choices.

Blahblahblahbblahblahblahblah EXCEPT

(A) **adventurers** blah blah blah
(B) blah blah **explorers** blah blah
(C) **frontiersmen** blah blah
(D) **advance scouts** blah blah
(E) **investors of capital** blah blah

Now which one of these types is not like the others? If you had been able to read the real SAT II question, which mentioned American fur traders and the

West, getting the answer would have been like taking candy from a baby. "Investors of capital" have nothing to do with "adventurers," "explorers," and "frontiersmen" or "advance scouts." So the exception, and the right answer, is **(E)**.

The differences in the answer choices of EXCEPT Questions are not always as stark as the ones in this example (especially since you didn't have to decipher the answer choices). Usually, the choice that sticks out does so because it is not in the same Era as the rest of the choices. Always connect to the Era first—the answer to the EXCEPT Question may be the anti-Era choice.

Let's look at another example.

All of the following were immediate social or economic consequences of the American Revolution EXCEPT

(A) increased opportunities for land settlement in the West
(B) reform of primogeniture inheritance laws
(C) expanded rights for women to hold property
(D) the opening of many areas of trade and manufacture
(E) the seizing of the Loyalist holdings

First, read the question and connect the Era. American Revolution: late 1700s, America breaks from Great Britain, main disputes are taxing and trading laws, most people live on the Atlantic coast. Answer choices (A), (D), and (E) are firmly within the Era, and a "Yes" means to eliminate it. Maybe (B) leaves you a little clueless, but if you had to choose between (B) and (C), which one of these things is least like the others? Which answer choice stretches the Era-boundaries? Obviously, choice **(C)** is the "No," the anti-Era exception, and the right answer. The first women's movement and women's rights did not become an issue until over a century later, in the late 1800s. Remember: On EXCEPT Questions, the anti-Era choice is right.

CHARTS, MAPS, AND CARTOONS

Scattered through the American History SAT II are charts, maps, and cartoons and questions about them which help to break up the monotony of the 95-question test. These questions are usually fun to answer, perhaps because they're a little distracting. Too bad there are only about five on the test. The chart questions tend to be very easy, while the maps tend to be harder. The difficulty of the cartoon questions depends on how well you can connect the cartoon to an Era. If you can, it's a piece of cake. If not, well . . . use common sense and guess. Often you are given two questions along with a graph or map. This is helpful, since if you have to spend some time deciphering the darned thing, you might as well get two questions-worth of points for it.

CHART-BASED QUESTIONS

Charts, tables, and graphs are really beautiful things, because they are almost always self-explanatory. They usually (not always) contain everything you need to know to answer the questions based on them. In that respect, they are giveaway points, unlike those on the rest of the test. To answer the question correctly, you merely have to pull the needed information from the illustration. If you are chart- or table-phobic, the best medicine is practice, practice, practice.

When you first approach a question with a chart or table, **don't look at the chart!** It's a waste of time to try to figure out the graph before you even know what you're looking for.

Read the question first. Sure, it's common sense, but since you usually hit the graph before the question, it's important to keep this in mind. When you do go to the graph, read its title next; it will quickly tell you what all those numbers and symbols are about. Here are some examples.

UNITED STATES INCOME TAX 1930–50 ($ millions)

	Individuals	Corporations
1930	$ 1,147	$ 1,263
1940	$ 982	$ 1,148
1950	$ 17,153	$ 10,854

ETS shows you the charts first, but skip over them! Read the question first. Then go back to the chart when you know what to look for.

The chart above gives the gross revenue from income taxes collected by the United States government in the years 1930–1950. The chart contains enough information to determine which of the following?

(A) In 1940, corporations paid a smaller percentage of their income to the government than did individuals.
(B) In 1950, the government received a higher proportion of its income from individuals than from corporations.
(C) The reduced rate of income tax indicated in 1940 was caused by the end of attempts to cure the Great Depression.
(D) Corporations did not pay a fair share of taxes in 1950.
(E) The increase in the income tax collected in 1950 was due to programs instituted by Dwight D. Eisenhower.

First read the question. The question asks you what can be determined from the chart. Then look at the chart. Only choice **(B)** can be determined from the numbers given in the chart. Choice (A) is tricky, but we do not know what percentage of each group's income went to taxes; we only know the totals. Choice (C) is incorrect because it is impossible to determine from the chart if the Great Depression caused the reduced rate of income tax. We don't know whether the rate of taxation changed (people could have been earning less money). Likewise, choice (E) is incorrect because nothing in the chart indicates the cause of the increase. Choice (D) is a judgment call, and that's never appropriate on chart questions.

Some chart-based questions do require knowledge of information not included in the charts themselves. Here's an example:

PERCENTAGE OF BLACKS IN
INTEGRATED SCHOOLS
IN 1964

Missouri	42.00%
Tennessee	2.72%
Alabama	0.007%
West Virginia	58.20%
Texas	5.50%

The figures above indicate that the states of
Tennessee, Alabama, and Texas will most likely be
in violation of which of the following Supreme
Court decisions?

(A) *Brown v. Board of Education*
(B) *Roe v. Wade*
(C) *Plessy v. Ferguson*
(D) *Marbury v. Madison*
(E) *Griswold v. Connecticut*

In this question you have to use both chart and Era techniques. Although none of the states listed has completely integrated schools, Tennessee, Alabama, and Texas have almost none of their black students attending "white" schools. These states would be in violation of the court decision that outlawed segregation, or answer choice **(A)** *Brown v. Board of Education*. The rest of the cases are from different Eras.

MAP-BASED QUESTIONS

Call it talent or call it cruelty, but Map Questions on the American History Test are confusing. Unlike questions referring to most graphs or charts, map queries may require you to know something history-based. Again, read the question first, then read the title of the map. If the question and map are self-explanatory, great—go for it. But you may find that the question is Era-based and then you would just follow the "Connect-to-the-Era" steps as usual. The map may also involve geography. Unfortunately, geography is not usually stressed in most high school history courses. Just do your best to eliminate wrong answers and guess.

Most important, don't get trapped into spending too much time on these questions. They can be confusing, and if you don't get the answer right away or if you have no clue what the map is supposed to mean, there is no use spending a lot of time on them. This time is stolen from other, easier questions that you could do better on. Remember, you have a lot of ground to cover in your one-hour time limit, so keep moving.

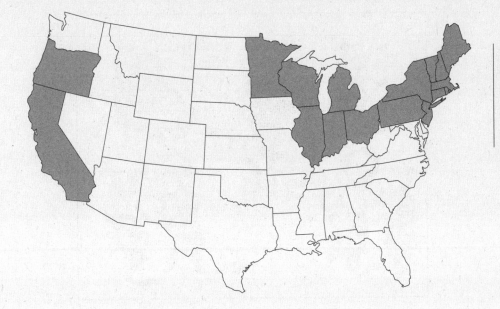

Don't get caught wasting time on maps. There are lots of points out there just waiting for you to grab them. If the map is tricky, guess and keep moving.

The map above shows the state-by-state results of the presidential election of 1860. Which of the following candidates won the majority of the votes in the states that are shaded here?

(A) Andrew Jackson
(B) James Monroe
(C) Abraham Lincoln
(D) Stephen Douglas
(E) Ulysses S. Grant

To answer this question correctly, it helps to know that the Civil War happened in the mid-1800s. This allows us to eliminate answer choices (A) and (B) immediately. Both Andrew Jackson and James Monroe were presidents in earlier Eras. Abraham Lincoln, answer choice (C), was president during the Civil War and the North (the anti-slavery states) supported him in his election. Looks like we have a winner here: the correct answer is **(C)**. Stephen Douglas lost to Lincoln in the election of 1860, and Ulysses S. Grant, though he became President later, was one of Lincoln's generals during the Civil War.

POLITICAL CARTOONS

The type of cartoons you will encounter on the American History SAT II are political cartoons, something like you might find on the editorial page of your newspaper. These are *always* Era-based and they will often give you the date that the particular cartoon appeared. More modern cartoons, say one from 1972, will probably be easier to recognize and to figure out than older ones, such as those from 1820, mainly because you are more familiar with the humor and the format. Approach cartoon questions just as you would any regular Era-based question and let common sense be your guide. Let's look at some examples.

Look for the visual clues in the cartoon to help you connect it to a particular Era.

The idea expressed in this nineteenth-century cartoon is that

(A) the *Dred Scott* decision led to some unusual political alliances in the election of 1860.
(B) Dred Scott was an influential statesman who orchestrated peaceful agreements among political rivals.
(C) music of the day had become too political to be enjoyed by most people.
(D) politicians should heed Dred Scott's example and should be willing to cater to special interest groups.
(E) the *Dred Scott* decision promised a renewed "Era of Good Feeling."

To answer this question, it is essential to connect to the Era of the cartoon. Maybe you recall that the *Dred Scott* decision was a controversy right before the election of 1860. Or maybe you recognize the character of Abraham Lincoln in the upper right hand corner. If you can connect this cartoon to the pre-Civil War era, you should be able to eliminate choices (B) and (C), since neither of these choices says anything about that Era (or any other Era). In choice (D), "special interest groups" refers to more contemporary issues, and in choice (E), the "Era of Good Feeling" refers to the period right after the War of 1812; there certainly weren't any good feelings during the Era right before the Civil War. Answer choice **(A)**, the right answer, is most firmly in the pre-Civil War era. To refresh your memory, the *Dred Scott* decision held that a black man could not be granted freedom even though he had been taken by his own "master" into a free part of the country. This astounding decision fueled tensions between the North and South, and motivated candidates from very divergent political groups to form alliances in the election of 1860.

Which of the following is the closest to the idea expressed in the cartoon above?

(A) The U.S. should intervene in the conflict between the working man and business interests.

(B) President Theodore Roosevelt's imperialistic foreign policy caused tension between him and American business interests.

(C) Uncle Sam, representing the American people, looks on disapprovingly as the president attacks a popular form of transportation.

(D) President Theodore Roosevelt is nobly trying to restrain the powerful railroad trusts.

(E) President Franklin D. Roosevelt extended the power of the government so that it could compete with commercial interests.

Take a Guess:

Q: Who was Joseph Smith?

(A) The fourteenth President of the United States.

(B) A Republican Senator from South Carolina who supported the abolitionist movement.

(C) Founder of the Mormons, publishing *The Book of Mormon* in 1830.

(D) A novelist whose works were widely read in the Take a guess:nineteenth century.

Again, connect to the Era and you will easily solve this question. The man wrestling with the railroad is Theodore Roosevelt. Remember, he was a president in the Progressive Era and one of his many nicknames was "The Trust-Buster." He was the first president to try to restrain the railroad monopolies. The American people were sick and tired of the unfair, powerful monopolies during this time, so you can eliminate choice (C). The cartoon itself gives no indication about foreign policy (eliminate (B)) and the drawing is definitely not of FDR (cross out (E)). Answer choice (A) might look tempting, but the cartoon and the Era should lead you to the correct answer choice **(D)**.

FACTOIDS — THE BAD NEWS

Unfortunately, many questions on the American History SAT II are based solely on little factoids, rather than on a general recognition of a particular Era. Because they are the toughest questions on the test, your goal is damage control. These questions are easy to spot; often the answer choices are just lists of people, states, or countries; or the question is short, asking about a particular book or trial, without giving a date or much information to go with it. Clearly, if you know the fact, these questions are not very hard, but of all the questions on the test, they tend to be the most knowledge-based. They also tend to ask about the more obscure facts in American history. Still, we have ways to reduce your losses on these questions.

Play your hunches

Take a Guess:

A: Even if you've never heard of Joseph Smith, you can still answer this question. If you think about the answer choices, there are good reasons to eliminate (A), (B), and (D). But even if you can eliminate one answer choice, you should still guess. (By the way, the answer is (C).)

These factoid questions are tough for everybody, but some students must get them right or they wouldn't be on the test. This means that it pays to play your hunches. The answer will probably not be something you've *never* heard of; it might just be about something you never thought was important enough to memorize. On this test, the correct answer will more likely be something you find vaguely familiar than something you've never heard of before. A corollary to this is to . . .

Go for the most famous person or thing

The correct answer will more likely be a famous person or thing, rather than someone or something obscure. This does not mean that if a president is listed in a group of choices, you should always select that answer. After all, we've had some pretty forgettable presidents. Again, if you are guessing, just go with your hunches. For instance, Abraham Lincoln may have been more famous than Daniel Webster, but Webster was more famous than Martin Van Buren. Of course, if you know that the famous person in the set is wrong, eliminate it and then go for the next most famous person.

And remember the golden rule:

IF YOU CAN ELIMINATE ANY CHOICE, GUESS

But if you can't eliminate any, skip the question. You don't want to waste time on a question that you have scarcely a chance of getting right. This is a long test and it is more worthwhile to try to finish, and get a crack at some questions that you can get right at the end, than to pull your hair out over hard questions. Check the American History SAT II Pacing Chart (page 13) to see exactly how many questions you can leave out in order to get your target score. (You may be happily surprised about how many you can comfortably guess on or skip.) Remember, it is always better for *you* to choose the ones you will skip rather than letting the College Board choose for you as you run out of time at the end.

REVIEW: THE QUESTIONS

1. Era Questions—Use the system.

2. EXCEPT Questions—Turn it into a Yes/No Question or use "One of these things is not like the others."

3. Graphs, Pics, and Cartoons—Read the question first; read the title second; use common sense.

4. Factoids—damage control.

If you can eliminate one answer, guess. If you have no idea, skip the question.

4

American History Review

INTRODUCTION

The following pages offer a brief introduction to the major Eras in American history. The test covers a fairly big chunk of time. Begin by studying the colonial period in the 1700s, with the establishment of the first English colony at Jamestown, Virginia. Then continue through the 1960s–1980s, with its social upheavals and ideological swings. Along the way you will refresh your memory about Jeffersonian vs. Jacksonian Democracy, the bloody clash between North and South, the westward expansion, the industrial revolution, two world wars, the Depression, and the Cold War. Remember, these descriptions are merely outlines, offering the key markers of each Era to help you master the SAT II questions. They are intended only as guides, not as substitutes for more comprehensive readings.

True or False?

Q: All of the American colonists wanted to start a war with England to win their independence.

ERA: THE COLONIAL PERIOD

1600s to Early 1700s

More than ten thousand years ago, the first Native American people migrated from Asia to North America across a land bridge (this is the currently accepted theory). In the eleventh century, a Norse (Viking) sailor, Leif Eriksson, reached North America. In 1492, Columbus sailed the ocean blue . . . and that is all the pre-colonial history you need to know. The American colonial history you need to know for the test starts in the early 1600s with the first English colony at **Jamestown, Virginia**.[1] Colonies of this time period were generally established for two reasons: **economic trading** and/or **social and religious freedom**. Commercial colonies, like Jamestown, were established by trading companies. Other types of colonies were initiated with royal charters, also known as **proprietary grants**.

The second English colony was founded by the **Pilgrims** at **Plymouth, Massachusetts**. These Puritan settlers, as you well know, came to the New World to escape religious persecution. The Pilgrims are remembered for designing the **Mayflower Compact**. This agreement was drafted to determine what the colony's civil laws would be once the pilgrims landed. Even though many groups came to the New World to practice their religion freely, they were not necessarily tolerant of other people's religious freedom. The Puritans set strict rules to govern their religious community.

Economics

In Colonial America, the regional climate had a lot to do with what each colony could and could not do to develop its economy. The New England terrain and climate was poorly suited for farming, so **New England** settlers depended on **domestic production of textiles, fishing, and sea trade**. **Southern** colonies could support **large-scale agriculture** because of their good soil and climate. Plantation systems were developed to produce single staple crops, like tobacco and, later, cotton—also known as **cash crops**, because they were sold as well as consumed by the growers. This type of farming was labor-intensive and was at first manned by

---

[1] Important names and events will be in bold type throughout the American History Review chapter.

indentured servants, people who had agreed to provide five years of labor in exchange for passage to America. Later, the system of indenture on plantations turned out to be insufficient to meet the demand for labor. This opened the door for the inhumane slave trade, which had been carried on by English merchants since at least the sixteenth century, and which increased steadily throughout the seventeenth, eighteenth, and nineteenth centuries.

Religion

Religion was the centerpiece of colonial life for many of the settlers. The established church groups were the Anglicans, who followed the Church of England (a breakaway from the Roman Catholic Church), and the Puritans, who followed Calvinist teachings. In addition to these, many other religious sects flourished, each with slightly different versions of Protestantism (the one colony founded by Catholics was Maryland). There is one religious factoid that the SAT II may want you to know. During the early 1700s, an evangelist, Jonathan Edwards, preached throughout the colonies and created a wave of religious fervor called the Great Awakening. His sermon "Sinners in the Hands of an Angry God" portrayed mankind as facing eternal damnation, and he thundered that people could only be saved by God's grace.

Despite the economic and religious differences among the colonies, the American colonies before the Revolution were very English in character. The advances in science, politics, and writing that occurred in the Enlightenment period in Europe greatly influenced the colonists.

ERA: TENSIONS LEADING TO THE AMERICAN REVOLUTION

EARLY 1700s TO 1775

Mercantile laws

England, like other European countries, believed strongly in the practice of mercantilism. Mercantilists believed that a nation's power was based on its ability to minimize the importation of foreign goods. The British Empire recognized that the colonies were good sources of both goods and services. Therefore, it monopolized the colonial trade, restricting the colonies from trading with other nation-states (France, Spain, the Netherlands and *their* colonies) through passage of the Navigation Acts and similar laws. These acts raised money by placing heavy taxes, called duties, on colonial goods traded with anyone outside the Empire. Such policies fomented anger among the colonists, because they couldn't make as much money with limited trade as they could with free trade, and as a result the colonists often openly disobeyed the laws.

The French and Indian War

At this time, American colonists felt threatened by the colonial settlements of France in the interior of the continent. France and Britain were long-time rivals, fighting numerous wars over the centuries. So now, of course, they fought wars

True or False?

A: False! Not all of the colonists were eager to fight a revolutionary war. Some colonists, known as Loyalists or Tories, actually stayed loyal to the British crown. Many colonists were unhappy with the way they were being treated by England, but they didn't necessarily want to be independent. Some were also afraid that England would win the war since it was more powerful.

in America, the principle bounty being the dominance of the fur trade, the rights to the North Atlantic fisheries, and the possession of the Ohio-Mississippi Basin. The French enlisted the Algonquin and the Iroquois Indian tribes to fight alongside them against encroaching English colonies. Some smaller wars led up to the large-scale **French and Indian War** in which England finally prevailed over the French. The British victory changed the boundaries of the two empires' worldwide possessions. French territory in America shrank. English territories expanded. The war had been enormously expensive and the British felt that the American colonists did not share equally the burden of the war costs. On the other hand, as American colonists no longer needed the strong defense against the French that the British provided, the colonists began to reconsider their role as subjects within the colonial system.

Taxation without representation

Directly following the French and Indian War, a new prime minister, George Grenville, was appointed to govern the American colonies. He sought a tighter control over them in order to raise revenues for England. In addition to stricter enforcement of existing trade laws, Grenville passed other unpopular laws. The **Sugar Act**, which placed high duties on certain foreign goods (not just sugar), basically forced the colonies to trade through England. The **Stamp Act** decreed that all legal and commercial documents, newspapers, and pamphlets should bear a stamp. The stamps were sold only by Grenville's Treasury at a cost that virtually doubled the colonists' tax burden. The Stamp Act was denounced by colonists, because it created a new tax to make revenue solely for the Empire, not the colonists themselves.

These laws generated uproar, not only because people thought that they were generally unfair, but because the colonists were not represented in England's Parliament when these laws were passed. Thus arose the revolutionary cry, **"No taxation without representation."** Many groups organized to protest the strict enforcement of these taxes. The **Sons of Liberty** were a particularly radical group that took to burning stamps and terrorizing British officials. England responded by lessening the severity of Grenville's Acts, but directly stated in the **Declaratory Act** that the mother country could tax the colonists in any way it saw fit.

A few years later, a new chancellor, Charles Townshend, worked to raise colonial taxes again. Similar protests arose, and this time even more boycotts and violence accompanied the new taxes. In the **Boston Massacre**, British soldiers who had been sent to the colonies to protect tax officials got into a brawl with colonial protesters, and the soldiers shot into a crowd, killing five civilians. Also under Townshend, Parliament passed the **Tea Act**, which removed mercantilist duties on tea exported to America by England's powerful **East India Company**. This drastically lowered the cost of that company's tea, which flooded the colonial market and undercut the price of tea sold by colonial merchants. These merchants still had to pay duties on other teas or smuggle tea (and risk imprisonment) to avoid the tax. The Tea Act prompted the **Boston Tea Party** protest. In this famous event, protestors dumped East India tea into Boston Harbor.

Translate the Answer Choice:

(C) imposed high duties on foreign goods
Translation: made it more expensive to buy stuff from other countries

Needless to say, England wasn't too happy with Boston's idea of a tea party and decided to punish the whole colony of Massachusetts with the so-called **Intolerable Acts**. Great Britain closed Boston Harbor until the city paid for the lost tea. The charter of Massachusetts was revoked and all of its elected officials were replaced with royal appointees. Town meetings were forbidden. And Bostonians were forced to feed and lodge the soldiers who would implement these policies with the passage of the **Quartering Act**.

These strict actions by England infuriated colonists and they decided to act. **The First Continental Congress** of 1774 was a gathering of representatives from all the colonies. The participants agreed to join together in a boycott of English goods. In addition, the Congress wrote up a list of grievances to present to the king. Very few colonists thought that these actions would ultimately lead to a military conflict. Nor did they anticipate the complete separation of the colonies from England in the American War of Independence.

ERA: INDEPENDENCE AND THE NEW UNITED STATES

1775 TO 1800

The American Revolution

A **Second Continental Congress** was scheduled to meet a year after the first one. Before it could commence, though, skirmishes broke out between the colonists and the British soldiers, known as redcoats, in Lexington and Concord, Massachusetts. Both England and the colonists extended separate plans of reconciliation, but the two sides reached no compromise. In July of 1775, England acknowledged an open rebellion in the colonies and the **American Revolution** officially started. Another year elapsed and the colonies declared that this would be a war of independence.

Several factors contributed to this original hesitancy:

1. The colonists felt attached to the mother country by language and culture.

2. It was difficult to build an intercolonial consensus on war goals.

3. Many colonists worried about the superior might of the British empire. Many others felt that even if the colonies did win, anarchy would reign without the ruling hand of the King.

On the other hand, many colonists expressed arguments in favor of separating from the mother country. A recent immigrant from England, **Thomas Paine**, summed up many of these arguments in his pamphlet *Common Sense*, which assailed the monarchy and appealed to the colonists to form a better government. With the **Declaration of Independence in 1776**, the American colonies made the "irrevocable" break with England.

General George Washington led the American troops against great odds. The British forces were larger in number, better trained, and supported by the wealth of England, the richest and most powerful nation in the world. Washington's strategic skills were invaluable to keeping the American forces alive during the war's early years. **France** was also a decisive ally for the Americans. Secretly supplying weapons and goods to the colonies, France, along with Spain and Holland, formally declared war against England. Another factor in America's favor was that the English greatly overestimated **Tory** or Loyalist support (that is, American support for the British) in the colonies and England approached the war as if they merely had to suppress a few reactionaries.

The weak Continental Congress

Finally, England no longer thought it worthwhile to fight the American colonies, especially as other European nations placed military pressure on them. American independence in the thirteen colonies was established and the **Articles of the Confederation** emerged from the Continental Congress as a framework for government. This document favored strong powers for the individual colonies, now referred to as states, but it did not establish the centralized federal offices necessary for national leadership. Consequently, the Articles soon proved to be an ineffective tool to mold the new nation. Under the Articles, the Continental Congress could not tax or raise funds for the nation; hence each state printed its own money. As a result, the federal government was dirt poor and reliable currency was difficult to obtain.

These factors led to an economic recession, prompting events such as **Shays' Rebellion**. In this incident, a debt-ridden band of farmers and war veterans violently protested and shut down the courts which had sent many of the poor to **debtor's prison**. Without military power, the Continental Congress could do nothing. The event symbolized the inherent weaknesses of the Continental Congress under the Articles of Confederation.

Federal government under the constitution

In 1787, the newly independent nation convened a **Constitutional Convention** where the **U.S. Constitution**, the foundation for our government, was written. Influential participants included **Alexander Hamilton, James Madison, and John Jay**. These men were self-proclaimed **Federalists**. Federalists believed in establishing a strong national government that would have the necessary power to supersede some state powers. The Constitution established the three branches of government: the **Executive**, or the Presidency, the **Legislature**, or the Congress (including both the Senate and the House of Representatives), and the **Judiciary**, or the Supreme Court and the lower federal court system. The branches were set up with a system of **checks and balances** so that none of the three branches could attain too much power. For example, the Supreme Court has the power to declare a law unconstitutional, the President has the power to veto a bill to stop it from becoming a law, and Congress has the power to override a President's veto. Originally, the Congress was the strongest element of the government because, with the **power of the purse**, Congress can raise and spend revenue. Also, Congress has the power to make laws. In the twentieth century, however, the Executive branch has developed into perhaps the stron gest branch with presidents like Franklin D. Roosevelt's pushing for a broader interpretation of the U.S. Constitution.

The Constitution was in many ways a difficult compromise among the various states' interests. One stumbling block to its formation was the question of representation among slave states. Each state had two Senators but representation in the House of Representatives was based on the number of people who lived in each state. The dilemma was this: How could you count slaves as both property (for taxation purposes) and people (for representation purposes)? The problem was "solved" with the **3/5 compromise,** which mandated that each slave be counted as 3/5 of a person when establishing the population of a state for representation. (Sad, stupid, and tragic, but this is our nation's history.)

The Bill of Rights, the first ten amendments to the Constitution, was also a compromise to urge states to ratify the document. Many smaller states wanted their civil rights spelled out to ensure that the new federal government would not infringe on them. Briefly, the rights guaranteed by the Bill of Rights are: freedom of religion, speech, and the press, the right to bear arms, the right to keep a soldier from living in your house, protection from unreasonable searches and seizures, the right to avoid self-incrimination during a trial, the right to a speedy trial by jury, and the right to due process. The Constitution was ratified and passed in 1789.

Rise of political parties

George Washington was named the first president. With others, he worked to formalize the structures described in the Constitution. Because of the financial difficulties faced by the new nation, Alexander Hamilton's position as the Secretary of the Treasury was especially important. Hamilton worked quickly to establish a financially sound federal government. He urged Congress to pass legislation that would dictate the **repayment of the national debt** in order to encourage foreign investment, the **establishment of a national bank**, and the **authority to print federal money**. Many, including Madison, one of the original framers, felt that these powers were not explicitly mentioned in the Constitution and were therefore unconstitutional. This first conflict regarding the Constitution led to the political definitions of a **"loose"** (Hamilton) **vs.** a **"strict"** (Madison) **interpretation** of the document.

The **Whiskey Rebellion** was similar in many respects to the earlier Shays' Rebellion. It was the first internal threat to the new government. Farmers, who were also whiskey producers, violently protested a large tax on whiskey and Washington dispatched 15,000 troops to squelch the uprising. Though it demonstrated the strength of the federal government, many felt that this use of power was excessive and revealed a bias toward the large, wealthy speculators who had lent the government money. These speculators were to be paid back from the proceeds of the whiskey tax. This unrest, coupled with ideological divisions over constitutional interpretation, helped forge the **Republican party**, led by Madison and **Thomas Jefferson**, as a challenge to Federalist control of the government. At the time, Republicans favored farmers and agricultural interests while the Federalists leaned toward manufacturing and commercial interests.

As the U.S. struggled to establish itself as a nation, its leaders had to contend with various threats from Great Britain, France, and Spain. Washington had been a strong advocate of **neutrality**, because he felt that the nation could not withstand a war in its fledgling state. Still, it was difficult for U.S. diplomats to reach agreements with, say, Great Britain, without angering France. In one infamous incident, known as the **XYZ Affair**,[2] France attempted to bribe U.S. negotiators and threatened to incite riots in the American states. Americans were indignant about the French agents' treatment of American representatives; the affair led to tensions between America and France that threatened to lead to war.

During this time, the **Alien and Sedition Acts** were passed, which (1) allowed the deportation of foreigners who seemed to be a threat to national security and (2) designated fines or imprisonment for persons who wrote "falsely and maliciously" against the laws of the government. Although the "sedition" aspect of this law ran counter to the First Amendment in the Bill of Rights, it was used to arrest and otherwise suppress Republicans who had been sympathetic to French interests. In attempts to repeal these laws Madison and Jefferson wrote the **Virginia and Kentucky Resolutions**. This would have given states the power to repeal unconstitutional laws. Though these resolutions did not gain national acceptance, they helped strengthen the Republican party and platform.

In the historic election of 1800, Thomas Jefferson, a Republican, won the Presidency, signaling the **first transfer of power** from one party to another. The new nation achieved this with much verbal infighting and mudslinging, but without bloodshed.

Know Your Rights!

Q: The Constitution guarantees the right to
(A) affordable housing
(B) free education
(C) health care
(D) not be forced to house a soldier

ERA: JEFFERSONIAN REPUBLICANISM

1800 TO 1816

Jefferson surrounded himself with loyal Republicans and stood up to the Federalist appointees in the Judiciary branch. The Republicans wanted to restrain the large federal government that had been built up by the Federalists in the preceding years. Part of Jefferson's philosophy was that farmers represented the noblest and most democratic aspects of American life. Often his policies favored their interests over the interests of business, trading, and manufacturing. Jefferson's presidency is best known for the **Louisiana Purchase**, which virtually doubled the size of America. Ironically, the purchase represented an expansion of the Federal powers he denounced.

Louisiana Purchase

So, why did the French sell us that big parcel of land? Well, **Napoleon Bonaparte** was in a jam; he had an empire to establish and he needed some cash. The French wanted to sell the land that Britain threatened to take away from them anyway (can't those two play nice for once?). Plus, a **slave revolt in Haiti**, ably led by **Toussaint L'Ouverture**, had depleted Napoleon's troops and supplies to a point where it seemed impossible for him to establish a foothold in the Western Hemisphere. When Jefferson sent emissaries to France, his primary

---

[2] XYZ stands for the code letters of the three French agents who tried to bribe the Americans.

concern was the control of the Mississippi River and the **Port of New Orleans**, invaluable trade routes for the Ohio Valley and western settlers. U.S. representatives were shocked to be offered the whole Louisiana territory. Although Jefferson was concerned about the constitutionality of such a large land purchase (remember, philosophically he was a "strict" interpreter of the constitution), he quickly acceded to the expansionist interests of the nation and supported Congress's approval of the deal.

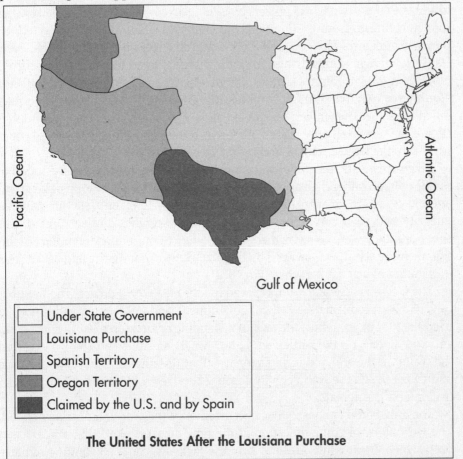

Under State Government
Louisiana Purchase
Spanish Territory
Oregon Territory
Claimed by the U.S. and by Spain

The United States After the Louisiana Purchase

Know Your Rights!

A: (D). The government now provides affordable housing, free education, and health care to many people, but these things aren't mentioned in the Constitution. Many rights that you may think are in the Constitution are actually laws that were passed much later. The Third Amendment, which is part of the Bill of Rights, actually says that no one can force you to have a soldier stay in your home during a time of war or otherwise.

The **Lewis and Clark Expedition** was funded by Congress soon after the Louisiana Purchase. These explorers, helped by Native American guides, travelled from St. Louis to the Pacific Ocean in a year and a half. Their expedition helped establish U.S. claims to the disputed Oregon territory. In effect, the period of westward expansion began at this point and continued throughout the nineteenth century. Because the Era of Western Expansion extends over such a long period of time, important events in the westward movement are covered in the Era in which they occur.

War of 1812[3]

During the early 1800s, Great Britain and France were at it again, fighting wars that affected the United States. The British were stopping U.S. ships and search-

---

[3] For the American History Subject Test, it is important for you to know the events leading up to and following any given American war, but it is unlikely that you will need to recall specific battles or dates. This book is written to reflect this tendency of the Subject Test writers.

ing them for British naval deserters. This was particularly troublesome because the British would often seize native-born or naturalized American citizens as well as runaway British sailors. The **Chesapeake Incident** was the most widely publicized episode of this "sailor kidnapping," formally known as **impressment**. The French also violated American neutrality rights by restricting trade and seizing U.S. ships and their cargoes while they rested in French harbors.

Jefferson and his successor, Republican **James Madison**, tried to avoid hostilities with these two world powers by issuing an **embargo**, which prohibited all foreign countries from trading with the United States until they respected national sovereignty. This embargo had a drastic effect on the Americans, especially New England merchants. Since the policy seemed to penalize Americans more than foreign interests, the embargo was repealed and replaced with the **Nonintercourse Act**. Though symbolically different, the result was the pretty much the same. The embargo restricted all foreign trade, whereas the Nonintercourse Act restricted only trade with Great Britain and France, but these countries were the largest traders in the world.

Like many wars, the impetus for a war declaration in 1812 was the mood of public opinion rather than a specific event. The **War Hawks**, a group of Westerners and Southerners who rallied for war against England, felt our national integrity had been compromised by the illegal searches and seizures of our ships, and they were concerned about the safety of our national borders. Madison, then President, was swayed by the War Hawks' popularity and asked for a declaration of war (guess when?) in 1812.

The U.S. was essentially unprepared to take on a world power. The Republicans had been reducing the Federal government, and military expenditures had been the first to go. Thus, the lack of a standing armed force led to some early embarrassments on the battlefield. Later, American ships had some success on the water. In the end, a crucial factor was that Britain was still fighting France and trying to subdue Napoleon in Europe. The Treaty of Ghent ended the war, declaring it a stalemate.

The only battle of consequence occurred after the war had officially ended. The technology of communication at the time delayed word that a treaty had been signed. Meanwhile, General **Andrew Jackson** won a resounding military victory at the **Battle of New Orleans**. News of this victory and the announcement of the peace treaty reached major cities at about the same time. Thus, it was popularly misunderstood that America had "won" the war with its military prowess. Jackson, the leader of the "victory" battle, went on to become a folk hero and president. (Just think, if CNN had been around...)

The War of 1812 caused significant regional division within the states. New Englanders opposed the war from the outset, since their livelihood was based on trade with Britain and other world powers. As noted before, the War Hawks consisted of mainly Westerners and Southerners. As the war pressed on and there were no significant victories, the Federalist party held a meeting, known as the **Hartford Convention**, to formulate and submit their grievances to Madison's administration. The Federalists announced their demands in Washington, D.C. just as news of Jackson's victory and the Treaty of Ghent signing reached the capital. The Federalist party was denounced as traitorous and their leaders returned to New England in disgrace. This marked the end of the Federalist party's impact on the national scene.

ERA: THE BEGINNINGS OF EXPANSION

Early Nineteenth Century: 1816 to the 1850s

President **James Monroe** led our country during the time immediately following the War of 1812. This time became known as the **"Era of Good Feelings."** The "good feelings" were in part due to the lack of political opposition to Republican policies and in part due to the afterglow of an apparent war victory. But, considering the militarism of the westward expansion and the mistreatment of Native American and African American people that continued through this Era, that phrase seems ironic at best.

Though the Monroe Era saw few party conflicts, the government was not completely Republican. John Marshall, a Federalist, helped mold the Judiciary into a powerful constitutional branch when he resided as the Supreme Court's Chief Justice. During his long tenure, the **Marshall Court** maintained an ideology of a strong national government even when that clashed with the Republican emphasis on state's rights.

> "The American continents, by the free and independent condition which they have assumed and maintain, are henceforth not to be considered as subjects for future colonization by any European powers."
> —President James Monroe, declaring what came to be known as the Monroe Doctrine

Adaptations to expansion

During this period, great numbers of people began moving west, drawn by the availability of cheap land and stories of rich natural resources. The **push to expand the western frontiers** influenced many of Monroe's domestic and international policies. Domestically, his administration negotiated the **acquisition of Florida** from Spain and the settlement with Great Britain for joint rights to the Oregon territory. To protect the North American hemisphere in particular, Monroe declared that any European interference in the Americas would be seen as a hostility to the U.S. This policy was called the **Monroe Doctrine**, and it greatly affected nineteenth- and twentieth-century international affairs.

The rapid growth of Southern and Western populations also fueled the **transportation revolution**. Since the Republicans did not believe in Federal involvement, most of the roads and canals were built or improved with state funding. The **Erie Canal of New York** became the model for the other states that were eager to improve transportation for commercial prosperity. The invention of the steamboat contributed to the transportation revolution, fueling interstate trade and thus interstate dependence. **Regional specialization** became more pronounced. New Englanders concentrated on manufacture, while the South maintained its plantation systems.

Sectional compromises

The Federalist Constitution was based on a delicate (and immoral) compromise between slave and non-slave states and, as westward expansion raised the issue of the entry of new states, the weaknesses of the constitutional compromise came to light. Remember, the 3/5 compromise was an agreement to balance the representation of slave states and free states in the Federal government. Northern interests wanted new western territories to be "free" and Southern interests wanted them to be "slave," either of which would upset the status quo. So during this period, **sectional politics**, North vs. South vs. West, gained importance in the national arena.

The **Missouri Compromise** (1820) was the first settlement to these new sectional disputes. Missouri, traditionally a slave state, had applied for statehood, but Northerners protested, fearing that slave states would outnumber free states. Representative Tallmadge of New York offered the **Tallmadge Amendment**, which specified that Missouri could enter if all children of slaves would become free when they reach the age of twenty-five. His measure was defeated but it touched off a heated controversy. The issue was not resolved until the free territory of Maine stepped forward for statehood. The compromise accepted both states, Missouri as slave and Maine as free. In addition to maintaining the Federal balance, the compromise banned slavery from all parts of the Louisiana Purchase north of the **36°, 30' Latitude**. These compromises set the tone for the next forty years leading up to the Civil War.

Literature

In the period between the War of 1812 and the Civil War, the arts flourished. There may be a few questions on the test specifically about literature of the time. English teachers like to say that a "truly American character" emerged in the literary works of the time. Below, we've listed a few names you should know. In their work, **Naturalist writers** pitted the individual against environmental or societal forces. They often questioned the effect of "civilization" on the individual. The work of **Transcendentalists** is described below.

During the mid-nineteenth century, reformer Dorothea Lynde Dix, a former school teacher, carried on a one-person crusade to improve the treatment of the mentally ill. Her efforts were instrumental in the establishment of hospitals and asylums.

Author	Work	Style
James Fenimore Cooper	"Leatherstocking" books *The Deerslayer*	Naturalist
Herman Melville	*Moby Dick*	Naturalist
Nathaniel Hawthorne	*The Scarlet Letter*	Naturalist
Ralph Waldo Emerson	"Nature" and other essays	Transcendentalist
Henry David Thoreau	*Walden*	Transcendentalist

Reform movements

During the early part of the nineteenth century, many people challenged religious and social institutions, often in attempts to lead a more "moral" life. These reform movements were enhanced by an optimism, a mood at least partially created by the expanding western frontier.

Leaders of the religious movements were often fire-and-brimstone evangelists who preached that individuals had to purge sin from their lives and actively seek salvation rather than depend on the local church or religious leaders to save them. But the followers of one movement, **Transcendentalism**, believed that God created people without evil and with the capacity to be perfect. Many intellectuals embraced this theory, the most influential being **Henry David Thoreau** and **Ralph Waldo Emerson**.

Some religious groups stressed values contrary to the dominant materialist culture, and this compelled them to congregate into isolated settlements. **The**

Shakers valued simplicity and hard work. One can see this reflected esthetically in their beautiful furniture. Another group, **the Mormons**, settled the state of Utah in the 1840s to escape persecution for their beliefs.

Social living experiments, also called **utopias**, came into being. The settlers of these communes shunned private property and other social institutions, even marriage, which they felt restricted individual freedom. To avoid chaos in the absence of law, they urged each person to work, think, and act for the sake of the community. These social experiments often didn't last very long.

Other idealists rejected utopianism. Rather than withdrawing into isolated communities, they sought to improve conditions in the existing society. They advocated **social reforms**, largely supported and often led by middle class women. Education reformers, like **Horace Mann**, pushed for **universal public education** of school-age children. **Dorothea Dix** crusaded to **improve the conditions of insane asylums and prisons**. The **temperance (anti-alcohol) movement,** started in the 1820s, was fueled by the moralist fervor of the time. The influence of women in these areas spurred them to reassess their own second-class status in the nation. Thus began the **women's rights** and **suffrage** movements.

The big daddy of all reform movements was the anti-slavery or **abolitionist crusade**. Some anti-slavery proponents were moderates, urging the gradual **emancipation** (setting free) of the slaves and "repatriating" them to Africa. A colony, **Liberia**, was founded for this purpose in the 1820s, but this didn't prove to be a viable or desirable solution. Other groups were more radical, like the **American Anti-Slavery Society**. The leader of this group, **William Lloyd Garrison**, wrote incendiary articles in his paper *The Liberator* and called for immediate and uncompromised freedom for slaves. **Frederick Douglass** was a vocal member of this group. Eventually their stance enticed loyal supporters. Still, many in the North (not to mention the South) did not wholeheartedly embrace the abolitionist crusade and often dismissed them as fanatics who threatened civilized society.

Party politics revisited

In the presidential election of 1824, Monroe stepped down, as was traditional after two terms, and a fight for the presidency ensued among three Republicans: **John Quincy Adams, Henry Clay, and Andrew Jackson**. In an electoral scandal, Jackson won a plurality of popular votes (the greatest number of votes, but less than fifty percent) but lacked the majority of electoral votes needed. When the vote went to the House of Representatives, Adams was awarded the presidency and he named Clay as his Secretary of State. Jackson felt that this was a corrupt political conspiracy and immediately began campaigning for the next election. This marked the **reemergence of party politics** in the previously united federal government of Republicans. Jackson supporters included **John C. Calhoun**, a powerful Southerner and current vice president to Adams, and **Martin Van Buren**. They called their coalition the **Democrats** and campaigned for a return to Jeffersonian ideals. Adams, Clay, and their supporters began calling themselves **National Republicans**.

True or False?

Q: During the early nineteenth century, a lot of people protested when Missouri wanted to enter the union because Missouri intended to become a slave state.

ERA: JACKSONIAN DEMOCRACY
1828 TO 1840

Andrew Jackson, waging a fierce campaign, was elected president by a landslide in 1828 with Martin Van Buren as his vice president.

Leader of the common man

Many political reforms had taken place during the 1820s and the vote was extended to many more people (more white men, that is). Andrew Jackson's popularity was built on his image as a "friend to the common man" and as the war hero of New Orleans. He was the first president who seemed to be "of the People" as opposed to aristocratic. In office, he surrounded himself with friends and supporters and advocated what was known as **the spoils system**. The phrase "to the winner go the spoils" meant that the winning political party should get all the political jobs in Washington.

Jackson molded his office into one of the strongest presidencies the young United States had experienced. He set a precedent by stretching the constitutional boundaries of the executive branch, and he used his popularity to build on his power. For instance, he used the **veto** to mold national policy, a step that had never been taken before. During his presidency, Jackson engaged in infamous confrontations with Native American tribes, Southerners, and bankers.

Jackson's confrontations

As a Westerner, Jackson favored selling land cheaply to settlers to further expand into the West. He advocated a complete "removal" of Indians, blatantly disregarding previous treaties that the U.S. government had made with many of the tribes. He signed a law called the **Removal Act of 1830** which mandated that the tribes surrender or die fighting. If Jackson was a "friend" to anyone, it was only to white men.

The **nullification crisis** refers to the conflict between South Carolina and the federal government over a taxation issue. South Carolina, led by Jackson's former supporter John C. Calhoun, defied a federal tariff on the importation of British goods. This tariff angered Southerners, who feared British retaliation against Southern cotton exports. Consequently, South Carolina declared the tariff null and void in its state. Southerners argued that their "state's rights" (to free commerce) outweighed any duty to the federal nation, and that they could choose to nullify any law they didn't like. Jackson acted quickly, concerned that South Carolina's blatant disregard of the federal law might lead to its secession from the Union. Declaring the state's action treasonous, Jackson asked Congress to authorize the **Force Bill** to send troops to defend the Union and federal law. Realizing that South Carolina would have to stand alone against the nation, Calhoun looked for a compromise. When Congress voted to lower the tax slightly, South Carolina backed down.

In Jackson's reelection campaign, a major issue was the rechartering of the **Second Bank of the United States**, a private bank that held all federal deposits. (The First Bank of the United States had been established by Alexander

---

True or False?

A: True! During the period before the Civil War, slavery was a very, very big issue. Northerners, who were anti-slavery, didn't want there to be more slave states than free states. The issue of Missouri's statehood was settled when Maine offered to enter the union as a free state, which balanced things out. This was called the Missouri Compromise.

Hamilton under George Washington.) Some historians feel the bank was financially sound and generally operated in the interests of the nation; others say it had speculated foolishly with deposits and behaved ruthlessly toward its smaller borrowers. Jackson assailed the institution as corrupt, unconstitutional, and a tool for the rich man's oppression of the common man. Jackson's enormous popularity won great voter approval for his veto of the recharter of the bank. When reelected, in a landslide, he sought to destroy the bank by ordering the transfer of federal monies to several small state banks, which came to be known as Jackson's "pet banks."

Jackson's strong will and firm stances on a variety of issues earned him some significant political enemies. Some people referred to him as "King Andrew I," a negative reference to the monarchy of England. Southerners were mortified by his actions in South Carolina. Northeasterners were annoyed by his constant berating of businessmen and merchants. This discontent helped forge a new political party, the **Whigs.** The leadership of this party had been National Republicans, but they changed the party name to more easily garner support from the Democrats. The Whig party was significant on the national scene for about twenty years but became weak because of its one-issue platform (that is, "We hate Jackson"). The Whigs could not satisfy the divergent interests of its members, especially as the rift deepened between North and South because of the slavery question.

Post-Jackson

Jackson stepped down after the customary two terms and handpicked his successor and former vice-president, Martin Van Buren. Van Buren, who narrowly won over Whig opposition, felt the full force of Jackson's banking policies during his administration. A boom in growth and industry led to crazy speculation, the widespread use of unsound credit, and the rise of unregulated banks that used risky lending procedures. This combination led to a crash of the financial market. The economic depression that followed was known as the **Panic of 1837**.

In the next election, the Whig party won with the **William H. Harrison** and **John Tyler** ticket. Tyler had not been a full-fledged proponent of the Whig party, but the Whigs put him on the ticket to bolster southern support. The Whigs were soon unhappy with this choice because Harrison became the first president to die in office (he got pneumonia at his inauguration) and Tyler assumed the Presidency.

The intense passions over presidential politics, marking the Jacksonian Era, diminished and remained subdued for about twenty years. The relatively mild statures of presidents during this time may have been a reaction to the strong (some thought overbearing) presence of Jackson in the White House. But it was also due to the state of the nation as it precariously avoided the slavery issue. This issue was the undercurrent for all sectional relations. While sectional strife was the definitive issue, no president or presidential candidate addressed that topic until Abraham Lincoln.

Pop Quiz

Q: Which one of these is not like the others?
  (A) The spoils system
  (B) Destruction of Native American tribes
  (C) Extended power of the executive branch
  (D) Support of Northern elites
  (E) Expansion of voting rights

ERA: SECTIONAL STRIFE—THE PATH TO THE CIVIL WAR - *Antebellum America*

1840 TO 1860

During Van Buren's term, Congress indefinitely tabled all discussions about the issue of slavery in a measure called the **Gag Resolution**. Supporters of the rule felt such debates were time-consuming and useless, while its few opponents thought it unconstitutional and corrupt to be forbidden to speak out against slavery. After eight years, the Gag Resolution was overturned.

North vs. South vs. West

The increasing sectional disagreements among the regions were due in large part to the differences in these regions' economies and cultures. The **North** was rapidly becoming an **industrialized economy**. With new factories springing up, urban centers grew with people migrating from the farmlands to the cities. Better transportation and communication systems were in demand to keep pace with industrial expansion. Railroad networks were built throughout the North, and the use of the telegraph aided in running this large network. Technological advances in farm equipment and farming methods also aided northern agriculture, allowing this region to produce staple crops at unprecedented rates.

The **South**, on the other hand, was like a region lost in time; the plantation system had remained largely unchanged since the colonial days. The **large-scale, labor-intense plantations** concentrated on **cash crops**, and the owners argued that this necessitated the use of slaves. Slavery became known as that "peculiar institution," and this euphemism sought to portray slavery as just something unique about the South rather than as something morally corrupt or depraved. Slavery might have declined in the South if it hadn't been for the invention of the **cotton gin**. The quick and easy removal of seeds from the cotton tufts, coupled with England's great demand for cotton, encouraged the South to focus on cotton growing, which in turn led to an increased demand for slave labor.

Meanwhile the **West** had its own ideology, but its territories were often used as bargaining chips in the powerful play between northern and southern interests. Mainly, Westerners supported territorial expansion, the concept called **Manifest Destiny**, which stated that it was divine will that America should stretch beyond its current boundaries until it governed the entire North American continent.

Texas, Oregon, and war

Presidents Tyler and **James K. Polk** were both supporters of western expansion. Polk had won on a campaign of "re-annexing Texas and re-occupying Oregon." This slogan glossed over the fact that, at the time, Texas was a Mexican province and the Oregon territory remained jointly held with Great Britain. Regardless of the potential for these policies to cause a war, expansion was popular with the electorate.

Texas had been colonized by Americans and had recently been given independent governance by Mexico. Soon after Polk's election, Texans requested

Pop Quiz

A: Choices (A), (B), (C), and (E) are connected to the presidency of Andrew Jackson. Choice (D) doesn't belong because Jackson characterized himself as a president of the people, winning popularity as a "friend to the common man."

annexation as a U.S. state. Thus, the pressure to add a free state to balance the slave/free state proportions in the Congress made it important that the Oregon territory become a state. The motto **"Fifty-four-forty or Fight"** referred to expansionist claims on the Oregon territory, and it meant that nothing but the entire region (or the latitude and longitude of "fifty-four-forty") would be acceptable. Yet, because of disputes near the Mexican border, Polk could not fight too much for Oregon, and the U.S. and Great Britain compromised on dividing the territory at the 49th parallel border.

Polk really wanted a war with Mexico. As an expansionist, he hoped to pressure the Mexicans into giving the U.S. substantial pieces of their territory, like California and the Southwest. Others, especially Northerners, opposed the war and feared that increased Southern acquisitions would overtly favor slave-state interests. The **Mexican-American War** officially began when Mexican troops, retaliating against Polk's pressures, crossed the Rio Grande into Texas. The war was not as swift as Polk would have liked, but it ended in his favor. With the **Treaty of Guadalupe-Hidalgo**, Mexico acknowledged the Rio Grande as the southern border of Texas and ceded the territories of California and New Mexico to the U.S. Soon after the acquisition of California, gold was discovered in "them thar hills," setting off the Gold Rush of 1849 and an unprecedented migration to the territory.

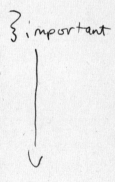

True or False?

Q: In 1861, the president supported the expansion of slavery into the western territories of the country.

New territories — New compromises

These new territories increased the tension between free and slave states in the populace and in Congress. Even as the Mexican-American War was being fought, representatives from the North and the South began disputing how this new territory would be organized, slave or free. The Gold Rush really forced the decision; in 1849, **California** requested admittance into the Union as a free state. President Tyler supported admittance; Southerners began serious talk of secession.

Henry Clay, by then an elder statesman, proposed several resolutions which came to constitute the **Compromise of 1850**. The ensuing arguments are sometimes referred to as **The Great Debate** and the notable participants were Clay, **Daniel Webster**, and **John C. Calhoun**. The compromise admitted California as a free state and maintained Texas as a slave state. The rest of the territory would be divided at the 37th parallel into New Mexico and Utah. These territories would be "unrestricted" and each locality would decide its own status. The slave trade in the District of Columbia would be abolished. The most significant resolution (and what kept the slave issue alive) was the new **Fugitive Slave Law**, which required citizens of any state to aide in the recovery of runaway slaves; citizens who refused would be fined or imprisoned. This sanction angered even moderate Northerners as a blatantly pro-slave state measure.

Although some thought that this compromise would settle the slave issue, it proved to be a temporary truce. In fact, in 1854, the **Kansas-Nebraska Bill** effectively repealed the Compromise of 1850. Stephen Douglas introduced the legislation, seeking quick acceptance of the Nebraska and Kansas Territories as states. (His own state of Illinois was interested in a proposed expansion of the railroad network into these areas.) Douglas suggested that each locality should decide the slave issue for itself. Passage of the bill widened the split between Northern and Southern interests. Increased opposition to slavery in the North grew and abolitionists felt more justified in speaking out against the status quo. Many local counties passed **personal liberty laws** that undermined the fugitive laws by disallowing their jails to be used for slave holding.

The Kansas-Nebraska Act helped set the stage for one of the first violent confrontations over the slavery issue. Because the fate of each locality in the Kansas-Nebraska region was decided by a popular vote, hundreds of pro-slavery and anti-slavery activists rushed into the territories to swing the decision. Often armed and ready to fight, Kansas became a literal battleground of the slave issue and was referred to as "bleeding Kansas." Beyond just advocating their cause, these activists sometimes attacked the settlements of their enemies and killed them. The most infamous incident was **John Brown's raid**, where Brown, a fanatical slavery opponent, led a group to murder five pro-slavery settlers. Later John Brown led another raid on the U.S. arsenal at **Harper's Ferry** (then in the state of Virginia) hoping to seize enough weapons to successfully arm a slave uprising. This time, John Brown was caught, tried for treason, and hanged.

True or False?

A: False! In 1861, Abraham Lincoln was president, and we all know that he represented Northern anti-slavery views.

A further attempt to resolve the slave crisis was made by the Supreme Court with the *Dred Scott* decision forwarded by **Chief Justice Roger B. Taney**. Dred Scott was a slave whose master had taken him into free territory whereupon Scott sued for his freedom. The Court decided that slaves and the descendents of slaves were not U.S. citizens and therefore could not have legal standing. Additionally, Taney ruled, slaves were property and protected as such by the slave owners' constitutional rights. This meant that slaves could not be taken from their masters regardless of a territory's "free" or "slave" status. This decision in effect nullified all of the previous compromises and permitted slave owners to take their "possessions" into any U.S. territory. Anti-slavery Northerners were angered and, instead of settling the issue, the decision further deepened sectional division.

During the **Lincoln-Douglas debates** of 1858, **Abraham Lincoln** entered the national scene as an anti-slavery Republican. He ran against the long-standing Senator Stephen Douglas in the U.S. Senate race in Illinois and challenged him to a series of debates. Lincoln deftly explained his belief that the nation's opposition to slavery could not be compromised and challenged the morality of Douglas's support of the *Dred Scott* decision and the Kansas-Nebraska Bill. Although Lincoln did not win the Senate race, he gained national prominence as an eloquent speaker for Northern views.

Sway of public opinion

In the North, some people were outspoken crusaders against the evils of slavery, but many more did not have a strong feeling about the issue. In the years following the Compromise of 1850, public opinion about slavery in the North was swayed by a few things. First, **Harriet Beecher Stowe** wrote a moving account of slavery called *Uncle Tom's Cabin* which brought the moral dilemma home to many middle-class citizens in the North. Although not an abolitionist's manifesto, the simple story galvanized anti-slavery sentiments. Also, blacks and whites organized the **Underground Railroad**, secretly and dangerously helping to transport runaway slaves to freedom in the North and in Canada, often in violation of federal laws. Though only a fraction of slaves were ever freed by this method, its existence played an important symbolic role in freeing slaves.

As noted previously, many presidents had avoided the slave question, but in the **election of 1860** the issue came to the forefront. The **Democratic party** was overwhelmingly pro-South and pro-slavery; the new **Republican party**, which nominated Lincoln, opposed slavery in the new territories; and a third party, a remnant of the Whig party called the Constitutional-Unionists, sought further compromise on the slave question. In the end, Lincoln carried only 40 percent of the popular vote and none of the slave states, but in the electoral college, he won the election handily. This election gave the Republicans control of the presidency and the House of Representatives, and the Democrats a majority in the Senate and the Supreme Court. As you can recall, Lincoln had not opposed slavery in the South, only in the new territories. Nonetheless, his election and his belief that the slavery issue must be decided one way or the other brought the country closer to Civil War.

Believe it or Not?

One factor that contributed to the onset of the Civil War was a novel written by the daughter of a Protestant Minister.

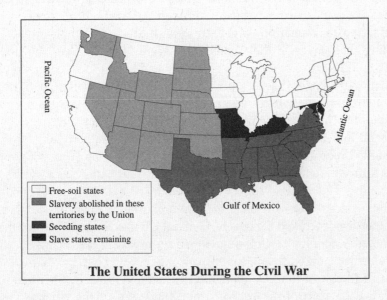

The United States During the Civil War

ERA: THE CIVIL WAR

1861 TO 1865

Secession from the Union

When Lincoln was elected, **South Carolina** proclaimed that its interests would not be represented in the new government and seceded from the Union. Very soon after, six other southern states (Alabama, Florida, Georgia, Louisiana, Mississippi, and Texas) also withdrew. These states formed the **Confederate States of America** and elected **Jefferson Davis** as their president. The Confederates seized all southern U.S. military locations, except Fort Sumter and Fort Pickens. Although some abolitionists cheered the departure of the Southern states, most Northerners wanted to **preserve the Union**. President Buchanan (Lincoln had not yet taken office) disagreed with the secession but did nothing to stop it.

As president, Lincoln declared the secession illegal and was determined not to lose the two remaining U.S. military sites in the South. He sent munitions to **Fort Sumter** and the Union's military leaders announced to the Confederates that they would have to acknowledge the authority of the federal government. If they wanted Fort Sumter, they would have to take it by force. **The Civil War** officially began when the Confederacy attacked Fort Sumter in April of 1861. Fort Sumter fell to the Confederates and Lincoln declared an "insurrection" in the Southern states that continued for four savage years—the bloodiest war in U.S. history.

War goals and battles

Believe it!

Harriet Beecher Stowe succeeded in spreading abolitionist (anti-slavery) ideas throughout America and the world when she wrote *Uncle Tom's Cabin*, a novel about the cruelty of slavery.

At first, the Civil War was fought not to free the slaves but to preserve the Union. Lincoln's primary objective was to defeat the Confederate forces and destroy their war-making capacities. Midway through the war, Lincoln announced the **Emancipation Proclamation**, largely to squelch divided opinions in the North. By stating that slaves in the Confederacy were "forever free," he hoped to strengthen the North's moral claim to victory and to employ the uprising slaves to military advantage. Indeed, upon this national proclamation, half a million slaves fled the plantations to the North. Lincoln also hoped to gain European support for the Union's cause with the Emancipation Proclamation.

General Robert E. Lee, the most prominent of the Southern military leaders, invaded the Union at **Gettysburg**. The mission failed, giving Lincoln an opportunity for a forceful defamation of the Confederacy. This battle was a turning point in the conflict. Union naval superiority led to a successful blockade of southern ports; the objective was to isolate the South and cut it off from supplies. This "starvation" tactic worked effectively. **General Ulysses S. Grant** became the foremost military leader for the Union and urged aggressive attacks on the South. Two decisive battles marked the defeat of the Confederacy. First, in what was called **Sherman's March to the Sea**, the Union General, **William T. Sherman**, cut an eight-mile-wide path of destruction from Tennessee to the Atlantic Coast of Savannah. He destroyed civilian property and everything in sight in order to "break the will" of the Confederate states. Grant then fought Lee's forces in Virginia and finally forced Lee to surrender at Appomatox in April of 1865.

ERA: RECONSTRUCTION

RIGHT AFTER THE CIVIL WAR

As you have heard and read before, the Civil War was a profoundly devastating event in the history of America. It grew out of, and deepened, bitter rifts between the North and the South, upsetting the social and economic structure of the entire country and leaving millions of Americans dead (it resulted in more American casualties than all the casualties from all other American wars combined).

Lincoln's plan vs. the Radical Republicans

Once it seemed certain that the North would win the Civil War, Lincoln devised a **plan of moderation** to deal with the South and their secession from the Union. That is, he wanted to "forgive and forget" as quickly as possible and allow the South to reenter the Union with relative speed and without harsh punishment. His plan was called the **10 percent plan**, because it allowed any state to reenter the Union if 10 percent of its voters took a loyalty oath to the Union. But his plan never got very far. A group of congressmen, known as the **Radical Republicans**, favored strong punishment for the South coupled with a long process of reunification.

Lincoln was assassinated before any of the Reconstruction plans got underway. **Andrew Johnson** succeeded him and, although he agreed with Lincoln's policies of moderation, he did not have Lincoln's political clout. Therefore, he was not an effective proponent of moderation. The Radical Republicans emerged as the most powerful group in the formulation of Reconstruction policy. With its influence in Congress, this group passed the **Reconstruction Acts** over the veto of President Johnson. These acts established the laws and procedures for the reinstatement of former Confederate states into the Union. The conflict between Johnson and Congress was so intense that **Congress impeached Johnson**, or brought him to trial. Johnson was acquitted, but only by one vote.

Civil rights: Good news/Bad news

For newly emancipated slaves, Reconstruction brought good news and bad. The good news was that the **Thirteenth Amendment**, which prohibited slavery, was passed. The bad news was that Southerners passed the **Black Codes**, rules which restricted blacks from many rights of citizenship. To nullify the Black Codes, Congress ratified the **Fourteenth and Fifteenth Amendments**, which strengthened the right of blacks to vote, and conferred citizenship and equal treatment before the law upon blacks. In addition, Congress passed—over Johnson's veto—a civil rights act which essentially stated the equal protection rights of the Fourteenth Amendment. But the amendments were not very effective. White Southerners used other methods to dissuade blacks from exercising their right to vote, including violence and intimidation from groups like the **Ku Klux Klan**, a **literacy test** (that many blacks could not pass because they had been denied an education under slavery), a **poll tax** (that many blacks could not afford to pay), prohibitive property requirements, and a **"grandfather clause"** that permitted any man to vote whose grandfather had voted. With the grandfather clause, uneducated or poor whites could vote, whereas uneducated or poor blacks, whose grandfathers had been slaves, could not.

Economics

Ending slavery was not just a moral issue for the South, but a serious economic issue. Slavery was the foundation of the plantation system. When the landowners lost their free labor, economic policies and procedures had to change. Large landowners divided up their land and "rented" it to black and white tenant farmers under the **sharecropper system**. The tenant farmer worked the plot of land and then paid half of his crop to the landowner as rent. He also usually owed the owner or a merchant some further portion for supplies and seed. As you might imagine, this system wasn't very profitable for the tenant farmer.

Pop Quiz

Q: If you had to answer a question about one of the facts on this page, and you didn't know the answer, what would you do?

Pop Quiz

A: Identify the Era that the question refers to, attack the answer choices, eliminate any anti-Era answers, and GUESS, GUESS, GUESS!

The weakening of the agricultural base in the South also opened the possibility for **increased industrialization** which had already begun in the North.

ERA: WESTWARD EXPANSION

1850 TO 1900: OVERLAPS THE ERAS OF SECTIONAL STRIFE, THE CIVIL WAR, AND RECONSTRUCTION

People on the move

This Era followed on the heels of the land purchases of the 1820s and 1840s. Western Expansion was fueled by the ideology of **Manifest Destiny**, which, as you read in the section on regional strife, held that America had a God-given right to expand from one ocean to the other, regardless of who was already living there (such as Native Americans). Two specific events really opened up the West and got all those people moving. First, the **Gold Rush of 1849** offered a strong economic incentive to get to "California or bust!" Second, the **Compromise of 1850** allowed the annexation of California as a free state.

The first industry of the West was **mining**, in which settlers tried to get rich quick by extracting precious minerals (gold was only one of them) from the ground. **Boomtowns** arose wherever mineral deposits were found. But these places often became **ghost towns** when the mines dried up. After the mining resources ran out, **cattle raising** and **farming** became profitable enterprises in the West. The large areas of flat grassland were suitable to both of these industries. The farmers and ranchers often violently competed for resources. In the end, the farmers, aided by government land gifts called **homesteads**, dominated most of the western lands.

Of course, the **Native Americans** continued to be a problem for the land- and resource-hungry settlers. In the 1880s, the U.S. government took a split position in dealing with the Native American tribes: the Department of the Interior supported some form of Native American independence through a reservation system, while the Department of War actively sought to rid the frontier of the "enemy." About this time, Helen Hunt Jackson wrote a humanitarian report, *A Century of Dishonor*, which exposed the inadequate reservation system. This spurred a mild reform movement which resulted in the **Dawes Act**. The act offered land and citizenship to the heads of Indian families in order to "civilize" them (that is, make them adopt white ways), but it also resulted in a loss to Indians of millions of additional acres. Its effect was to open more land for the settlers. The **Burke Act** tried to rectify the problems of the Dawes Act, but it wasn't very effective either.

Farmers' grievances

One inescapable condition of agricultural production is the law of **supply and demand**. The more efficient farming methods become, the more crops grow. But a large supply brings the cost of the crops down, often to prices so low that farmers cannot make a living. A farmer can also be caught in a **cycle of debt**. He

Common Sense POE

Q: The spirit of Manifest Destiny and westward expansion encompassed which of the following?
What do you think of this answer choice?
(C) Assimilation of Native American people into various aspects of frontier society.

borrows money to buy seed, machinery, and supplies, hoping that a good crop will enable him to pay the debts and make a little extra for living expenses. But if the farmer doesn't get a good crop, he has to borrow again for next year, thereby getting even deeper into debt. These problems faced by western farmers led to the **coinage debate**.

Basically, farmers felt like they were providing an invaluable service to the country, but they did not earn a decent wage for their hard labor. **The Grange** was the first large-scale organization of farmers; Grangers soon gained political power in the West. As explained above, farmers were in constant debt; therefore, they supported the production of more money. But such a monetary policy causes **inflation**, because the more dollars that circulate in society, the more merchants raise their prices (including the prices of farm supplies). In other words, the more dollars there are, the less they're worth. As prices go up, farmers demand that the government print even more money. It's a vicious cycle. Money could be produced by printing paper dollars, each of which would be backed by a gold dollar in the U.S. Treasury (a **gold standard**), or **by coining silver money**. The gold standard was the safest form, but it would limit the amount of dollars in circulation. Grangers therefore opposed this policy. Some farmers went so far as to call for the printing of **greenbacks**, or paper dollars that were not backed by anything but the credit of the government. They formed the **Greenback party**, but most farmers favored the more moderate, still inflationary, silver standard. They requested the **free and unlimited coinage of silver**. For years the government vacillated between wholly rejecting silver coinage and appeasing the farmers by buying silver.

In the 1870s and 1880s, a new political group called the Populist party (or People's party) emerged and campaigned for many farmers' issues, advocating a **silver standard of 16 to 1** (16 silver ounces to 1 gold ounce). The Populist party came to be a working man's party, as it sought the support of wage laborers of the industrial Northeast. Although the group seemed radical at the time, many of its policies, such as graduated income tax, an eight-hour work day, a national post office, the direct election of U.S. Senators, and a secret ballot, were accepted in the twentieth century. (Other tenets, such as nationalizing the telegraph system and seizing lands owned by corporations and "aliens" were never accepted.)

The height of the Populist movement was the **Election of 1896**, when both the Populists and the Democrats nominated **William Jennings Bryan** as their candidate. At the Democratic convention, Bryan made a famous and impassioned speech in favor of the silver standard saying, "You shall not press down upon the brow of labor this crown of thorns, you shall not crucify mankind on this cross of gold." Bryan's opponent was the Republican industrialist, **William McKinley**; the ideological difference in the campaign was clear. Bryan was the pro-farmer, pro-labor candidate with strong support in the West and the South, whereas McKinley was the pro-business choice with strong support in the North. McKinley won the election and Bryan's loss served to demoralize the farmer and labor movements.

Common Sense POE

A: Trash that answer choice! Westward expansion meant getting rid of the Indians to make room for pioneer settlers. Some people wanted to squeeze the remaining Indian tribes onto reservations and some wanted to eliminate them altogether. Any answer choice that describes positive action toward Native Americans during the nineteenth century is probably wrong.

ERA: THE INDUSTRIAL REVOLUTION

1865 TO THE EARLY TWENTIETH CENTURY

Following the Civil War, many factors contributed to the rise of industrialization and manufacturing. Remember these important ones: **abundant natural resources**, **large labor supply** (ex-soldiers, freed slaves, immigrants, women, and children), **improved transportation** (railroads), and other **new technologies**.

Big business

The term "big business" refers to the large corporations that first developed as a result of industrialization. While it was generally believed that free competition in the marketplace produced fair prices for consumers, corporations were interested in **maximizing their profits** (which often meant maintaining unfair prices) and saw competition as hurtful to them. So, to reduce competition with other big businesses, "captains of industry" would get together and set prices for the industry, thus forming a **monopoly** or a **trust**.

As industrialization spread, two prominent attitudes contributed to the popular support of big business. One was the economic theory of **laissez-faire**, which roughly means, "let them do what they want." The idea is that government has no right to interfere with private enterprise and should follow a "hands-off" policy in dealing with businesses and their activities. But despite its official non-interference policy, the government gave them considerable economic support through **grants of land, loans, and high tariffs**. (A tariff adds money to the price of a competitive imported good, thus allowing American producers to keep their prices higher than they would if the prices on imports were lower.)

The second idea that contributed to businessmen's stature was the theory of **social Darwinism**. Like Darwin's biological evolutionary theory, this social ideology maintained that life was a struggle in which only the fittest would and should survive. Wealthy businessmen were seen as the embodiment of "the fittest." This rationale was used against social reform, because it maintained that those who lived in poverty deserved their plight (they were "unfit") and that reformers were countering the "natural order."

Remember that **railroads** were big back then, and their owners were deeply involved in corruption and political manipulation. It was crucial to everyone to be able to move goods and people across the nation, and the railroad owners were quick to take advantage of the situation. Eventually, the railroad industry became one of the first businesses to be regulated.

Regulation and anti-trust legislation

By around the 1880s, voters—chafing under an unbridled laissez-faire policy—began to call on the government for help. Small producers complained that big businesses were pushing them out of the market, farmers complained about increased transportation prices, and consumers demanded protection from high prices and the restoration of free, or non-monopolistic, trade. Anti-trust laws were passed at first by state legislatures, and later by the federal government. But political corruption often made it very difficult to enforce any restrictions on business interests.

If your head hurts from cramming facts, take a step back and look at the big picture. If you have a good sense of what happened in a particular era, then don't sweat it. Whether you remember one factoid or another won't make or break your score.

A **trust** is the collective control of an industry by a small group of separate corporations working together. A **monopoly** is the control of an entire industry by a single corporation.

To regulate the railroads, some states set **maximum rate laws**, establishing the highest price a railroad could charge. Congress initially declared those laws unconstitutional. About a decade later, in response to an increasingly louder public outcry, the federal government passed its first legislation to control the actions of business, the **Interstate Commerce Act**, which forbade railroads from forming monopolistic price agreements and outlawed some of their discriminatory pricing practices. This act proved hard to enforce.

The **Sherman Antitrust Act**, the one piece of antitrust regulation you have to remember, made it illegal for any business to restrain trade by trust or conspiracy. But, for around a decade or so of the law's existence, the government did not, or could not (the act was vaguely worded), aggressively enforce the provisions. None of the U.S. presidents of the time were willing to strongly oppose business interests.

Organized labor

As mentioned above, the industrial revolution could never have taken place without the large supply of labor available to business for a relatively low price. The term "organized labor," refers to the groups or **unions** that tried to represent the interests of workers as they bargained for higher wages and better working conditions. As business and industry grew, so did these labor unions. Some influential unions were the **Knights of Labor**, the **American Federation of Labor (AFL)**, led by **Samuel Gompers**, and the **Industrial Workers of the World (IWW)**, often referred to as "Wobblies," a militant anti-capitalist group. Often the conflicts between labor and management resulted in strikes and boycotts, as dissatisfied, often exploited workers walked off the job. Most people sympathized with the individual grievances of workers but were often scared by the sometimes violent repercussions of organized labor's strikes and protests.

The **Haymarket Riot** is one historical protest that ended in violence. At a mass meeting organized to protest police treatment of striking workers (officers had killed two striking workers the day before), someone threw a bomb, killing several policemen and injuring many more. The police charged the crowd, killing even more people. In the end, labor leaders were blamed, and some who weren't even there were convicted of inciting the riot. The result was a sharp decrease in any public sympathy for union interests and an increase in fear and skepticism towards the union groups. (Public antipathy for immigrants, who made up a notable percentage of union membership, was also used by the police to whip up anti-union sentiment.)

> "Year by year man's liberties are trampled underfoot at the bidding of corporations and trusts, rights are invaded and laws are perverted."
> —Samuel Gompers, leader of the American Federation of Labor

ERA: INDUSTRIALISM AND POLITICS

1865 TO 1900: OVERLAPS WITH THE INDUSTRIAL REVOLUTION

Following the Civil War, with the assassination of Lincoln and the impeachment proceedings against the presidency of Andrew Johnson, the nation experienced a serious leadership crisis. Many factors contributed to the political and social chaos, including factional disagreements among and within political parties, the movement and resettlement of thousands of people, and the rapid rise of big business and industrialization. Before we explore the major events, let's quickly review the presidents of this time and their actions.

Scandalous presidents

Ulysses S. Grant was the general who led the Union Army to victory in the Civil War, but he was inexperienced as a politician or statesman. His tenure as president was riddled with scandal and corruption. Among the worst scandals of the time were "Black Friday," "The Whiskey Ring," and "The Belknap Scandal."

The **Election of 1876** produced the most disputed voting results of any election before or since. Demonstrating a clear weakness in the electoral college system, Samuel J. Tilden won the popular vote (he got more actual votes) but did not have a majority of electoral college votes. A compromise, sometimes called the Compromise of 1877 or the **Hayes-Tilden compromise**, was devised where Rutherford B. Hayes was given the presidency, and Tilden supporters, many of whom were southern Democrats, were promised the **removal of Federal troops** from the South. This withdrawal marked the end of Reconstruction, and, without the military presence, the white majority in the South further disenfranchised the freed blacks.

After Hayes' term in office, the first administration of **Grover Cleveland** signaled an end to many of the scandals that had plagued the government. He supported measures to improve the workings of the government, including revitalizing the idea of public service. During his reelection campaign, he argued strongly that tariffs should be lowered. Recall that tariffs are taxes placed on imports; the foreign manufacturers who make these imports then have to raise their prices to cover the tax. American manufacturers who don't pay the tariffs, could therefore keep their prices higher than they would otherwise but lower than the prices of the imports, without worrying about lower-priced foreign goods. These tariffs are called **protective tariffs**, because they protect American businesses from having to compete with potentially lower-priced foreign goods. One effect of these tariffs is higher prices to American consumers. Cleveland lost the next election in a close race to Benjamin Harrison.

The most interesting thing about Harrison's administration was **William McKinley** (you read about him in the section on westward expansion), a powerful, pro-business Republican U.S. Representative. He guided the legislation of the **McKinley tariff** that raised taxes on many goods by about 50 percent. Some consumer goods were on a "free list" which remained untaxed, but voters were still outraged by the policy. This was one cause of the Democratic landslide of the next election cycle.

In a history-making election, Cleveland was reelected to a second term over Harrison in 1892. This time his luck ran out: Harrison had dropped an economic depression in his lap. **The Panic of 1893** lasted for most of Cleveland's second term.

In the United States presidential elections, majority rules—usually. In 1876, Rutherford B. Hayes was elected president by winning a majority of the electoral college votes. Unfortunately, Samuel J. Tilden won the popular vote, meaning more people actually voted for him. The situation was resolved through the Hayes-Tilden compromise. (Hayes became president.)

McKinley and imperialism

The election of 1896 was notable for several reasons, some of which were mentioned in the Era of western expansion. Cleveland, blamed for the Panic of 1893, was not chosen to represent the Democrats in the presidential race. Instead, the farmers of the South and the West forged an alliance with the laborers of the East in support of a young, dynamic candidate, **William Jennings Bryan** (you read about him in the section on western expansion, and saw this election from another perspective). McKinley ran with strong Republican support despite the tariff fiasco. In the end, McKinley and pro-business interests of the Republicans won the presidency.

The **Spanish-American War** was a war that truly did not have to happen. Cuba's insurrection against Spain was the primary event leading to the war. At first, Americans wanted to stay out of the conflict (although they supported Cuban independence). Both Cleveland and McKinley supported peaceful platforms. But tabloid newspaper accounts (**"yellow press"**) of the war falsified stories and photographs of Spanish "atrocities," which helped to turn public opinion toward favoring a war. One famous incident was **the sinking of the** *Maine*, a U.S. battleship. An explosion left 260 Americans dead, but the cause or responsible agent was never found. Although it could have been an accident, or the act of a Cuban revolutionary, the press " tried and convicted" Spain of bombing the *Maine*.

McKinley issued a warning and strict conditions to Spain soon after the event. Although Spain accepted McKinley's terms, Congress had already moved to mobilize for war, and thus, war broke out. The war itself was relatively brief. The U.S. was well-armed and won the war with relatively few casualties. Military highlights of the war include a strong Navy, led by Commodore Dewey, and the **Rough Riders**, a cavalry unit, led by **Theodore Roosevelt** in **the Battle of San Juan Hill**. The Treaty of Paris ended the war. Spain gave up all claims to Cuba, which emerged independent, and the U.S. acquired Puerto Rico, Guam, and the Philippines.

Under McKinley, the U.S. continued its **expansionist policies** and became more involved in international affairs. There are two other events that the test may ask about concerning this period, and they both concern our **trade relationship with China**. At this time, foreign powers (Germany, Japan, Great Britain, France, and Italy) tried to maintain **spheres of influence**, or geographical areas over which they had special influence, in China. To crack Europe's monopoly, John Hay, the U.S. Secretary of State, orchestrated the **Open Door Policy,** which established the joint right of these nations to trade with and within China. (Think "Open Door" as in "the door was open to everybody.") Then, within China, the **Boxer Rebellion** broke out. The Boxers were a Chinese nationalist group that wanted to get rid of all the foreigners. Led by the U.S., an armed force of several European nations came in to suppress the Boxers, restore the rule of the Peking dynasty, and ensure that China would be open to U.S. and European trade. Hay was very influential in restoring "order" in China; some foreign powers had wanted to partition the country into colonies based on the spheres of influences.

ERA: THE PROGRESSIVE ERA

1900 TO 1920

After decades of political scandals and big-business corruption, people were ready for a change. The reform movement of the early twentieth century, or the **Progressive Era**, commenced. **Presidents Theodore Roosevelt, William Taft, and Woodrow Wilson** were very powerful in directing the reform movement, but social factors also influenced this time period.

Literary muckrakers

A group of writers called **muckrakers** dedicated themselves to stirring public opinion by exposing the corruption of politicians and businessmen. By informing people of the widespread wrongdoings, they were influential in getting popular support of reform platforms. Among the important muckraking authors were **Ida M. Tarbell**, whose *History of the Standard Oil Company* condemned the monopolistic tactics of that corporation, and **Upton Sinclair**, whose novel *The Jungle* exposed unsafe conditions in Chicago's meatpacking plants.

True or False?

Q: A great deal of corruption and dishonesty in American politics and business came to an end at the beginning of the twentieth century.

The continuing struggle: Women's rights, blacks' rights, and the "New" immigrants

Suffrage means the right to vote, and the **Women's suffrage movement** sought to gain that right for female citizens. (Although a constitutional amendment extending voting rights to women was sent to Congress in the 1880s, the **Nineteenth Amendment** wasn't passed until 1919). You should remember two feminists in particular, **Susan B. Anthony** and **Elizabeth Cady Stanton**. During this time, increased numbers of women began to work outside the home and, in some cases, to pursue higher education. The majority of these women, though, worked either as domestic servants or in factories for wages equaling about half of a man's wage.

By the turn of the century, whatever civil rights advances blacks had made in the Reconstruction Era had vanished and the ruling system was again **"white supremacy."** **Racial segregation** (division on the basis of race) was legalized under what were called the **Jim Crow laws**. A famous Supreme Court decision, *Plessy v. Ferguson*, ruled that laws requiring "separate but equal" facilities for whites and blacks were constitutional. The facilities that were justified under this ruling were separate, but they were anything but equal.

Despite this institutional oppression, many strong black leaders emerged during the Progressive Era. The **National Association for the Advancement of Colored People (NAACP)** and the **National Urban League** were multiracial groups founded to combat racial discrimination. Within the black community, opinion was widely divided over which path to take in the pursuit of equal rights. **Booker T. Washington** advocated that blacks should refrain from "agitating" the white majority, and instead strive to achieve economic equality through job training and diligent work. He believed that once economic parity was achieved, political and social rights would follow. In contrast, **W.E.B. DuBois** (who helped to found the NAACP) argued that, while job training was beneficial, black people should aggressively demand political, social, and economic rights immediately.

He urged the "talented tenth" of the community to assume scholarly and leadership roles in the crusade for equality.

Between 1880 and 1920, America experienced its largest influx of immigrants ever. Twenty-four million people, mostly from southern and eastern Europe, moved to the U.S. The new immigrants settled in cities and dramatically changed the social, cultural, and economic landscape of the areas in which they lived.

Roosevelt and the Square Deal

The Roosevelt of this period was Teddy, (not to be confused with the later Roosevelt, Franklin Delano). **Teddy Roosevelt's** administration's platform was the **Square Deal**, which referred to the equal treatment and fairness he felt all Americans deserved.

As President, Roosevelt revived the regulations of business that had not been adequately enforced, like the Sherman Antitrust Act and the Interstate Commerce Act. An example of his influence was the **Northern Securities Case,** which broke up a strong railroad monopoly. Teddy Roosevelt was also an **environmental President**, favoring the establishment of the National Park system, advocating a system to manage the use of natural resources, and establishing the **National Conservation Commission**. The combination of the muckrakers' writings and Roosevelt's memories of the Spanish-American War (where the canned meat was literally more fatal than enemy bullets) stirred legislation to protect consumers and to safeguard food and drug packaging. This resulted in the **Pure Food and Drug Act** and the **Meat Inspection Act**.

Taft—Moving to the right

Roosevelt handpicked William Howard Taft as his successor. While Taft was certainly not as exciting or dynamic as Roosevelt, he did continue the legacy of reforms, especially in regard to railroad regulation. Taft, as President, tried to reconcile the liberal and conservative factions of the Republican party, but he leaned decidedly to the right. Taft's willingness to compromise, to the Progressives' dismay, was shown in his reaction to the Payne-Aldrich Tariff. A high tariff of about 57 percent had been in place since McKinley, and both Roosevelt and Taft sought to have it lowered. As you know, high tariffs result in higher prices for consumers. When the tariff bill was finally passed, tariffs were lowered only slightly. Taft still signed it. This told the public that Taft was no Roosevelt and he quickly began to lose support. Taft's most visible reforms were in governmental organization. He established the **graduated income tax** and created the Department of Labor and Commerce.

Aggressive foreign policy (Roosevelt and Taft)

Despite the renewed emphasis on domestic problems, the U.S. had established itself as a world power and Roosevelt presented himself as an aggressive foreign-policy president. His motto was, "Speak softly, but carry a big stick." This came to be known as **"big-stick" diplomacy**.

Because of Pacific land acquisitions from the Spanish-American War, the U.S. felt it necessary to gain free access to the Pacific by sea. So, after a lot of negotiating, the U.S. set out to build the **Panama Canal** in a brand new county called Panama, which had been carved out of Colombia following an insurrec-

True or False?

A: True! During the Progressive Era (1900–1920), a group of journalists and writers known as muckrakers went about exposing all the nasty abuses of power and money that went on during the end of the nineteenth century. They stirred up public opinion and helped win public support for various social reforms.

tion. (Some historians believe the U.S. helped to foment the insurrection.) Our increased interests in the Panama Canal zone, the Caribbean, and all of Latin America spurred Roosevelt to reinterpret the Monroe Doctrine to justify the United States' right to intervene in the domestic and foreign affairs of this area. The doctrine, called the **Roosevelt Corollary**, didn't win us any friends in the region. Far from being satisfied with playing politics in Latin America, Teddy was highly involved in many foreign policy issues pertaining to Europe and its holdings, and he helped negotiate the end of the Russo-Japanese War.

Taft continued Roosevelt's foreign policy activism, but he did so in a style much more suited to his temperament. Instead of openly aggressive tactics, Taft used economic incentives to win influence in Latin America and elsewhere. This came to be known as **"dollar diplomacy."** With this policy, Taft hoped to increase U.S. trade to these regions, stabilize their governments, and maintain the balance of power among U.S. interests and the interests of other foreign nations in these regions.

Woodrow Wilson

As noted above, Roosevelt and Taft were reformers, but Wilson outdid them. While the earlier presidents wanted to regulate trusts and unfair business practices, Wilson wanted to abolish trusts and do away with all business privileges and corruption. He was also opposed to the protective tariffs that had been a staple of Republican administrations. The **Underwood Act**, passed shortly after Wilson came into office, was the first tariff designed to bring in revenue rather than protect businesses. The effects of this bill are hard to measure, since World War I started soon after its enactment and international trade changed dramatically.

Two major pieces of legislation emerged to regulate business from Wilson's first administration. First, the **Federal Trade Commission** was established to prevent businesses from misrepresenting their products (i.e., selling a product called "Mrs. Jones's Beef Stew" when the soup had no beef in it) and causing unfair competition. Second, the **Clayton Antitrust Act** was designed to fill in the gaps of the Sherman Antitrust Act and give more power to the courts in regulating business monopolies. Even with these measures, business interests remained very powerful and often escaped the rule of law. Wilson also supported the rights of labor and increased aid to farmers.

Banking reform was established under Wilson with the **Federal Reserve Act**. Essentially, the act made credit more flexible so that money could be more easily transferred to different parts of the country. Also, it made currency itself more elastic so that the supply of money could be altered—made available for circulation—to suit the borrowing needs of banks. The banks had lent out too much money (they overspeculated) to businesses that were failing. By gaining access to more credit, the banks hoped to forestall future "panics."

ERA: WORLD WAR I

1914 to 1920

For the SAT II, the events that lead up to a war and the peace plans that follow afterwards are more important than what actually happened during the fighting.

War broke out in Europe in 1914, and because of a lot of secret alliances among the European nations, most were drawn into the fight within a few months. Britain, France, and Russia led the **Allies**; Germany and Austria-Hungary led the **Central Powers**. Wilson and many Americans desperately wanted to stay out of the war and maintain **U.S. neutrality**. Circumstances, however, made this increasingly difficult to do.

Although Wilson tried to mediate between the Allies and the Central Powers with calls of **"Peace without victors,"** no one in Europe was willing to listen. American popular sentiment rested more with the Allies, a tendency further exaggerated by aggressive **German policies of submarine warfare**. Basically, Germany felt that it could destroy any ship within the war zones surrounding Great Britain and Ireland, whereas we felt that they had to, under international law, treat neutral and merchant ships differently. The **sinking of the *Lusitania***, a luxury passenger liner, was an example of German submarine tactics—it was sunk without a warning or search of the ship. The incident killed 1,198 people, 128 of them American, and turned public opinion against Germany. A similar, though less severe incident, involving a French passenger ship, the *Sussex*, further worried the U.S. When the U.S. issued an ultimatum to Germany, they responded with the *Sussex* **pledge** that they would not sink commercial vessels without warning or without attempting to save human lives. Though things cooled for a while, these acts of aggression aroused concern in the U.S. over its preparedness to enter war if necessary.

In the election of 1916, Wilson ran on the slogan: "He kept us out of war," and won despite a deep national rift over whether or not the U.S. should enter the conflict.

In early 1917, Germany announced that it would resume its unrestricted submarine warfare in war zones and, soon after, torpedoed five American merchant ships, killing all hands. Also, the **Zimmerman Telegram**, a diplomatic message from Germany to Mexico, surfaced, which suggested that if an alliance between them was made, and if the United States entered the war, Germany would help Mexico "reconquer [its] lost territory in New Mexico, Texas, and Arizona." Needless to say, this last bit of info enraged the government. Wilson asked Congress to declare war on Germany in 1917.

Wilson did not want to portray America as a ruthless aggressor and his war message was colored with high moral aspirations. Notable mottoes called the war an effort to make the world **"safe for democracy"** and to forge **"a peace founded upon honor and justice."**

Peace negotiations

Although Wilson had been a spokesman for a fair peace agreement, it was very hard for the **victorious Allied Powers** to suppress their nationalistic objectives. Indeed, many of the Allied nations entered the war under the assumption that

Pop Quiz

Q: What was America's policy at the onset of both World War I and World War II?

victory would give them specific land gains. Wilson forwarded a plan that he proclaimed "the only possible program" for maintaining peace after the war. It was entitled the **Fourteen Points Plan**. (Guess why.) Many of the points dealt with reduced armaments, freedom of the seas, and other aspects of international relations. The fourteenth point was the most dramatic, calling for a "general association of nations" that would work to assure the political independence of all nations.

This association came to be known as the **League of Nations**. Wilson had trouble selling this plan not only to the nationalistic Allies, but also to the strongly Republican U.S. Congress. The Republican Senate was especially peeved because they felt he wrote his plan without due consultation with them.

Thus, the Fourteen Points did not fare well at the negotiations in Paris. The **Treaty of Versailles**, which set the terms of the peace, dealt a harsh and burdensome punishment to the Central Powers, mainly Germany. Initially, the treaty did establish a League of Nations, excluding the Central Powers and Communist Russia, and it was hoped by some that this body would lessen the force of the other, punitive aspects of the treaty. After Wilson's diplomatic struggles in Paris, he came home to even more trouble—the **U.S. Senate refused to ratify the Treaty**. It's a long and complicated story, but basically the Republicans in Congress did not like the idea of the League of Nations at all. The opposition was led by **Henry Cabot Lodge**. Wilson tried to appeal to the nation and gain popular support, but he fell ill during the process. (It probably wouldn't have made a difference even if he had remained healthy.) The United States' rejection caused further treaties to be drawn, none of which mandated a League of Nations, and by this time, Warren G. Harding had reached the White House.

Pop Quiz

A: American policy was to stay out of it! The U.S. remained neutral at the beginning of both World Wars until certain events (the sinking of the *Lusitania* and the Zimmerman Telegram in World War I, and the bombing of Pearl Harbor in World War II) caused them to get involved.

ERA: THE ROARING TWENTIES

1920 TO 1929

Conservatives in office

After the war and the post-war disagreements, the Republican party called for a **"return to normalcy"** and won landslide victories. Normalcy, however, meant a return to the corruption of **powerful big businesses**, a rollback of many Progressive reforms, and an increasing disregard of international ties in favor of **isolationism**.

Warren G. Harding was happy to let the Republican Congress and his cabinet lead the nation, a stance that resulted in scandals as his compatriots betrayed him and the country. One major scandal to remember is the **Teapot Dome scandal**, which involved the Secretary of the Interior taking bribes to allow certain companies oil-drilling rights. Harding died of a stroke as these allegations and others were coming to light.

Calvin Coolidge, who succeeded Harding, quickly worked to cooperate with investigations of corruption, thus gaining public admiration for his personal integrity. His deft political skill plus the general prosperity of the time lead

Coolidge to an easy victory in the following presidential election. The Coolidge Administration was attuned to the needs of American industry and commerce. When Coolidge chose not to run for reelection, **Herbert Hoover**, his Secretary of Commerce, was nominated to run. Again, the Republicans won easily and Hoover became president. He was seen as a man of efficiency and skill who would run the government like a well-oiled machine.

Roaring restrictions (Or: Let it all hang out but do it my way)

The 1920s were largely a reaction to the Progressive Era and World War I. Liberal reforms and restraints on businesses in the previous decade were dismissed as radical, and the ideals of Wilson and his peace plan were cast as restrictive of personal freedom. People seemed to have shifted their interests to personal gratification, preferring to "kick up their heels" and have fun. Also, this was the decade of **Prohibition of alcohol**, which generated a vast market in illegal liquor. The prevalence of bootlegging and speakeasies demonstrated the irreverence of most people to the moralism of government. The attitude was that business and people should be able to do what they wished without government interference.

The loosening social structure led to many new freedoms for women, who had recently gained the right to vote. Black Americans also gained some social respect as they returned from military service in World War I and some economic advantages from relatively high paying jobs in the northern war industries. During the war, tens of thousands of blacks migrated from the South to the North, seeking these higher paying jobs. A movement of **black nationalism** began under the leadership of **Marcus Garvey**, who believed in worldwide black unity. Not believing in racial integration, he supported a back-to-Africa program. Though his program never succeeded, his personal appeal and persuasiveness helped to increase black pride.

The post-war period was also an era of many restrictions, especially on immigration and political activism. Afraid of an impending human flood washing over the U.S. following the destruction of Europe in the war, Congress instituted **immigration quotas** that allowed only a small fraction of people to enter America from Europe (immigration from Asia had already been prohibited). Although these measures were meant to be temporary, the quotas remained intact until the 1960s; these quotas would have a measurable effect on people trying to escape from persecution in Europe in the mid-1930s.

The new stance of **American isolationism** also led to a very strict definition of what was "American" and what was good for America. Labor unions and other progressive groups were often painted as communist (the Russian Revolution took place in 1917), which fanned the flames of an intense anti-radical and **anti-communist** sentiment. Know two terms that exemplify this mania: **the Red Scare**, the general panic that dangerous communists might be lurking under every bed, and **the Palmer Raids**, in which Attorney General A. Mitchell Palmer conducted raids, often violating constitutional rights, to arrest suspected communists. Also, in response to the increased opportunities for blacks as well as the xenophobic aura of the time (Catholics, Jews, and foreigners were added to the hate list), the **Ku Klux Klan's** membership soared throughout the 1920s.

Another famous example of the cultural clashes of the 1920s is the John T. Scopes trial, or the **Scopes Monkey Trial**. The case revolved around the issue of teaching Darwin's theory of evolution in schools. But it tested the divide between fundamentalist Christian beliefs and current scientific beliefs. William Jennings Bryan argued the fundamentalist case, while **Clarence Darrow** defended Scopes, the teacher. Although Scopes lost the case, weaknesses were exposed in the fundamentalist position that led to its popular decline and growing respect for the tenets of modern science.

Cultural renaissance

Despite, or maybe because of, many social restrictions, this period is considered a **golden age** for many American art forms. Indeed, many American artists took up residence as **expatriates** in Europe to enjoy a more liberal and intellectual climate. The writer Gertrude Stein characterized these expatriates as the **"lost generation."** Black Americans and their artistic works greatly added to this cultural wellspring; their contributions are recognized as **the Harlem Renaissance**. Jazz, often touted as the "only truly American art form," flourished at this time. The following chart presents a few of the key cultural works of the Era.

Pop Quiz

A: Choices (A), (B), (D), and (E) are all associated with the 1920s. Choice (C) is out of place because the Era following World War I was a period of American Isolationism, which meant we didn't want to get involved with problems in foreign countries.

Art Form	Artist	Work
Novels (works of realism and naturalism	F. Scott Fitzgerald Ernest Hemingway Sinclair Lewis	The Great Gatsby The Sun Also Rises Babbit
Poetry (realistic) (experimental)	Robert Frost T.S. Eliot	Collected Poems The Waste Land
Drama (realistic)	Eugene O'Neill	Strange Interlude
Music	Louis Armstrong Bessie Smith	jazz blues

ERA: THE GREAT DEPRESSION AND THE NEW DEAL

THE 1930S TO WORLD WAR II

The crash

The decade from 1919 to 1929 was one of stunning growth and prosperity. The three Republican administrations, led by Andrew Mellon in the Treasury Department, greatly favored business, giving it tax breaks and supporting high protective tariffs. Businesses boomed, buying on credit became widespread, and a great number of **highly speculative (i.e., risky) investments** were being made on the stock market. Everything seemed fine until it all ended on **Black Tuesday, October 29, 1929**, when the stock market crashed and about $30 billion worth of stocks were wiped out.

Thus began the period known as **the Great Depression**, and its immediate results were widespread **unemployment**, widespread **business failures**, a drastic drop in the Gross National Product and in the personal income of almost everyone. Hoover genuinely believed that market mechanisms and **individual initiative** (entrepreneurship) would pull the nation out of the depression, so he did not enact much government assistance for the problem.

After a couple of years, Hoover did pass a bill to establish the **Reconstruction Finance Corporation (RFC)**, which was designed to lend government money to banks and other private business enterprises. Later that year, the **Relief and Construction Act** was passed to give communities emergency relief. These actions were too little, too late. **Hoovervilles**, communities of rundown shacks where thousands of homeless squatted, became the symbol of the Hoover administration's failures to counter the effects of the Great Depression.

To be fair to Hoover, the market crash was an event unlike any other in the nation's history; other "depressions" were short-lived and past experience had backed Hoover's incorrect belief that "prosperity [was] right around the corner."

Pop Quiz
Q: What was the New Deal?

Franklin D. Roosevelt and the New Deal

If prosperity contributed to the carefree and laissez-faire attitudes of the 1920s, the Great Depression, by contrast, caused many people to reconsider the role of government. They were quite ready for the government to take some responsibility for the economic well-being of the nation and its people. This dramatic shift in public opinion was punctuated by the **election of 1932**, as the new Democratic President **Franklin D. Roosevelt (FDR)** ushered in an unprecedented era of reform. (He easily won reelection to a second term, so you can think of 1932 to 1940 as all one Era under the New Deal.)

Relief, recovery, reform

The three R's: That's the key to thinking about the New Deal.

During his first **Hundred Days** in office, a time frame he set for himself, FDR promised quick work to do something about the state of the nation. He wanted to provide **relief** in the form of money, jobs, or loans; he wanted to spur **recovery** by passing legislation to assist business and agriculture; and he wanted to **reform** banking and other economic institutions to make them more stable. Regardless of the effect of his programs, he projected strong leadership and instilled in the country a new confidence. His skill as an orator and a charismatic politician may have helped the country as much as his specific programs. His famous words at his inauguration were, "You have nothing to fear but fear itself."

The **New Deal** marked the first time that the government seriously introduced elements of a modified **planned economy**, a system in which the government helps to influence economic developments, rather than just letting the market system determine everyone's fortune. The theories of **John Maynard Keynes** were an important part of New Deal philosophy. He argued that the nation could "spend its way back to prosperity," with the government doing the spending, thereby countering the destructive effects of laissez-faire economics.

During the 1930s and 1940s, FDR established numerous economic programs; some failed while others succeeded. A few important ones are contained in the following chart, but you just need to remember that any legislation during this period dealt with trying to end the Depression and get people back on their feet economically.

	Program	Function
CCC	Civilian Conservation Corps	Provided work for unemployed young men.
NIRA	National Industrial Recovery Act (National Recovery Administration)	Established codes for fair competition; the idea was to keep prices down and employment up.
WPA (PWA)	Works Project Administration Public Works Administration	Both programs gave people jobs; some went to writers and artists, some for building roads and hospitals.
AAA	Agricultural Adjustment Act	Paid farmers to reduce their production, hoping this would bring higher prices for farm goods.
TVA	Tennessee Valley Authority	A government owned business to help produce and distribute electrical power services to a large number of people.

Pop Quiz

A: The New Deal was a series of reform, recovery, and relief programs begun by President Franklin D. Roosevelt during the 1930s to help Americans recover from the Great Depression.

FDR's banking reforms consisted of establishing the **Federal Reserve Board** to influence interest rates and therefore dampen inflation or spur growth; the **FDIC** to insure personal bank deposits; and the **Securities and Exchange Commission (SEC)** to regulate the trading of stocks and bonds. The administration also passed the first laws guaranteeing **minimum wage, unemployment insurance, and Social Security**.

Art in hard times

Art form/Artist	Importance
Novels	
John Steinbeck William Faulkner	Stories that focused on poverty and social injustice.
Modern Dance	
Martha Graham	Dance that focused on an outpouring of emotion with a minimal amount of staging and music.
Movies	The popularity of movies exploded. For a small sum, people could escape their troubles in glamorous fantasy.
Radio	Very popular as family entertainment. Approx. 90 percent of families owned a radio in 1940.

Know this book! The American History SAT II loves John Steinbeck's *The Grapes of Wrath*. It's about the migration of a family (the Joads) from their homestead in Oklahoma to California during the Great Depression.

Helped with some money from the WPA, writers, artists, and musicians produced numerous works of art at this time that reflected the stricken state of the country. Novels tended to stress the abject poverty of many Americans; movies and radio offered lighthearted distractions. Be familiar with a few of the cultural works of the time.

ERA: WORLD WAR II

1939 TO 1945

Things started to look bad in Europe around the mid-1930s. Hitler had risen to power in **Nazi Germany**, Italy was under the **fascist regime of Mussolini**, and the rest of the **Allied powers** and the U.S. were playing the wait-and-see game. Nobody, except maybe Hitler, wanted a replay of World War I, so compromises and negotiations took place even as the German and Italian aggressors (known as the **Axis Powers**) followed their own agenda, trampling many beneath their boots. In Germany and Poland, furthermore, Hitler began his policy of **genocide**, often referred to as the **Holocaust**, killing six million Jewish people and seven million other human beings, including Gypsies and homosexuals. Great Britain and France declared war on Germany in 1939. While the United States' sympathy was with the Allies, we remained neutral.

> "No matter how long it may take us to overcome this premeditated invasion, the American people, in their righteous might, will win through absolute victory."
> —President Franklin D. Roosevelt, speaking to Congress the day after the Japanese bombed Pearl Harbor.

Neutrality, at first

The ideal of isolation was still strongly held in the United States, and Congress initially took measures to avoid the problems that led up to our entry into World War I. The first **Neutrality Acts** (1935–37) mandated that weapons could not be sold, nor loans given, to the warring nations, and that U.S. citizens could not travel on the ships of countries at war. Later, in 1939, the act was revised to allow weapon sales on a **"cash and carry"** basis, meaning that friendly nations could come to the U.S. and buy supplies, so long as they shipped the weapons themselves, thereby avoiding placing U.S. ships at risk. Public opinion, it should be noted, was turning more towards helping the Allies win the war, but staying out of it ourselves. The **Lend-Lease Act** of 1941 expanded the power of the president to lend, lease, sell, exchange, or do whatever he wanted to get arms and supplies to nations that served the United States' best interests, namely the Allies.

Near this time, in 1940, Roosevelt ran for an unprecedented third term of his presidency, with the argument that it would be dangerous to switch leaders during a worldwide conflict. He won, but not by the large margins that he had previously enjoyed.

In 1941, Roosevelt met with Winston Churchill, the British Prime Minister, to discuss the Allied war aims. He also gave U.S. merchant ships carrying weapons the OK to shoot German submarines on sight—hardly typical of a nation at "peace." Isolationists in the U.S. were outraged, but the debate was soon put to rest.

During the late 1930s, Japan was a strong aggressor in the Pacific, having invaded China. When Japan joined the Axis powers in 1940, its aggression increased. On **December 7, 1941**, the "day that will live in infamy" as FDR noted, the

Japanese bombed Pearl Harbor. The nation was shocked and declared war on Japan. A few days later, Germany and Italy declared war on us, and we returned the declaration.

The home front

The United States had been preparing somewhat for the possibility of war, but the mobilization of forces, including weapons, soldiers, and other war materials after **Japan attacked Pearl Harbor** was phenomenal and the key to the Allied success. Once the U.S. government declared war, nearly everyone supported the war effort. The country's entire economic and social structure adapted to meet that effort. A few noteworthy events: **rationing** and price-fixing were accepted for meat, sugar, gasoline and other staples; **women went to work** at war factories by the thousands ("Rosie the Riveter" became a popular cultural icon), doing jobs that had previously been considered "men's work"; the sale of **war bonds** and a large scale revision of tax laws were instituted to finance the war. In the midst of the war came the Election of 1944, when Roosevelt was elected to a fourth term and **Harry S. Truman** became his vice president. A few months later, Roosevelt died in office and Truman led the nation to the conclusion of the war and into the next era.

War ends, peace talks begin

As with the other wars, it isn't necessary to remember the different battles, but you should know how the war ended and how peace negotiations were handled.

The war in Europe was over in May, 1945, as **Allied troops marched into Berlin** from both sides, the U.S. and Great Britain from the west, and the Soviet Union from the east. Hitler supposedly committed suicide upon hearing of his imminent defeat. The U.S. then wanted to speed up the defeat of Japan in the Pacific region. After issuing an ultimatum to Japan to surrender unconditionally, the **U.S. dropped an atomic bomb on Hiroshima**, then dropped another bomb, three days later, on **Nagasaki**. The two cities were obliterated and nearly a quarter of a million people were killed or wounded. Japan surrendered.

Even before the war was over, the Allied Powers set about forging an agreement concerning the would-be defeated powers of Germany and Japan. Three main issues were **occupation, prosecution of war criminals, and establishing peace treaties**. Still, the negotiations dragged on for several years, complicated by the tensions between the Western Allies and the Communist Soviet Union. This was shown most dramatically as the occupation of Germany was negotiated. A **divided Germany** emerged from the talks, with the **Federal Republic of Germany** as the Western-influenced sphere, and the **German Democratic Republic** as part of the Eastern bloc. The infamous **Nuremberg Tribunal** was held to prosecute high- and low-level Nazis for their war crimes, including international aggressions and their systematic attempts to exterminate the Jewish people. As for Japan, **General Douglas MacArthur** ruled the occupied nation and its territories until a U.S.-Japan peace treaty was signed in the early 1950s. On a positive note, through these many post-war conferences and negotiations, the **United Nations** was established in 1946 with representatives from fifty-one countries.

ERA: POST-WAR — COLD WAR

AFTER WORLD WAR II

Truman and the Fair Deal

Truman had some uncomfortable shoes to fill as he succeeded Roosevelt as president. Not only would it have been hard to match the charisma and personality of FDR, but many people, Republicans especially, felt that the Democrats had had an unnaturally long stay in the White House. So, even though Truman tried to continue the reforms of the New Deal, renamed as the **Fair Deal**, he met a lot of resistance from the Republican Congress. In fact, when the election of 1948 came around, everyone was convinced that Truman would lose, but he won by a tiny margin. In his victory, Truman felt vindicated and continued to push for reforms of education, health care, and civil rights. Still, the Republican Congress was powerful enough to block his efforts. In the next election, Truman chose not to run, and Republican moderate and World War II hero, **Dwight D. Eisenhower**, won the White House.

The Cold War abroad

Immediately following the world war (and the dropping of two atomic bombs), **tensions between the Western Allies and the Soviet Union** deepened. The term **Cold War** means that even though there was no fighting, relations between the nations were very hostile. In Europe, the Soviet Union controlled most of Eastern Europe, which was characterized as being **"behind the iron curtain."** The U.S. had good relations and influence among the Western European nations. The presence of atomic weapons was a strong impetus to keep passions cooled, since a war could mean worldwide nuclear annihilation, or Mutual Assured Destruction (MAD).

Basically, the Cold War represented deep mutual suspicion. The U.S. (and its allies) and the Soviet Union (and *its* allies) each viewed the other as trying to take over the world. In fact, both nations did become actively involved in the affairs of numerous other countries, supporting or opposing revolutions, funding and arming insurrections, and establishing "puppet governments."

Directly after World War II, Truman responded to the threat of the Soviet Union with a policy of **"containment"** that became known as the **Truman Doctrine**. This policy set the tone for the Cold War and pledged U.S. economic and military support to help "free peoples" resist the Soviet "aggression." Soon after, Truman's Secretary of State, George C. Marshall, argued that the best way to "protect" nations from succumbing to communism was to help them become economically and politically strong. The **Marshall Plan** provided grants and loans to war-torn European nations. It was targeted against "hunger, poverty, desperation, and chaos." Soon, this economic support helped bring Western Europe to a strong post-war recovery and aided their stiff opposition to communist expansion.

Another show of Western strength was the formation of **NATO** (North Atlantic Treaty Organization), which declared the twelve nations of Western Europe would stand together in an attack on any one of them. The communist,

Pop Quiz

Q: Has the fear of Communism in America ever been as great as the period of McCarthyism during the 1950s?

Eastern European nations countered with the formation of a similar coalition known as the **Warsaw Pact**.

The **Korean War**, which occurred under Truman, became a stage on which Cold War hostilities were played out. After World War II, Korea had been divided into North Korea, under Soviet control, and South Korea, under American occupation. Following the withdrawal of both Soviet and U.S. troops, North Korea, led by Soviet-trained military leaders, attacked South Korea without provocation, presumably to unify the country. Led by America, the United Nations Security Council, in the absence of the Soviet delegate, declared North Korea an aggressor and sent a force led by General MacArthur to the region. The U.N./U.S. forces had initial successes, but when the newly communist China sent in troops, the conflict seemed like it was going to get even messier. Armistice talks began but dragged on for two years.

Eisenhower was elected near the end of the Korean War, and his administration was firmly entrenched in the Cold War ideology. During his presidency, the Middle East emerged as a new arena for U.S.-Soviet politics. An early **crisis** in the region erupted at the **Suez Canal** in Egypt. It began when Israel, which was formally established as a nation only a few years earlier, attacked Egypt in the hope of destroying bases from which Arab militants harassed Israeli settlements. Meanwhile, England and France, angry about Egypt's recognition of Communist China, withdrew plans to build a **dam** on the Suez Canal. In response, Egypt's President Nasser seized the assets of the European company that owned and ran the Canal. Britain and France then joined the attack on Egypt in what many decried as a resurgence of the old pre-war imperialism.

Thus the Cold War atmosphere, coupled with new Middle East power struggles, contributed to small "hot" wars. Following the withdrawal of England, France, and Israel (under U.S. pressure), Eisenhower asked Congress to commit economic and military resources to the region in an effort to undermine communist influence there. This policy became known as the Eisenhower Doctrine.

Also under Eisenhower, the **Space Race** began when the Soviets launched the first-ever space satellite, *Sputnik*. The space race, which became a show of technological bravado between the U.S. and the Soviet Union, was a direct result of Cold War tensions.

The Cold War hits home

The period following World War II was colored with fear and sometimes exaggerated perceptions of the Soviet Union and the communist threat. People were worried about communist infiltration of the government and about double-agent-like spies who might be stealing state secrets. Many government employees were forced to resign following probes into their lives. In several highly publicized cases, once respected figures were jailed for treason. Two people, the **Rosenbergs**, were executed for spying.

In the vanguard of the deep anti-communist sentiment in the country was **Senator Joseph R. McCarthy**, who led a "crusade" to rid the government of communists, suspected communists, "fellow travelers," or "sympathizers"— labels the senator affixed to virtually anyone who disagreed with him. (Don't

Pop Quiz

A: Yes. After World War I, and the Russian Revolution in 1917, there was great fear that radical communists were trying to take over the U.S. government. This period was known as the "Red Scare." It was a "scare" because no one was really trying to take over the government. The fear of communism was partially due to a distrust of foreigners in general, and it was also spurred on by Attorney General A. Mitchell Palmer, who was in many ways as bad as McCarthy.

confuse him with Senator Eugene McCarthy, a liberal who ran unsuccessfully for president two decades later.) Joseph McCarthy's tactics, which became known as **McCarthyism**, were ruthless, and his claims were often unsubstantiated. McCarthy's demise came when his bullying tactics were shown and televised as part of a Senate Committee investigation of Army spies. When popular opinion turned against him, the Senate voted to "censure" his actions as unbecoming of his office.

After World War II, Congress seemed to be motivated by strong anti-labor, anti-union sentiments. Through that war, labor had forgone wage increases in order to support the nation's war effort. When it was over, inflation had risen dramatically and workers demanded compensation. But the Republican Congress sided with management and passed tough legislation that restricted organized labor tactics. One such bill, the **Taft-Hartley Act**, enjoyed public support as labor unions seemed to have a tinge of the dreaded communist ideology. The law passed over Truman's veto. In response, and to strengthen their numbers, the two most powerful labor union coalitions joined to form the **AFL-CIO** (American Federation of Labor-Congress of Industrial Organizations).

Post-war affluence

The decade following World War II brought general affluence and a good standard of living to Americans. Also, when soldiers returned from World War II, they and their spouses got down to the business of attempting to realize the American dream and making babies, lots of babies. The explosive increase in the number of kids was known as the **"baby boom."**

Even with this affluence, many groups of Americans remained economically disenfranchised and had substantially lower living standards, particularly in the black community. These differences worsened with the development of suburbs, as whites left the cities for less congested greener areas. As they left, of course, they took their buying power (and tax payments) with them. Blacks and other minority groups came to make up increasingly larger proportions of the cities' populations. This physical separation of the racial groups, accompanied by a relatively stagnant income for blacks, contributed to some of the tensions that would erupt in the 1960s.

Civil rights

Indeed, in the South, these physical separations were encoded into law. During this period, these laws came into serious question. *Brown v. Board of Education of Topeka* (1954) was a famous and important Supreme Court decision that helped open the door for civil rights change. Under the 1896 Supreme Court ruling *Plessy v. Ferguson*, public schools and other institutions were legally segregated under the doctrine of "separate but equal." In reality, the white schools and facilities far surpassed those for blacks. In the 1954 decision, **the Supreme Court** unanimously reversed this decision and declared this policy **unconstitutional. Chief Justice Earl Warren's** decision stated that **"separate educational facilities are inherently unequal"** and ordered that all public schools **desegregate**. This ruling helped to steel the black community and they began to organize openly against the contemptible segregation that pervaded Southern society.

"We conclude that in the field of public education the doctrine of 'separate but equal' has no place. Separate educational facilities are inherently unequal."
—Chief Justice Earl Warren, who wrote the unanimous opinion in the case of *Brown v. Board of Education of Topeka*

Rosa Parks, a black woman, initiated the **Montgomery Bus Boycott** by refusing to give up her seat on a bus to a white man. Her subsequent arrest led to a protest. The black community united under the leadership of **Martin Luther King, Jr.**, and refused to ride the buses. The boycott continued for months until the Supreme Court ruled that segregated seating was unconstitutional. Many members of the Southern white community did not like this upheaval of their stratified society. A widely publicized incident was **the confrontation at Little Rock**, Arkansas, as the city's board of education selected nine black students to enroll at the previously all-white Central High School. The governor of the state ordered the Arkansas national guard to bar the black students from the building. President Eisenhower declared the governor's action to be in violation of federal law. When the governor withdrew the national guard, an angry white mob sought to bar the students. Finally, Eisenhower sent federal troops to protect the black students and the soldiers remained through the entire school year. Furthermore, Eisenhower supported the **Civil Rights Acts of 1957 and 1960** which sought to remove the voting barriers that many southern states had put into practice and also to help minimize the violence that had been directed towards blacks (e.g., the bombing of black churches and schools).

ERA: THE 1960S

CULTURAL AND SOCIAL REVOLUTION

Kennedy/Johnson and the Great Society

John F. Kennedy, elected in a close contest against Richard M. Nixon, brought a feeling of optimism to the nation with his youthful idealism and sense of individual responsibility. He forwarded several progressive pieces of legislation that got minimal support from Congress. He did succeed in establishing the **Peace Corps**, a volunteer organization that sends teachers and technical assistance to developing countries.

Kennedy was assassinated while riding in a Dallas motorcade. When **Lyndon B. Johnson**, who had been vice president, ascended to the presidency, he outlined noble goals for the nation and asserted that the government should play more of a role in making people's lives better. He coined this vision **the Great Society**, promising a country in which poverty, disease, lack of education, and racial discrimination would and could be eliminated. No doubt, this was a tall order to fill, but Johnson did make some inroads into correcting some inequity in housing, schools, and civil rights. His most remembered legislation was the **Economic Opportunity Act**, which was billed as **"the war on poverty."** The major flaw in Johnson's program was that he was trying to fund a real war, the Vietnam war, at the same time as his war on these social evils. Among other problems, the war effort consumed billions of dollars.

Cuba and Vietnam—Hot Cold War

The Cold War heated up under Kennedy when Cuba, led by Fidel Castro, became the close-to-home stage for U.S.-Soviet tensions. The **Cuban Missile Crisis** was the closest thing to a nuclear showdown that this country has ever experienced. Cuba, which had recently overthrown the U.S.-supported dictator Batista, repelled an American-financed invasion at the **Bay of Pigs**. Fearing additional invasions, it sought and received Soviet military and economic support. A U.S. spy plane discovered that the Soviets and the Cubans were building offensive missile bases in Cuba. Kennedy ordered a blockade of all Soviet ships coming into the area and demanded that the bases be dismantled. The Soviets refused. As the U.S.S.R. and the U.S. moved dangerously close to nuclear war, Khrushchev, the Soviet premier, agreed to dismantle if the U.S. pledged not to invade Cuba. The situation defused.

The ultimate Cold War policy gone bad was the nation's approach to **Vietnam**. Though it is basically a story of the communists vs. the anti-communists, remembering the different players in this war can get a little complicated. **North Vietnam** was communist-controlled and the government of **South Vietnam** was anti-communist. The **Viet Cong** was a group of communist guerillas who had the support of North Vietnam and had also infiltrated into South Vietnamese territory. In the early 1960s, the Viet Cong and the North Vietnamese led raids on the capital of South Vietnam, **Saigon**, and many of its surrounding towns, in a battle to unify their country. Many of the towns were completely destroyed, but the South Vietnamese did not rise in rebellion against their own government, nor did they join the ranks of the communists (as the Viet Cong had hoped). Kennedy, at the request of the South Vietnamese government, sent U.S. support in the form of weapons and military advisers. He was motivated by the prevailing **domino philosophy**, which held that once one country "fell" to communism, others in the region would also swiftly fall, like a stack of dominos. The nearness of Communist China and the Soviet Union terrified the U.S. (After the murder of the South Vietnamese president, South Vietnam sustained a succession of corrupt dictators.)

Though it began with modest support to the South Vietnamese, the U.S. commitment to Vietnam escalated through the 1960s and early 1970s. During the Johnson administration, further military commitments were made to the region with the **Gulf of Tonkin Resolution**. In spite of some South Vietnamese government victories, the **Tet Offensive** of 1968 showed that neither side could easily win. Politically, this attack of the Viet Cong and North Vietnamese on Saigon and hundreds of other South Vietnamese towns reinforced the American people's reluctance to continue the war. Most of the domestic opposition to the war, however, was a result of moral outrage. Many Americans came to view their own country, not the North Vietnamese or the Viet Cong, as the aggressor. The peace process began under Johnson but stalled. Under Nixon, the war officially ended, although American troops still occupied the area until 1975. In the end, the Vietnam War lasted over twelve years and became a symbol of the lack of leadership and the **lack of clear goals** in our foreign policy and relationships with communist nations.

Although the Vietnam War lasted over twelve years and cost the lives of more than 50,000 American soldiers, Congress never officially declared war.

A different war at home

At home, unrest continued to grow: the **Civil Rights Movement** came into full swing as blacks demanded equal treatment, many young people vehemently **opposed the Vietnam War** and U.S. military policy, **hippies** emerged, and women's rights became an issue voiced by feminists in the **women's liberation movement** towards the end of the decade. An infant **environmental movement** began to stir.

In the 1950s, progress had been made in confirming and strengthening some civil rights for blacks, but starting in the early 1960s, things really began to heat up. Blacks became more forceful in claiming their rights and denouncing their "second-class citizen" status. Under the leadership of the Rev. Dr. Martin Luther King, Jr., the protesters embraced the tactic of **non-violent resistance** to achieve their goals. They engaged in several types of demonstrations. **Sit-ins** involved blacks going into "white only" restaurants and other establishments, sitting down and not leaving as service was denied them. On **Freedom Rides**, blacks and their white supporters rode interstate buses to test the in-state legislation passed in the 1950s. Freedom riders encountered hostility and violence as the buses rode into "white only" bus terminals; but with this demonstration, the government explicitly ordered that interstate buses be desegregated, and airplanes and trains voluntarily followed suit. Another form of demonstration was the **mass demonstration or march**; the famous example of this was the **March on Washington** to show support for civil rights legislation that had been advanced by Kennedy. It was the largest group that had ever assembled in the nation's capital and it held that record for over twenty years. During this protest, Dr. Martin Luther King, Jr., gave his well-known "*I Have A Dream*" speech.

After many forced delays by Southern Congressmen, the **Voting Rights Act of 1964** was signed by President Johnson. It mandated strengthened voting protections for blacks and prohibited discrimination in public accommodations, housing, and employment. The strength of the law was tested the next year in **Selma, Alabama**, a city that had a large population of blacks, of whom only a few were registered to vote. The local police violently suppressed groups demonstrating for their voting rights and prevented them from trying to register. The next year, Johnson signed even stronger legislation to protect voting, **the Civil Rights Act of 1965**.

Although King and his supporters advocated non-violence, many of the whites who opposed them, including the local police forces, were openly and frequently violent. One famed incident in **Birmingham**, Alabama, showed police using firehoses, nightsticks, cattle prods, and dogs to disband the non-violent protesters. The incident was televised, offering the opportunity for many people, especially those in the North, to see violent racial hatred. It helped generate much sympathy and support for the civil rights movement among whites.

Violence towards the black protesters spurred division within the ranks of the civil rights movement. The NAACP and Martin Luther King, Jr., continued to advocate non-violent protest, but more militant black groups felt as if these groups were sending their young people to slaughter. **Malcolm X**, who acted as the chief spokesman for the **Nation of Islam** (sometimes referred to as the Black Muslims), favored complete separation of the races, although he eventually broke with the Nation of Islam and altered his separatist views toward the end of his short life. **CORE** (Congress on Racial Equality) and **SNCC** (Student Non-Violent Coordinating Committee) represented people who had switched allegiance from King and came to advocate armed self-protection. The **Black Panthers** were another group advocating armed self-defense. These groups often used the term **Black Power**, not only in reference to the idea that blacks should arm themselves for an "imminent" revolution against the white power structure, but in reference to the empowerment that comes from self-pride.

Vietnam became an increasingly **unpopular war**, perhaps the most unpopular war in America's history. Folks at home didn't much understand it or care about it until Johnson escalated our military and personnel commitments and then **reinstated the draft**. It was also the first war to be nationally televised. People could see in their own living rooms the horrible effects of the war on their sons, and the horrible things that their sons were being ordered to do to others. TV served to de-glamorize war and to undermine our government's assertions that we were winning and that it would soon be over. Public protest and acts of resistance increased after the U.S. widened the war by invading Cambodia. At **Kent State** university, during an anti-war protest in 1970, national guardsmen fired on the demonstrators, killing four students. A shocked nation became even angrier about the war and loudly called for its end.

ERA: THE 1970S AND 1980S

Tricky Dick

Richard Nixon was the bridge from the 1960s to the 1970s. He came into office promising to end the Vietnam War after Johnson chose not to run again for President because of the whole war disgrace. Actually, Nixon wavered for a while, and our involvement in the war slowly fizzled out through 1973, 1974 and 1975. Nixon used a **policy of détente** in foreign relations, meaning a policy of lessened hostilities. Thus he reached **trade agreements with Communist China** and began a tradition of **arms-negotiations with the Soviet Union**.

Nixon built his political base on what he called the **"Silent Majority,"** which supposedly encompassed those Americans who were tired of big government, tired of the cultural and social unrest, and tired of concerns about racial strife. Domestically, he took a dramatically different turn from the Kennedy-Johnson Era. He disapproved of and cut many social and economic welfare programs. He also instituted conservative economic programs as the nation began feeling the economic weight of Johnson's combined social and military commitments.

Relatively popular, Nixon easily won reelection in 1972. His downfall was caused by the **Watergate scandal** during his second term. The president had used his influence to direct a group of people to break in to the Democratic National Headquarters at the Watergate Hotel, and to wiretap the premises. He sought to discover the Democrats' strategy for the 1972 presidential election. This was not only unbecoming for a president; it was also illegal. As the scandal came to light, **Nixon resigned** his office (the only president in history to do so) rather than face impeachment.

Every question has five answer choices. Four of them are wrong. Find the wrong answers and get rid of them! Remember: If you can eliminate even one answer choice—guess!

During the 1970s, the Arab nations that controlled most of the world's oil supply refused to ship oil to any Western countries, including the United States. This boycott created an energy crisis that hit hard on America. As a result of the oil embargo, gasoline prices skyrocketed and people waited on long lines to fill up their cars.

Ford/Carter/Reagan

The SAT II does not venture very far into history after Richard Nixon. Essentially, this part of history is of too recent memory, and it is harder for historians, let alone high school teachers and high school textbooks, to decide what was really important. You will probably not see more than one or two questions dealing with the mid-1970s and 1980s, but here are a few basic facts.

Gerald Ford succeeded Nixon, but later lost to a Democrat, **Jimmy Carter**. The presidencies of Ford and Carter were plagued by a **troubled economy** and by an **energy crisis**. Neither Ford's nor Carter's policies alleviated the economic trouble, and under Carter, the nation faced **double-digit inflation**—higher prices, especially for gasoline—as well as steep unemployment. Because of an oil shortage manipulated by the Middle East cartel, **OPEC**, which controlled much of the world's oil deposits, the Middle East became an even more important arena of foreign policy. Though Carter had some foreign policy success (he helped negotiate an Egyptian-Israeli peace treaty), he left office in defeat. By the 1980 election, fifty-two American citizens had been held hostage in Tehran for over a year, captured in the course of an Iranian civil war.

Defeating Carter, **Ronald Reagan** began a legacy of conservatism in politics and economics. His **"trickle-down"** economic plan advocated cutting taxes on the rich so that their subsequent investments would drip down to the poorer classes. This policy, coupled with massive spending on the military and severe cutbacks for social programs, created a short-lived financial boom in the 1980s, which lasted until the stock market plummeted in 1987.

REVIEW OF THE ERAS

Now that you've reviewed American history, quiz yourself to find out how much you remember. Next to each Era, write down a few things about it. This will give you practice in the "Connect-to-the-Era" thinking you will need on the American History SAT II.

THE COLONIAL PERIOD

_____

_____

_____

_____

_____

TENSIONS LEADING TO THE AMERICAN REVOLUTION

_____

_____

_____

_____

_____

INDEPENDENCE AND THE UNITED STATES

_____

_____

_____

_____

_____

JEFFERSONIAN REPUBLICANISM

_____

_____

_____

_____

_____

THE BEGINNINGS OF EXPANSION

_____

_____

_____

_____

_____

JACKSONIAN DEMOCRACY

_____

_____

_____

_____

_____

SECTIONAL STRIFE—THE PATH TO THE CIVIL WAR

_____

_____

_____

_____

_____

THE CIVIL WAR

_____

_____

_____

_____

_____

RECONSTRUCTION

_____

_____

_____

_____

_____

_____

_____

_____

TION

_____

_____

_____

_____

INDUSTRIALISM AND POLITICS

_____

_____

_____

_____

_____

THE PROGRESSIVE ERA

_____
_____
_____
_____
_____

WORLD WAR I

_____
_____
_____
_____
_____

THE ROARING TWENTIES

_____
_____
_____
_____
_____

THE GREAT DEPRESSION AND THE NEW DEAL

_____
_____
_____
_____
_____

WORLD WAR II

_____
_____
_____
_____
_____

POST-WAR—COLD WAR

_____
_____
_____
_____
_____

THE 1960s

_____
_____
_____
_____
_____

THE 1970s AND 1980s

_____
_____
_____
_____
_____

5

The Princeton Review
American History and
Social Studies Subject Test I

THE PRINCETON REVIEW AMERICAN HISTORY AND SOCIAL STUDIES SUBJECT TEST I

The test that follows is a simulated American History Subject Test.
In order to get a good estimate of your score, you should take this exam under test conditions.

- Give yourself an hour to do the test when you are not going to be bothered by anyone. Unplug the phones and tell your parents to tell your friends that you are not home.

- Clear away a space to work in. You want no distractions.

- Have someone else time you. It's too easy to fudge the time when you are keeping track of it yourself.

- Tear out the answer sheet provided in the back of the book. This way, you will get the feel for filling in all those lovely ovals.

- Don't worry about the complicated instructions; just pick the correct answer.

- Instructions for grading the exam are on page 108.

GOOD LUCK!

AMERICAN HISTORY AND SOCIAL STUDIES SUBJECT TEST I

SECTION 1

Your responses to the American History and Social Studies Subject Test questions must be filled in on Section One of your answer sheet (the box on the front of the answer sheet). Marks on any other section will not be counted toward your American History and Social Studies Subject Test score.

When your supervisor gives the signal, turn the page and begin the American History and Social Studies Subject Test. There are 100 numbered ovals on the answer sheet and 95 questions in the American History Subject Test. Therefore, use only ovals 1 to 95 for recording your answers.

AMERICAN HISTORY AND SOCIAL STUDIES TEST I

<u>Directions</u>: Each of the questions or incomplete statements below is followed by five suggested answers or completions. Select one that is best in each case and then fill in the corresponding oval on the answer sheet.

1. One result of the Tea Act of 1773 was

   (A) a sharp decline in tea exports from British East India
   (B) an increase in the price of coffee beans
   (C) a drop in profits among American colonial tea merchants
   (D) an immediate violent response from the American colonists
   (E) a disruption of British trade in tobacco and sugar

2. Which of the following played an important role in encouraging American colonists to rebel against the British government?

   (A) Thomas Paine
   (B) George Washington
   (C) George Rogers Clark
   (D) Voltaire
   (E) Cotton Mather

3. The addition of the Bill of Rights to the United States Constitution was most strongly endorsed by believers in

   (A) women's rights
   (B) abolition
   (C) imperialism
   (D) states' rights
   (E) Manifest Destiny

4. The government body most responsible for raising federal revenue is

   (A) the Senate
   (B) the House of Representatives
   (C) the Executive
   (D) the General Accounting Office
   (E) the Supreme Court

5. Which of the following best describes the difference in economy between the Northern states and the Southern states before the outbreak of the Civil War?

   (A) The North relied upon manual labor while the South did not.
   (B) Northern factories employed young free whites while Southern factories employed slaves of both sexes.
   (C) The South was primarily agricultural while the North relied upon industry.
   (D) The standard of living in the South was higher than that in the North.
   (E) The North offered more employment opportunities to blacks than did the South.

6. The completion of the Erie Canal led to the economic growth of which of the following cities?

   (A) Boston
   (B) Baltimore
   (C) Richmond
   (D) Philadelphia
   (E) New York

7. Which of the following states were settled by pioneers who shared the same religious beliefs?

   I. Pennsylvania
   II. Virginia
   III. Utah

   (A) I only
   (B) II only
   (C) I and II only
   (D) I and III only
   (E) I, II, and III

GO ON TO THE NEXT PAGE

8. Laissez-faire capitalism was an idea espoused by

   (A) moderate socialists
   (B) mercantilists
   (C) free-market industrialists
   (D) abolitionists
   (E) labor unions

9. Which of the following would be most useful in determining the political views of American women in the 1870s?

   (A) voting returns from the presidential elections of 1876
   (B) membership rolls of the major political parties
   (C) diaries and published works by women indicating political viewpoints
   (D) comparable viewpoints of French women of the same period
   (E) voting returns of American men of the same period

10. All of the following contributed to the growth of manufacturing during the middle of the nineteenth century EXCEPT

   (A) the completion of the transcontinental railroad
   (B) the development of labor-saving machines
   (C) the perfection of the assembly line
   (D) an increase in the discovery and use of natural resources
   (E) increased production made possible by the economies of scale available to large companies

IMMIGRATION 1881-1920

Year	Total in Thousands	Rate[1]
1881–1890	5247	9.2
1891–1900	3688	5.3
1901–1910	8795	10.4
1911–1920	5736	5.7

[1]Annual rate per 1,000 U.S. population. Rates computed by dividing the sum of annual immigration totals by the sum of annual United States population totals for the same number of years.

11. Which of the following can be inferred from the above table?

   (A) More immigrants arrived in the United States between 1911 and 1920 than during any other period from 1881 to 1920.
   (B) The period between 1891 and 1900 marked the lowest rate of immigration between 1881 and 1920.
   (C) Political persecution in Europe led to a rise in immigration to the United States between 1881 and 1920.
   (D) World economic factors led to a rise in immigration from East to West.
   (E) During the years between 1881 and 1920, the United States government provided incentives to draw immigrants to the United States.

12. Theodore Dreiser and Upton Sinclair can best be described as

   (A) naturalists
   (B) futurists
   (C) transcendentalists
   (D) romantics
   (E) evolutionists

GO ON TO THE NEXT PAGE

13. The efforts of the United States government to rectify the problems of the Great Depression led to increases in all of the following EXCEPT

  (A) the role of government in managing the economy
  (B) the role of government in supporting the arts
  (C) the regulation of the banking industry
  (D) the use of presidential power in creating government agencies
  (E) the abolition of the sale or manufacture of alcohol

14. Which of the following presidents signed the Antipoverty Act into law?

  (A) Harry S. Truman
  (B) Franklin D. Roosevelt
  (C) Lyndon B. Johnson
  (D) Herbert Hoover
  (E) Theodore Roosevelt

15. The term "shuttle diplomacy" is most closely associated with

  (A) the Yom Kippur War of 1973
  (B) the Six-Day War of 1967
  (C) the Cuban Missile Crisis
  (D) the Camp David Accords
  (E) the Bay of Pigs incident

16. Native American tribes living prior to the arrival of Columbus could best be described as

  (A) uniform in language and religious beliefs
  (B) isolated from one another
  (C) diverse in customs and culture
  (D) nomadic herders of livestock
  (E) eager to assist European settlers

17. One of the principle reasons for the creation of the colony of Georgia was to

  (A) establish cotton plantations
  (B) introduce religious freedom to America
  (C) create a haven for political refugees
  (D) provide economic opportunities for freed slaves
  (E) rehabilitate debtors and criminals

18. The taxes imposed upon the American colonies in the late 1700s were a direct result of

  (A) expenses incurred by the British during the French and Indian War
  (B) efforts of the colonists to exert influence over British politics
  (C) a loss of control over British colonial holdings
  (D) a desire on the part of France to turn the colonists against the British government
  (E) war-reparations that Britain owed to the French government

19. The Neutrality Proclamation passed by George Washington's administration reflected the president's desire to

  (A) delay renewed hostilities with Great Britain
  (B) avoid entangling alliances
  (C) exert influence over Central and South America
  (D) attract foreign investment in American business
  (E) increase the country's population

20. One goal of the calling of the Constitutional Convention in 1787 was to

  (A) facilitate interstate trade
  (B) provide Americans with guaranteed freedoms
  (C) keep the British from interfering in United States politics
  (D) promote states' rights
  (E) define the role of religion in American politics

GO ON TO THE NEXT PAGE

21. Which of the following shaped United States government policy in South America?

    I.   The Monroe Doctrine
    II. The Roosevelt Corollary
    III. The Wilmot Proviso

    (A) I only
    (B) II only
    (C) I and II only
    (D) II and III only
    (E) I, II, and III

22. The so-called "Tariff of Abominations" (1828) was notable because

    (A) the taxes that it proposed were endorsed by the southern states
    (B) some of the money raised by these tariffs would go to the British treasury
    (C) the revenues would benefit Northeastern industries at the expense of some southern states
    (D) the tariff's revenues would be distributed equally to all states
    (E) the tariff was the result of a compromise among all three branches of government

23. The Panic of 1837 was most likely precipitated by all of the following EXCEPT

    (A) unregulated lending practices on the part of Andrew Jackson's "pet banks"
    (B) Andrew Jackson's refusal to re-charter the Bank of the United States
    (C) Andrew Jackson's passage of the Specie Circular denying the use of credit to buy land
    (D) a change in the standard for setting the value of United States currency
    (E) overconfidence in the strength of the real-estate market

24. Which of the following phrases was coined in the mid-nineteenth century to describe the American desire for westward expansion?

    (A) Social Darwinism
    (B) 44° 40' or Bust
    (C) Manifest Destiny
    (D) Gold Rush
    (E) Popular Sovereignty

25. A major cause of the Spanish-American War was

    (A) the expansion of Spanish sea power in the Atlantic
    (B) the historic relationship between the United States and France
    (C) President McKinley's desire to spread the influence of the United States in the Caribbean
    (D) the refusal of the Spanish regime to recognize the independence of Puerto Rico
    (E) the capture of the Alamo by General Santa Ana

RURAL AND URBAN POPULATION IN
AMERICA FROM 1940–1970
(in thousands)

	Rural	Urban
1940	57,246	74,425
1950	54,230	96,468
1960	54,054	125,269
1970	53,887	149,325

26. Based on the chart above, all of the following can be inferred about the period between 1940 and 1970, EXCEPT

    (A) the percentage of people living in urban areas increased between 1940 and 1970.
    (B) the number of people living in rural areas has decreased since 1940.
    (C) more people lived in rural areas in 1940 than did in 1970.
    (D) agriculture had ceased to be an important aspect of American life by 1970.
    (E) more people lived in the United States in 1970 than in 1940.

27. The ratification of the eighteenth amendment led to

    (A) universal suffrage for women
    (B) voting rights for former slaves
    (C) the establishment of a Federal income tax
    (D) a ban on the manufacture and sale of alcoholic beverages
    (E) the guarantee of equal protection under law for all Americans

GO ON TO THE NEXT PAGE

28. The Constitutional amendment restricting the executive branch to a two-term limit was passed by Congress during the presidency of

    (A) Franklin D. Roosevelt
    (B) Harry S. Truman
    (C) Dwight D. Eisenhower
    (D) Lyndon B. Johnson
    (E) Richard M. Nixon

29. The Social Security Act of 1935

    (A) protected workers from unfair dismissal
    (B) led to the establishment of the Tennessee Valley Authority
    (C) insured depositors against bank failures
    (D) created public works projects for unemployed workers
    (E) provided insurance for retired persons over 65

30. The Constitution gives the executive branch of the government the power to do which of the following?

    (A) Appoint Supreme Court justices
    (B) Levy taxes
    (C) Declare wars
    (D) Spend government funds
    (E) Enact laws

31. Since 1950, a common criticism of the presidential election system has been that

    (A) few candidates can acquire enough popular support from voters to decisively win an election
    (B) candidates who do not win a majority of electoral votes can still become president
    (C) the Constitution provides no method for choosing a president in the event that no candidate wins a clear majority
    (D) the electoral college system makes it possible for a candidate to win an election without receiving the majority of popular votes
    (E) thinly populated states wield too much power in the electoral college

32. Which of the following is a right guaranteed by the United States Constitution?

    (A) The right to violate unjust laws
    (B) The right to a free public education system
    (C) The right to affordable housing
    (D) The right to form an organization opposing the government
    (E) The right to live on federally controlled land

33. Which of the following Puritan political traditions is still valid today?

    (A) Freedom of worship
    (B) Freedom of expression
    (C) Community participation in government
    (D) Public humiliation of criminals
    (E) Universal suffrage

34. All of the following were founders of American colonies EXCEPT

    (A) William Penn
    (B) John Winthrop
    (C) James Oglethorpe
    (D) Christopher Newport
    (E) William Bradford

35. In which of the following ways did some of the American colonies attract new settlers?

    I. By offering certain desirable rights unavailable to people in Europe
    II. By offering free or inexpensive land to settlers
    III. By pooling the resources of all the colonies to pay the passage of new settlers

    (A) I only
    (B) II only
    (C) I and II only
    (D) II and III only
    (E) I, II, and III

GO ON TO THE NEXT PAGE

36. "There is something very absurd in supposing a continent to be perpetually governed by an island. In no instance hath nature made the satellite larger than its primary planet."

    The above statement is an example of

    (A) the application of natural law to political theory
    (B) the Loyalist policy toward the American colonies
    (C) Federalism
    (D) Puritan political thought
    (E) civil libertarianism

37. In his sermon "Sinners in the Hands of an Angry God," Jonathan Edwards delivered which of the following messages?

    (A) Man is essentially evil and has no hope for redemption.
    (B) God has already predetermined the fate of all of his creatures.
    (C) God is an irrational being who cannot be reasoned with or pleased.
    (D) God has no role to play in the future of America.
    (E) God saves the souls of men through His grace alone.

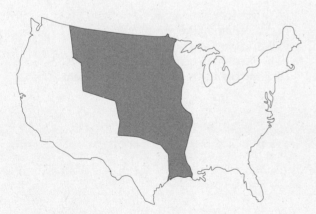

38. The shaded region of the map above represents land acquired from

    (A) Britain
    (B) Spain
    (C) France
    (D) Canada
    (E) the Iroquois Confederacy

39. Which of the following parties was formed in opposition to the policies of Andrew Jackson?

    (A) The Republicans
    (B) The Know-Nothings
    (C) The Copperheads
    (D) The Whigs
    (E) The Democratic Republicans

40. James Fennimore Cooper's "Leatherstocking Novels" deal mainly with

    (A) the difficulties faced by the early explorers of the American continent.
    (B) the lives of men and women on the North American frontier.
    (C) the attitudes of British political figures towards the American colonies.
    (D) the settlement of California by Spanish colonists.
    (E) the achievements of immigrants in nineteenth-century New York.

41. The controversy surrounding the admission of Texas to the United States arose from

    (A) a border dispute with the newly created Republic of Mexico
    (B) the creation of a large, pro-slavery state
    (C) the violation of a long-standing treaty with Spain
    (D) the displacement of large numbers of Native American inhabitants of Texas
    (E) the inclusion of Spanish-speaking people in the Texas state government

42. The completion of a national railroad network in the United States led to an increase in all of the following EXCEPT

    (A) industrial production in the United States.
    (B) the proportion of female settlers on the west coast.
    (C) cargo traffic on canals and waterways.
    (D) revenues for eastern railroad monopolies.
    (E) forced migration of Native American peoples.

GO ON TO THE NEXT PAGE

43. "You shall not press down upon the brow of labor this crown of thorns, you shall not crucify mankind upon a cross of gold."

    The statement above made by William Jennings Bryan in 1896 was intended as a defense of

    (A) the American labor movement
    (B) the American farmer
    (C) persecuted religious minorities
    (D) advocates of school prayer
    (E) evolutionary theorists

44. Which of the following works drew attention to the need for reform in the meat packing industry?

    (A) *Uncle Tom's Cabin*
    (B) *The Scarlet Letter*
    (C) *The Jungle*
    (D) *The Crucible*
    (E) *The Red Badge of Courage*

45. The nomination of Theodore Roosevelt as the presidential candidate for the "Bull Moose" party led to the election of which of the following presidents?

    (A) William McKinley
    (B) William Howard Taft
    (C) Franklin D. Roosevelt
    (D) Woodrow Wilson
    (E) Calvin Coolidge

46. A provision of the Quota Act of 1924 led to

    (A) an increase in the export of American goods
    (B) a decrease in voter registration
    (C) the creation of affirmative action programs
    (D) a refusal to admit immigrants from Japan
    (E) an increase in tariffs placed on European imports

47. Which of the following was a direct result of the "Red Scare" of the 1920s?

    (A) The passage of the McCarran Act
    (B) The victory of the Bolshevik party in the Russian Revolution
    (C) The formation of the Congress of Industrial Organizations
    (D) The trial and execution of the Rosenbergs
    (E) The arrest of 4,000 suspected communists

48. "We cannot allow the natural passions and prejudices of other peoples to lead our country to destruction…We are on the verge of a war in which the only victor would be chaos and frustration…A war which cannot be won without sending our soldiers across an ocean to fight and to force a landing on a hostile coast against armies stronger than our own. We are on the verge of war, but it is not yet too late to stay out."

    The opinions in the speech above were most likely expressed by

    (A) an interventionist
    (B) an isolationist
    (C) a Federalist
    (D) an internationalist
    (E) a Loyalist

49. Which of the following was NOT created during the administration of Franklin D. Roosevelt?

    (A) The Works Progress Administration
    (B) The Tennessee Valley Authority
    (C) The Public Works Administration
    (D) The Interstate Highway system
    (E) The National Recovery Administration

50. The first amendment of the Bill of Rights of the United States Constitution guarantees all of the following EXCEPT

    (A) freedom of religion
    (B) freedom of the press
    (C) the right to assemble peacefully
    (D) the right to bear arms
    (E) the right to petition the government

GO ON TO THE NEXT PAGE

51. Which of the following is an example of the policy known as "dollar diplomacy"?

   (A) The United States Congress places limits on interstate trade in order to control local governments.
   (B) The United States government offers financial rewards to countries in order to achieve its foreign policy goals.
   (C) American multinational corporations represent United States government interests in other countries.
   (D) Government officials sell arms to foreign countries in order to raise money for covert military operations.
   (E) The government abandons the gold standard as a measure of the value of United States currency.

52. The purpose of a filibuster is to

   (A) justify the passage of unpopular legislation
   (B) delay or block the passage of a piece of legislation
   (C) explain a piece of legislation for the benefit of voters
   (D) exclude the Executive branch of government from the legislative process
   (E) override a presidential veto

53. The Constitution describes the form and function of all of the following EXCEPT

   (A) the Presidency
   (B) the Congress
   (C) the Supreme Court
   (D) the Vice Presidency
   (E) the Cabinet

54. Each of the following presidents came to prominence as wartime generals EXCEPT

   (A) Dwight D. Eisenhower
   (B) Ulysses S. Grant
   (C) Andrew Jackson
   (D) Theodore Roosevelt
   (E) George Washington

55. The admission of Missouri into the United States was made possible by

   (A) a cash payment to the French, who laid claim to the land
   (B) the admission of Maine, a state which outlawed slavery
   (C) the admission of Texas, a state which laid claim to Missouri territory
   (D) the creation of the Confederate States of America
   (E) the opening of the American West

56. All of the following political decisions were results of the debate over slavery and abolition EXCEPT

   (A) the Wilmot Proviso
   (B) the Missouri Compromise
   (C) the Compromise of 1850
   (D) the Kansas-Nebraska Act
   (E) the Civil Rights Act

57. Transcendentalist literature is characterized by which of the following?

   (A) An emphasis on technological progress
   (B) A mistrust of religious ideas
   (C) A heavy reliance on mythological imagery
   (D) A belief in the importance of the human spirit
   (E) A desire to emulate European literature of the time

58. The Dred Scott decision led to the nullification of

   (A) the Missouri Compromise
   (B) the Emancipation Proclamation
   (C) the Fugitive Slave Law
   (D) the Three-Fifths Compromise
   (E) the Intolerable Acts

GO ON TO THE NEXT PAGE

59. The United States exercised which of the following policies in gaining access to the land where the Panama Canal was built?

  (A) The Monroe Doctrine
  (B) The Roosevelt Corollary
  (C) Nativism
  (D) Strict constructionism
  (E) Cultural imperialism

60. An immigrant arriving in New York City between the years 1880 and 1920 was most likely born in

  (A) East Asia
  (B) Northern Europe
  (C) Southern or Eastern Europe
  (D) Latin America
  (E) West Africa

61. All of the following campaigned for women's suffrage EXCEPT

  (A) Susan B. Anthony
  (B) Elizabeth Cady Stanton
  (C) Lucretia Mott
  (D) Harriet Beecher Stowe
  (E) Amelia Bloomer

62. All of the following may have contributed to the stock market crash of October 29, 1929, EXCEPT

  (A) the lack of sufficient cash reserves in the banking system
  (B) the overvaluing of the stock market
  (C) the unrestricted purchase of stock on credit
  (D) the speculative investment of large amounts of money
  (E) the lack of insurance for bank depositors

63. Before 1913, the Constitution gave the federal government the right to do all of the following EXCEPT

  (A) enter into treaties with foreign governments
  (B) appoint ambassadors
  (C) regulate commerce among the states
  (D) levy taxes on personal income
  (E) to declare war

64. The Korean conflict was considered a "police action" because

  (A) the Supreme Court found the U.S. Army's recruiting practices unconstitutional
  (B) the President did not endorse the participation of American troops
  (C) Congress never formally declared war against North Korea
  (D) the United Nations forced the U.S. government to enter the war
  (E) the war was fought between two sovereign states

65. The successful launch of *Sputnik* in 1957 led to

  (A) an increased interest in the United States space program
  (B) a decline in the popularity of Dwight D. Eisenhower
  (C) a decrease in tensions between the Soviet Union and the United States
  (D) a decline in funding for United States defense
  (E) government suspicion of the "military-industrial" complex

66. The activities of Senator Joe McCarthy led to

  (A) the creation of the Hollywood blacklist
  (B) the censorship of televised senate proceedings
  (C) the investigation of suspected communists in the U.S. Army
  (D) the 1968 riot at the Democratic convention
  (E) the creation of the House Un-American Activities Committee

GO ON TO THE NEXT PAGE ➡

67. In the United States, the distribution of federal welfare benefits is determined by

    I. the national government
    II. the state governments
    III. private, non-profit organizations

    (A) I only
    (B) II only
    (C) I and II only
    (D) II and III only
    (E) I, II and III

68. The Oregon Territory was acquired in the 1840s through

    (A) a compromise with the British government
    (B) a treaty with the local Native American inhabitants
    (C) the diplomatic efforts of Lewis and Clark
    (D) a cash transaction with Russia
    (E) an extension of the terms of the Louisiana Purchase

69. The Mormons settled the region now known as Utah under the leadership of

    (A) Joseph Smith
    (B) Brigham Young
    (C) Millard Fillmore
    (D) James Buchanan
    (E) Horace Greeley

70. The Emancipation Proclamation was designed to accomplish all of the following EXCEPT

    (A) giving southern slaves an incentive to take up arms against their Confederate masters
    (B) appeasing the slave-owners in states that stayed loyal to the Union in the Civil War
    (C) gaining the support of European powers in the battle against the Confederates
    (D) increasing public support for abolition in the Northern states
    (E) imposing a penalty on secessionist states

71. United States policy toward Native American tribes in the West during the 1880s can best be described as

    (A) inconsistent
    (B) conciliatory
    (C) clearly defined
    (D) assimilationist
    (E) separatist

72. Which of the following was NOT a factor in the growth of American cities in the mid-nineteenth century?

    (A) A sharp rise in immigration
    (B) The lure of newly created jobs in industrial centers
    (C) A decline in the population of farmers
    (D) Government incentives to resettle in urban areas
    (E) The scarcity of natural resources in rural America

73. Which of the following was sought by reformers during the Progressive era?

    (A) Laws against racial discrimination
    (B) The creation of the Securities Exchange Commission
    (C) The creation of industrial trusts
    (D) More frequent use of referendums
    (E) A discontinuation of the use of paper money

GO ON TO THE NEXT PAGE

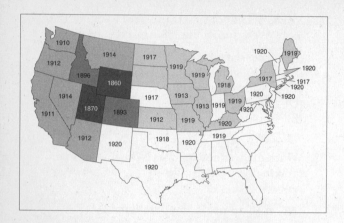

74. The best title for the map above would be

 (A) The Admission of States to the Union
 (B) The Settlement of North America
 (C) The Passage of Woman Suffrage Laws by State
 (D) The Repeal of Prohibition Laws by State
 (E) The Passage of Desegregation Laws by State

75. The Sherman Antitrust Act had its greatest effect on

 (A) business and industry
 (B) woman suffragists
 (C) the military
 (D) former Confederate states
 (E) America's allies during the Second World War

76. The period between 1918 and 1941 is best known for the development of which of the following art forms?

 (A) Transcendental poetry
 (B) Jazz music
 (C) Impressionist painting
 (D) Postmodern architecture
 (E) Folk music

77. "We are impressed by a medium in which a man sitting in his living room has been able for the first time to look at two oceans at once."

The statement above made by a television journalist most likely refers to

 (A) the impact of mass-communication technology on the general public
 (B) the results of government censorship in the mass media
 (C) the difficulties faced by travelers in the early twentieth century
 (D) the lack of information available to the average television viewer
 (E) the influence wielded by the media on political affairs

78. All of the following were writers of the Harlem Renaissance EXCEPT

 (A) James Weldon Johnson
 (B) Countee Cullen
 (C) Langston Hughes
 (D) Henry Louis Gates, Jr.
 (E) Zora Neale Hurston

79. The Viet Cong's Tet Offensive of 1968

 (A) illustrated the weakness of the North Vietnamese forces
 (B) was the first major victory enjoyed by the Viet Cong
 (C) was a major political setback for Lyndon B. Johnson
 (D) increased support among Americans for the Vietnam War
 (E) drew the Chinese into the Vietnam War

GO ON TO THE NEXT PAGE

80. One result of the Marshall Plan of 1948 was

    (A) the shipment of food, raw material and machinery to post-war Europe
    (B) the airlift of vital supplies to blockaded West Berlin after the Second World War
    (C) the division of Germany into four administrative zones
    (D) the withdrawal of the United States from foreign affairs
    (E) the admission of China to the United Nations

81. In 1939, the official United States policy toward the Second World War was

    (A) direct military involvement whenever necessary
    (B) non-military support of Britain, France and the Soviet Union
    (C) neutrality and isolation
    (D) appeasement of the Axis powers
    (E) manipulation of the European political process

82. Rachel Carson's book *Silent Spring* was significant because it

    (A) brought the dangers of DDT and other pesticides to the attention of the American public
    (B) made a decisive case in favor of woman suffrage shortly before the ratification of the nineteenth amendment
    (C) was the first book by a female author published in the United States
    (D) led to the passage of the strict legislation to protect the ozone layer
    (E) was awarded the Pulitzer Prize in 1968

83. "Laws permitting, and even requiring, their separation in places where they are liable to be brought into contact do not necessarily imply the inferiority of either race to the other…."

    The above passage was probably taken from which of the following Supreme Court rulings?

    (A) *Brown v. Board of Education*
    (B) *Gideon v. Waingwright*
    (C) *Plessy v. Ferguson*
    (D) *Marbury v. Madison*
    (E) *Miranda v. Arizona*

84. All of the following are ideas advocated by *The Federalist Papers* EXCEPT:

    (A) republican government works best in small communities.
    (B) wider representation decreases the opportunities for tyranny.
    (C) individual states will grow increasingly hostile to one another.
    (D) the army should be under Federal control.
    (E) a republican government must balance its power among different branches.

85. The "spoils system" favored by President Andrew Jackson led to

    (A) the establishment of the Food and Drug Administration
    (B) the development of negative campaign tactics still in use today
    (C) the distribution of government jobs to members of the president's party
    (D) the increase in legal discrimination based on race
    (E) the defeat of American troops in the War of 1812

86. Which of the following reforms is associated with Jacksonian Democracy?

    (A) Improved public education
    (B) Education for women
    (C) The rise of abolitionism
    (D) Improved treatment of the insane
    (E) The creation of child-labor laws

87. Radical Reconstruction differed from Lincoln's original plans for reconstruction in that

    (A) the Radical plan sought to punish secessionist states
    (B) Lincoln's plan did not call for the abolition of slavery
    (C) Lincoln's plan denied southern soldiers the right to vote in federal elections
    (D) the Radical plan favored the creation of "separate-but-equal" status for free blacks
    (E) the Radicals did not want to disband the Confederate bureaucracy

GO ON TO THE NEXT PAGE

THE UNDECIDED POLITICAL PRIZE FIGHT.

Reprinted by permission of the Library of Congress

88. The cartoon above refers to

(A) the onset of the Civil War
(B) the Lincoln-Douglas debates
(C) Lincoln's inability to capture the presidency
(D) the Federal government's lack of faith in its citizens
(E) a mistrust of the electoral process

89. "I have never been a quitter. To leave office before my term is completed is abhorrent to every instinct in my body, but as president I must put the interests of America first. America needs a full-time president and a full-time Congress, particularly at this time, with the problems we face at home and abroad. Therefore, I shall resign from the presidency, effective at noon tomorrow...."

The speech quoted above was delivered during

(A) the 1940s
(B) the 1950s
(C) the 1960s
(D) the 1970s
(E) the 1980s

90. All of the following are examples of post-First World War isolationism in the United States EXCEPT

(A) non-involvement in the affairs of foreign nations
(B) refusal to join the League of Nations
(C) the "Red Scare"
(D) suspension of trade with European nations
(E) a reduction in military funding

91. The Teapot Dome scandal is an example of

(A) an effort on the part of the Taft administration to weed out government corruption
(B) widespread financial misconduct during the presidency of Warren Harding
(C) efforts made by American colonists to protest unfair taxation
(D) the desire of Congress to be recognized as the most influential branch of government
(E) the methods used by Harry Truman to pass his Fair Deal legislation

92. The recovery programs instituted by President Roosevelt during the Depression were significant because

(A) they encouraged government participation in the economic development of the nation
(B) they received little cooperation from industrialists and businessmen hurt by the stock market crash
(C) they required the involvement of foreign governments in rebuilding the United States economy
(D) they were important to the success of British and French forces during the Second World War
(E) they caused Roosevelt's political opponents to gain popularity

GO ON TO THE NEXT PAGE

93. The North Atlantic Treaty of 1949 established

    (A) an alliance among the nations of Western Europe and North America
    (B) a return to the isolationism of the 1920s
    (C) lend-lease agreements for the supply of war materiel to the Allied forces
    (D) lasting peace with the nations of the Communist world
    (E) the framework for the United Nations

94. Which of the following is a complete and accurate list of the Allied nations in the Second World War?

    (A) The United States, France, and Italy
    (B) The United States, Britain, and the Soviet Union
    (C) The United States, Britain, and Japan
    (D) The United States, Germany, and Italy
    (E) Germany, Italy, and Japan

95. All of the following took place during the administration of Lyndon Johnson EXCEPT

    (A) the passage of the Civil Rights Act
    (B) the Gulf of Tonkin incident
    (C) the outbreak of the Vietnam War
    (D) the passage of the Anti-Poverty Act
    (E) the arrest of the Watergate burglars

STOP
IF YOU FINISH BEFORE TIME IS CALLED, YOU MAY CHECK YOUR WORK ON THIS TEST ONLY.
DO NOT TURN TO ANY OTHER TEST IN THIS BOOK.

HOW TO SCORE THE PRINCETON REVIEW
AMERICAN HISTORY AND SOCIAL STUDIES SUBJECT TEST I

When you take the real exam, the proctors will collect your text booklet and bubble sheet and send your answer sheet to New Jersey where a computer (yes, a big old-fashioned one that has been around since the 1960s) looks at the pattern of filled-in ovals on your answer sheet and gives you a score. We couldn't include even a small computer with this book, so we are providing this more primitive way of scoring your exam.

DETERMINING YOUR SCORE

STEP 1   Using the answers on the next page, determine how many questions you got right and how many you got wrong on the test. Remember, questions that you do not answer don't count as either right answers or wrong answers.

STEP 2   List the number of right answers here.   (A) _____

STEP 3   List the number of wrong answers here. Now divide that number by 4. (Use a calculator if you're feeling particularly lazy.)   (B) _____ ÷ 4 = _____

STEP 4   Subtract the number of wrong answers divided by 4 from the number of correct answers. Round this score to the nearest whole number. This is your raw score.   (C) (A) ____ – (B) _____ = _____

STEP 5   To determine your real score, take the number from Step 4 above and look it up in the left column of the Score Conversion Table on page 110; the corresponding score on the right is your score on the exam.

ANSWERS TO THE PRINCETON REVIEW
AMERICAN HISTORY AND SOCIAL STUDIES SUBJECT TEST I

Question Number	Correct Answer	Right	Wrong	Question Number	Correct Answer	Right	Wrong	Question Number	Correct Answer	Right	Wrong
1	C	___	___	33	C	___	___	65	A	___	___
2	A	___	___	34	E	___	___	66	C	___	___
3	D	___	___	35	C	___	___	67	B	___	___
4	B	___	___	36	A	___	___	68	A	___	___
5	C	___	___	37	E	___	___	69	B	___	___
6	E	___	___	38	C	___	___	70	B	___	___
7	D	___	___	39	D	___	___	71	A	___	___
8	C	___	___	40	B	___	___	72	D	___	___
9	C	___	___	41	B	___	___	73	D	___	___
10	C	___	___	42	C	___	___	74	C	___	___
11	B	___	___	43	B	___	___	75	A	___	___
12	A	___	___	44	C	___	___	76	B	___	___
13	E	___	___	45	D	___	___	77	A	___	___
14	C	___	___	46	D	___	___	78	D	___	___
15	A	___	___	47	E	___	___	79	C	___	___
16	C	___	___	48	B	___	___	80	A	___	___
17	E	___	___	49	D	___	___	81	B	___	___
18	A	___	___	50	D	___	___	82	A	___	___
19	B	___	___	51	B	___	___	83	C	___	___
20	A	___	___	52	B	___	___	84	A	___	___
21	C	___	___	53	E	___	___	85	C	___	___
22	C	___	___	54	D	___	___	86	A	___	___
23	D	___	___	55	B	___	___	87	A	___	___
24	C	___	___	56	E	___	___	88	B	___	___
25	C	___	___	57	D	___	___	89	D	___	___
26	D	___	___	58	A	___	___	90	D	___	___
27	D	___	___	59	B	___	___	91	B	___	___
28	B	___	___	60	C	___	___	92	A	___	___
29	E	___	___	61	D	___	___	93	A	___	___
30	A	___	___	62	E	___	___	94	B	___	___
31	D	___	___	63	D	___	___	95	E	___	___
32	D	___		64	C	___	___				

THE PRINCETON REVIEW AMERICAN HISTORY AND SOCIAL STUDIES SUBJECT TEST I SCORE CONVERSION TABLE

Recentered scale as of April 1995

Raw Score	Scaled Score	Raw Score	Scaled Score	Raw Score	Scaled Score
95	800	60	650	25	430
94	800	59	640	24	430
93	800	58	640	23	420
92	800	57	630	22	410
91	800	56	630	21	410
90	800	55	620	20	400
89	800	54	610	19	390
88	800	53	610	18	390
87	800	52	600	17	380
86	800	51	590	16	380
85	800	50	590	15	370
84	800	49	580	14	360
83	790	48	580	13	360
82	790	47	570	12	350
81	780	46	560	11	340
80	780	45	560	10	340
79	780	44	550	9	330
78	770	43	540	8	330
77	760	42	540	7	320
76	750	41	530	6	310
75	740	40	530	5	310
74	740	39	520	4	300
73	730	38	510	3	290
72	730	37	510	2	290
71	720	36	500	1	280
70	710	35	490	0	280
69	710	34	490	−1	270
68	700	33	480	−2	260
67	690	32	480	−3	260
66	690	31	470	−4	250
65	680	30	460	−5	250
64	680	29	460	−6	240
63	670	28	450	−7	230
62	660	27	440	−8	230
61	660	26	440	−9	220
				−10 through −25	210

6

The Princeton Review American History and Social Studies Subject Test II

THE PRINCETON REVIEW AMERICAN HISTORY AND SOCIAL STUDIES SUBJECT TEST II

The test that follows is a simulated American History Subject Test.
   In order to get a good estimate of your score, you should take this exam under test conditions.

   ◆   Give yourself an hour to do the test when you are not going to be bothered
       by anyone. Unplug the phones and tell your parents to tell your friends
       that you are not home.

   ◆   Clear away a space to work in. You want no distractions.

   ◆   Have someone else time you. It's too easy to fudge the time when you are
       keeping track of it yourself.

   ◆   Tear out the answer sheet provided in the back of the book. This way, you
       will get the feel for filling in all those lovely ovals.

   ◆   Don't worry about the complicated instructions; just pick the correct
       answer.

   ◆   Instructions for grading the exam are on page 133.

GOOD LUCK!

AMERICAN HISTORY AND SOCIAL STUDIES SUBJECT TEST II

SECTION 1

Your responses to the American History and Social Studies Subject Test questions must be filled in on Section One of your answer sheet (the box on the front of the answer sheet). Marks on any other section will not be counted toward your American History and Social Studies Subject Test score.

When your supervisor gives the signal, turn the page and begin the American History and Social Studies Subject Test. There are 100 numbered ovals on the answer sheet and 90 questions in the American History Subject Test. Therefore, use only ovals 1 to 90 for recording your answers.

AMERICAN HISTORY AND SOCIAL STUDIES TEST II

<u>Directions</u>: Each of the questions or incomplete statements below is followed by five suggested answers or completions. Select one that is best in each case and then fill in the corresponding oval on the answer sheet.

1. The most important cash crop in seventeenth-century Virginia was

   (A) tobacco
   (B) corn
   (C) wheat
   (D) barley
   (E) grapes

2. Which of the following was LEAST often considered in determining an individualís voting status in a colonial legislature?

   (A) The person's race
   (B) The person's gender
   (C) Whether or not the person was born in the colonies
   (D) Whether or not the person owned property
   (E) The colony in which the person resided

3. The concept of "virtual representation" is best summarized by which of the following?

   (A) Because colonial governors represented the king of England, they could exercise all the powers of the monarchy.
   (B) British colonists in America were represented in Parliament by virtue of the fact that Parliament represents all British subjects, whether or not they are allowed to vote.
   (C) Native Americans should be allowed to file lawsuits in U.S. federal courts even though they are not citizens of the United States.
   (D) Wealthy Southern landowners should be allowed to hire others to serve, in their places, in the Confederate army.
   (E) Because a flag stands for the country it represents, the Pledge of Allegiance is, in effect, a loyalty oath to the United States.

4. The election of 1824 is often called the first "modern election" because it was the first

   (A) to occur following the ratification of the Bill of Rights
   (B) that was decided by voters in the Western states
   (C) to utilize voting booths
   (D) in which a candidate chosen by party leaders did not win the nomination
   (E) in which African Americans were allowed to vote

5. The first to use the presidential veto extensively was

   (A) George Washington
   (B) Thomas Jefferson
   (C) Andrew Jackson
   (D) William Henry Harrison
   (E) James Buchanan

6. Congress brought impeachment proceedings against Andrew Johnson primarily because

   (A) Johnson sought to block the harsher aspects of Congressional Reconstruction
   (B) Johnson's Republican policies had fallen out of favor with the Democratic majority
   (C) Johnson repeatedly vetoed Congressional aid packages aimed at reestablishing the South's economic independence
   (D) a Congressional committee discovered that Johnson had accepted bribes from Western gold speculators
   (E) it was rumored that Johnson was too ill to execute the office of the presidency effectively

GO ON TO THE NEXT PAGE

7. Which of the following best describes the "muckrakers" of the Progressive era?

   (A) Politicians who slandered opponents in order to win elections
   (B) State prisoners who, working in chain gangs, cleaned state roads
   (C) Journalists whose reports exposed corruption in government and business
   (D) Novelists who wrote historical fiction about the Civil War era
   (E) Social scientists who analyzed all human behavior in the context of Freudian theory

8. "In good time we are going to sweep into power in this nation and throughout the world. We are going to destroy all enslaving and degrading capitalist institutions and recreate them as free and humanizing institutions."

   The statement above best represents the ideology of

   (A) Radical Republicans of the 1870s
   (B) American Socialists of the 1910s
   (C) Isolationists of the 1920s
   (D) New Deal Democrats of the 1930s
   (E) McCarthyites of the 1950s

9. Many of the programs Franklin D. Roosevelt initiated during "the first hundred days" had been discontinued by 1936 because of

   (A) adverse Supreme Court decisions
   (B) overriding Congressional legislation
   (C) unfavorable public opinion poll results
   (D) contradictory executive orders
   (E) the successful completion of their mission

10. The development of the interstate highway system was accompanied by a sizable population shift from

    (A) Western states to Eastern states
    (B) cities to suburbs
    (C) rural areas to large urban centers
    (D) single-family housing to apartment buildings
    (E) Southern states to Midwestern states

11. Lyndon Johnson's social programs were known collectively as the

    (A) American System
    (B) Second New Deal
    (C) New Frontier
    (D) Great Society
    (E) 1,000 Points of Light

12. In the sixteenth century, Spain was the dominant colonial force in the New World because

    (A) no other European nations knew of the existence the Americas
    (B) other European countries lacked both the necessary capital and manpower to colonize the New World
    (C) Spanish settlers adopted the indigenous religions and cultures of the New World
    (D) Spain had negotiated with other countries for the exclusive rights to settle the New World
    (E) the Spanish Armada controlled the Atlantic Ocean

13. The fundamental difference between the Congregationalist and Separatist wings of the Puritan movement was that

    (A) one group settled in the northern colonies, the other in the South
    (B) only one group wanted to split from the Anglican church
    (C) only one group advocated the separation of church and state
    (D) one group believed the Bible was factually accurate, the other believed it was not
    (E) one group remained in England, the other emigrated to the New World

GO ON TO THE NEXT PAGE

14. Which of the following statements about indentured servants in the seventeenth century is NOT correct?

    (A) The majority of those who were indentured did not survive their terms of servitude.
    (B) The majority of British immigrants in the southern colonies were indentured servants.
    (C) Terms of indenture were usually seven years, after which indentured servants received their freedom and, often, a plot of land.
    (D) Indentured servants served under the exact same conditions as did African slaves.
    (E) The majority of indentured servants were males between 14 and 29 years old.

15. The Sugar Act of 1764 was designed to

    (A) encourage colonists to import more sugar from Great Britain
    (B) strengthen the colonial economy by increasing the duty England paid on imports
    (C) raise revenues to offset the costs of the French-Indian War
    (D) improve relations among the English, French, and Spanish colonists in the New World
    (E) prevent the impressment of American colonists to the British navy

16. The system under which national and state governments share constitutional power is called

    (A) federalism
    (B) nationalism
    (C) idealism
    (D) autocracy
    (E) oligarchy

17. The transition of the American economy from a subsistence economy to a market economy was largely the result of two inventions by Eli Whitney. Those two inventions were the

    (A) automobile and the cotton gin
    (B) telephone and the telegraph
    (C) repeating rifle and interchangeable machine parts
    (D) cotton gin and the electric light
    (E) cotton gin and interchangeable machine parts

18. The Embargo Act of 1807 resulted in all of the following EXCEPT

    (A) the near-collapse of New England's import-export industry
    (B) the alleviation of French and British harassment of American ships
    (C) the cessation of legal trade with Canada
    (D) an increase in smuggling of British goods into the United States
    (E) a sharp decrease in the value of American farm surplus

19. Which of the following factors contributed LEAST to the demise of the Federalist Party?

    (A) Throughout the early nineteenth century, party leadership shifted from moderates to extremists.
    (B) The loss of the presidency in 1800 disrupted the unity of the party.
    (C) The resolutions of the Hartford Convention caused those outside the party to view the Federalists as traitors.
    (D) The party's power base was New England, a region that grew less powerful politically as more states were added to the Union.
    (E) Dissension over the Kansas-Nebraska Act split the party along regional lines.

20. The Compromise of 1850 included all of the following provisions EXCEPT

    (A) Admission of California to the Union, as a free state.
    (B) Creation of two new territories, Utah and New Mexico.
    (C) Repudiation of the concept of popular sovereignty.
    (D) Prohibition of slavery in the District of Columbia.
    (E) Strengthening of the fugitive slave law.

GO ON TO THE NEXT PAGE

21. Signs such as the one shown in the photograph were imposed and enforced by

    (A) Radical Reconstructionists
    (B) the Fourteenth Amendment to the Constitution
    (C) the Taft-Hartley Act
    (D) the Wilmot Proviso
    (E) Jim Crow laws

22. The Open Door Policy was primarily aimed at increasing sales of American goods in

    (A) Vietnam
    (B) Eastern Europe
    (C) France
    (D) China
    (E) Brazil

23. The majority of Japanese-Americans imprisoned in internment camps during World War II

    (A) were native-born Americans
    (B) were employees of the Japanese government
    (C) lived on Pacific islands
    (D) had expressed their primary allegiance to Japan during the 1940 census
    (E) worked in the munitions industry

24. During World War II, the availability of consumer goods to civilians

    (A) increased greatly, because the war invigorated the economy
    (B) increased slightly, because some citizens were overseas serving in the armed forces
    (C) remained at the same level it had been at prior to the war
    (D) decreased slightly, causing prices to rise; only the poor were substantially effected
    (E) decreased greatly, to the point that the government had to ration most necessities

25. Which of the following best summarizes the primary motivation for U.S. involvement in the Vietnam War?

    (A) Vietnam was the source of many strategic minerals essential to American industry.
    (B) The domino theory held that the fall of Vietnam to Communism would lead to a Communist takeover of the region.
    (C) The United States was obliged to commit troops under the NATO charter.
    (D) The United States sent troops to the region in order to prevent a Japanese invasion of Vietnam.
    (E) The United States sent troops to Vietnam in response to the India-Pakistan Wars.

26. The political party an individual chooses to join is most influenced by

    (A) the region in which the individual lives
    (B) the amount of money the individual has
    (C) which party the individualís parents belonged to
    (D) whether the individual completed high school
    (E) whether the individual is self-employed

GO ON TO THE NEXT PAGE →

27. During the early seventeenth century, the British valued their American colonies primarily as

    (A) markets for raw goods produced in England's West Indian colonies
    (B) producers of livestock and fresh fruits and vegetables
    (C) manufacturing centers
    (D) population centers from which the British military could draft soldiers
    (E) conduits of trade with Native American artisans

28. The Articles of Confederation were flawed in all of the following ways EXCEPT

    (A) They did not create a chief executive office of the government.
    (B) They did not empower the government to levy taxes.
    (C) They did not grant the national government the right to regulate commerce.
    (D) They made the admission of new states to the union impossible.
    (E) They required the unanimous consent of the states for all national legislation.

29. Which of the following does NOT describe a beneficial economic result of the construction of the Erie Canal?

    (A) The success of the Erie Canal sparked a boom in canal construction across the country, providing jobs for thousands.
    (B) The canal greatly decreased the cost of moving cargo from the Midwest to New York City.
    (C) The building and maintenance of the canal provided a foundation for the economies of several cities along its banks.
    (D) The availability of the canal greatly eased traffic along the congested Mississippi River, especially in the South.
    (E) By creating greater access to a port city, the canal facilitated more trade with Europe.

30. Which of the following is true of the Indian removal policy pursued by the United States during Andrew Jackson's presidency?

    (A) It met with great popular resistance in the states.
    (B) It was implemented with the cooperation of all Indian tribes involved.
    (C) Its implementation violated Indian rights as defined by the Supreme Court.
    (D) It was less harsh than the policy pursued by the previous administration.
    (E) Its focus was the relocation of Indians living in the Northeastern states.

31. The United States took control of the Oregon Territory by

    (A) annexing it from Mexico during the Mexican War
    (B) expelling the Russian army, which occupied the territory
    (C) bartering American-held colonies to France, which owned the Oregon Territory
    (D) buying it from the Native Americans who lived there
    (E) negotiating a settlement with Great Britain, which also laid claim to the area

32. The Reconstruction Act of 1867 required Southern states to do all of the following to gain readmission to the Union EXCEPT

    (A) Allow blacks to participate in state conventions and elections
    (B) Ratify the Fourteenth Amendment to the Constitution
    (C) Pay reparations and provide land grants to all former slaves
    (D) Rewrite the state constitution
    (E) Submit the state constitution to the U.S. Congress for approval

GO ON TO THE NEXT PAGE →

33. The cartoon above depicts Theodore Roosevelt as

    (A) a militant imperialist
    (B) a *laissez-faire* economist
    (C) an overseas advocate of American exports
    (D) a trust-buster
    (E) an environmentalist

34. In his book *The Souls of Black Folks*, W.E.B. Du Bois challenged Booker T. Washington's views concerning the advancement of African-Americans in American society. The difference between the two men's positions can be best summed up as the difference between

    (A) despair and optimism
    (B) violence and pacifism
    (C) religiousness and atheism
    (D) democratic and totalitarian ideals
    (E) confrontation and accommodation

35. Which of the following correctly states Woodrow Wilson's position on Germany's use of U-boats during World War I?

    (A) Wilson demanded that all U-boat attacks be stopped because he believed that they violated international law.
    (B) Wilson opposed only the use of U-boats against British ships.
    (C) Wilson supported the U-boat attacks, because their primary targets were British ships.
    (D) Because the U-boats were built by American manufacturers, Wilson actively campaigned for their use.
    (E) Because the U-boats traveled underwater, their existence was secret and Wilson did not learn of them until after the war ended.

36. "I have no trouble with my enemies. I can take care of my enemies in a fight. But my friends . . . they're the ones who keep me walking the floor at nights!"

The president who made this statement presided over an administration besmirched by the Teapot Dome Scandal, among other instances of corruption. He was

    (A) George Washington
    (B) Franklin Pierce
    (C) Woodrow Wilson
    (D) Warren G. Harding
    (E) Dwight D. Eisenhower

37. In *Gideon v. Wainwright,* the Supreme Court ruled that the government must

    (A) enforce federal laws guaranteeing African-Americans the right to vote
    (B) provide defense lawyers to felony defendants who are too poor to hire attorneys
    (C) prevent businesses from establishing monopolies in essential services, such as food production
    (D) overturn laws aimed at discriminating against unpopular religious groups
    (E) advise criminal suspects of their right not to incriminate themselves

GO ON TO THE NEXT PAGE

38. The sites of colonial cities were chosen primarily on the basis of their proximity to

    (A) gold mines
    (B) coal reserves
    (C) wild game
    (D) mountains
    (E) waterways

39. Which of the following is true of the Townshend Acts?

    (A) They halved the number of English military and government officials in the colonies.
    (B) They did not impose any new taxes on the colonists.
    (C) They stripped the colonial legislatures of the "power of the purse" by altering the method by which tax collectors were paid.
    (D) They offered the colonists direct representation in Parliament if they, in return, would renounce the Declaration of Independence
    (E) They repealed the Tea Act.

40. Throughout the nineteenth century, United States senators were chosen by

    (A) popular election
    (B) the House of Representatives
    (C) the president
    (D) their state governors
    (E) their state legislatures

41. Which of the following is NOT true of the reform movements of the 1830s?

    (A) Their memberships were dominated by women.
    (B) They were concentrated primarily in the Midwest.
    (C) Many were inspired by the Second Great Awakening.
    (D) Their alliance with the Whigs was stronger than their alliance with the Democrats.
    (E) Most reform groups were devoted to improving the lots of disenfranchised groups.

42. Which of the following is NOT a nineteenth-century American novel?

    (A) *Moby Dick*
    (B) *For Whom the Bell Tolls*
    (C) *The Last of the Mohicans*
    (D) *The Adventures of Huckleberry Finn*
    (E) *The Scarlet Letter*

43. During the 1840s, the greatest number of immigrants to the United States were born in

    (A) Ireland
    (B) Cuba
    (C) Japan
    (D) Russia
    (E) Canada

44. In the early 1850s, many Northern states passed personal liberty laws in response to the

    (A) political platform of the Know-Nothing Party
    (B) growing popularity of the concept of Manifest Destiny
    (C) Fugitive Slave Act
    (D) Emancipation Proclamation
    (E) Haymarket Square Riot

45. The Populists wanted the government to increase the amount of money in circulation because they believed that doing so would result in

    (A) a recession, which would allow banks to increase the number of mortgage foreclosures
    (B) a drop in the wholesale price index, which would spur international trade
    (C) price stagnation, which would encourage foreign investment in American manufacturing
    (D) inflation, which would make it easier for farmers to repay their loans
    (E) universal employment for adults

GO ON TO THE NEXT PAGE

46. In the early twentieth century, the United States government asserted its right to intervene in Latin American politics if it felt that instability in the region threatened U.S. security. That assertion is known as the

   (A) domino theory
   (B) Roosevelt Corollary to the Monroe Doctrine
   (C) "mutually assured destruction" strategy
   (D) "good neighbor" policy
   (E) doctrine of social Darwinism

47. All of the following contributed to the Senate's defeat of the Treaty of Versailles EXCEPT

   (A) President Wilson's unwillingness to compromise with the Senate
   (B) the opposition of the British and French governments to the treaty
   (C) post-war isolationism among conservatives
   (D) widespread skepticism about the potential effectiveness of the League of Nations
   (E) criticism that the treaty punished Germany too harshly

48. Members of which of the following groups would have been LEAST likely to switch allegiances, from the Republican to the Democratic party, because of the New Deal?

   (A) African-Americans
   (B) the poor
   (C) economic conservatives
   (D) city dwellers
   (E) union members

Paid Civilian Employment of the Federal Government, 1911–1970

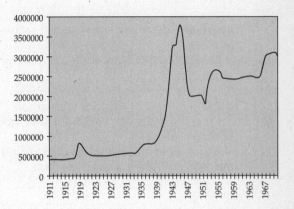

49. Which of the following hypotheses best accounts for the trends in federal employment of civilians shown in the graph above?

   (A) The government grows most rapidly during wartime.
   (B) Growth in the federal government closely mirrors the growth of the population of the United States.
   (C) The growth and reduction of the federal government is primarily a function of which party controls the White House.
   (D) By employing those who would otherwise remained unemployed, the government engineered the country's recovery from the Great Depression.
   (E) Increases in the number of rights guaranteed to citizens is always accompanied by an immediate growth in the size of government.

GO ON TO THE NEXT PAGE

50. In deciding to drop atomic bombs on Japan, President Truman was probably LEAST influenced by his

    (A) misconception that the bomb was no more destructive than other conventional weapons of the era
    (B) fear that the Soviet Union would join the war against Japan
    (C) certainty that an invasion of Japan would result in numerous American casualties
    (D) belief that it was the best way to force a quick Japanese surrender
    (E) desire to demonstrate to the rest of the world the power of America's new weapon

51. The difference between a "cold war" and a "hot war" is that, during a "cold war,"

    (A) neither side publicly acknowledges its animosity toward its enemy
    (B) United Nations armed forces are used to maintain treaties
    (C) opponents differ over religious, rather than political, ideals
    (D) the opposing sides are military superpowers
    (E) opposing sides do not engage in military combat

52. Anne Hutchinson was banished from the Massachusetts Bay colony because she

    (A) campaigned for women's suffrage
    (B) argued that all colonists should have the right to bear arms
    (C) believed that one could communicate with God without the assistance of the clergy
    (D) organized a boycott of British goods
    (E) sold provisions and weapons to local Native Americans

53. Most historians regard the First Great Awakening as a response to

    (A) Enlightenment ideals
    (B) the English Civil War
    (C) the Industrial Age
    (D) World War I
    (E) the Great Depression

54. "I hold it that a little rebellion, now and then, is a good thing, and as necessary in the political world as storms in the physical."

    The statement above was made by Thomas Jefferson in response to

    (A) Bacon's Rebellion
    (B) the War of 1812
    (C) the Louisiana Purchase
    (D) Shays' Rebellion
    (E) the Embargo Act of 1807

55. The XYZ affair resulted in

    (A) a reversal of American public sentiment toward France
    (B) an American declaration of war against English settlers in Canada
    (C) the mass relocation of Southwestern Indians
    (D) the establishment of the First National Bank
    (E) the Missouri Compromise

56. Although Texas petitioned for admission to the Union in 1836, the United States did not annex the territory until 1845. Of the following issues, which two were most responsible for that delay?

    I. Concern for the rights of Native Americans in the region
    II. Slavery
    III. Widespread popular antagonism toward expansion of any type
    IV. Fear of provoking war with Mexico

    (A) I and III
    (B) I and IV
    (C) II and III
    (D) II and IV
    (E) III and IV

GO ON TO THE NEXT PAGE →

57. The site of the photograph above is most probably

   (A) Rhode Island in the 1830s
   (B) Ohio in the 1850s
   (C) Nebraska in the 1880s
   (D) Illinois in the 1910s
   (E) Louisiana in the 1940s

58. A historian wanting to analyze quantitative data concerning how Americans earned their living during the 1880s would probably find the most useful information in which of the following sources?

   (A) The diary of a man who worked several jobs during the decade
   (B) United States census reports
   (C) Employment advertisements in a large city newspaper
   (D) Letters from a mid-level government bureaucrat to a friend overseas
   (E) Lyrics to popular songs from that era

59. The American takeover of the Philippines after the Spanish-American War was immediately followed by

   (A) the establishment of democratic self-rule on the islands
   (B) a transfer of control of the islands to Japan
   (C) a Philippine referendum calling for admission to the United States
   (D) a protracted armed insurgence by Philippine nationalists
   (E) a second war, between the United States and England, for control of the island

60. The Progressive movement received the greatest support from which of the following constituencies?

   (A) middle-class city dwellers
   (B) land-owning farmers
   (C) migrant farm workers
   (D) Southern Democrats
   (E) Western cattle ranchers

GO ON TO THE NEXT PAGE

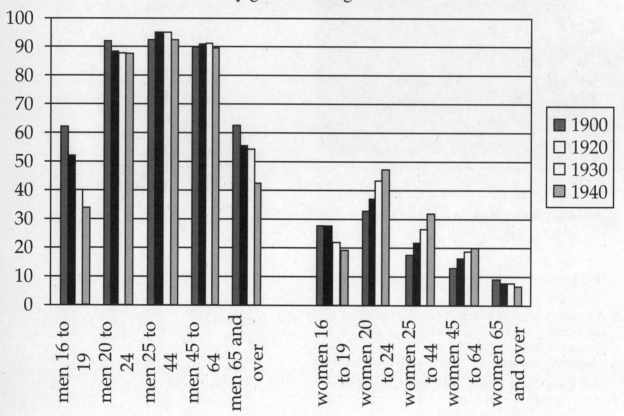

Percentage of population in labor force 1900–1940,
by gender and age

61. The data presented in the chart above best supports which of the following conclusions?

(A) Preparations for the United States' entry into World War II increased employment rates for all segments of the American population.

(B) Young people chose to pursue full-time education in increasing numbers between 1900 and 1940.

(C) Child labor laws enacted during the Progressive era essentially put an end to the employment of people under the age of 16.

(D) Between the years 1920 and 1930, most men left agricultural jobs to pursue work in manufacturing.

(E) Between 1900 and 1940, men between the ages of 25 and 64 who did not work simply did not look hard enough for jobs.

GO ON TO THE NEXT PAGE

62. Which of the following novels does NOT take African-American alienation from the cultural mainstream as one of its central themes?

    (A) Ralph Ellison's *Invisible Man*
    (B) Richard Wright's *Native Son*
    (C) F. Scott Fitzgerald's *The Great Gatsby*
    (D) Zora Neale Hurston's *Their Eyes Were Watching God*
    (E) James Baldwin's *Go Tell it On the Mountain*

63. Most historians believe that Franklin Roosevelt decided to run for an unprecedented third presidential term primarily because he

    (A) was convinced that the U.S. would soon enter World War II
    (B) hoped to establish a precedent of three-term presidencies
    (C) believed that only he could prevent the Communist takeover of Cuba
    (D) wanted Harry Truman to succeed him but believed Truman was not yet ready to take over the presidency
    (E) knew that he would die within weeks of his reelection

64. In response to a 1957 court order to integrate Little Rock public high schools, the state of Arkansas

    (A) closed the city's high schools for two years
    (B) initiated the nation's first state-funded school busing program
    (C) integrated schools in the city of Little Rock, but not in smaller towns
    (D) allowed blacks and whites to attend the same schools, but held segregated classes
    (E) negotiated a compromise with the court, allowing the state ten years to complete the integration process

65. Which of the following states the central idea of the 1963 book *The Feminine Mystique*?

    (A) The United States military, having succeeded at racial integration, should also integrate the two genders.
    (B) Cultural forces conspire to discourage women from pursuing careers and to encourage them to seek fulfillment in domestic life.
    (C) Mentally, psychologically, and physically, women are fundamentally no different from men.
    (D) Those who pursue abortion rights do so in support of a larger, politically subversive agenda.
    (E) The economic circumstances that, in many families, require both spouses to work full-time are bringing about the destruction of the American family.

66. The primary purpose of the War Powers Resolution of 1973 was to

    (A) provide the U.S. Army with enough funding to win the Vietnam War
    (B) allow the president to suspend the writ of habeas corpus during times of war
    (C) empower military leaders to overrule presidential orders
    (D) pardon all Americans who had refused military service during the Vietnam War
    (E) make it more difficult for the president to unilaterally commit American troops overseas

67. Bacon's Rebellion is one of the earliest examples of

    (A) a potentially violent conflict resolved through peaceful negotiation
    (B) armed conflict between French and British colonists
    (C) an act of pacifist civil disobedience
    (D) a populist uprising in America
    (E) a colonial protest against unfair tariffs imposed by the British

GO ON TO THE NEXT PAGE

68. Of the following, which did mercantilists consider most important to a country's economic well-being?

    (A) Full employment
    (B) A favorable balance of trade
    (C) The establishment of a large national debt at moderate interest rates
    (D) Free trade
    (E) The extension of civil liberties to as many people as possible

69. Which of the following argued for a "broad constructionist" interpretation of the Constitution?

    (A) Thomas Jefferson
    (B) Alexander Hamilton
    (C) James Madison
    (D) Benjamin Franklin
    (E) Thomas Paine

70. The "Lowell system" was established for the primary purpose of

    (A) clearly defining and distinguishing the roles of the local, state, and national governments
    (B) promoting abolitionism in the southern states
    (C) calculating the net worth of the United States' gross national product
    (D) rehabilitating non-violent criminals
    (E) enticing rural New England women to work in textile mills

71. In the years immediately following the declaration of the Monroe Doctrine, the doctrine's goals were achieved primarily because

    (A) the American military imposed a blockade on all European ships traveling to the Western Hemisphere
    (B) American merchants reinforced the doctrine with a boycott of goods produced in countries that violated its goals
    (C) the British navy prevented Spain and Portugal from retaking their colonies in Central and South America
    (D) American and European diplomats negotiated a treaty reiterating the Monroe Doctrine's objectives
    (E) a prolonged European economic depression made it impossible for any European nation to intervene in the Western Hemisphere

72. Andrew Jackson opposed supporters of the doctrine of nullification for all of the following reasons EXCEPT

    (A) he believed they had misinterpreted the Virginia and Kentucky Resolutions, on which their doctrine was based
    (B) Jackson feared that nullification, if accepted, would threaten the stability of the Union
    (C) nullification supporters believed the states could unilaterally interpret the Constitution; Jackson disagreed
    (D) the nullification movement was led by Jackson's political enemy, John C. Calhoun
    (E) Jackson believed that the federal government, not state governments, should exert the most influence over the lives of citizens

73. Settlement houses were established as a means of combating problems caused by

    (A) migrant farming
    (B) the Dust Bowl
    (C) strip mining
    (D) nuclear radiation
    (E) urban poverty

74. "[The wealthy man is required] . . . to consider all surplus revenues which come to him simply as trust funds, which he is called upon to administer . . . in the manner which . . . is best calculated to produce the most beneficial results for the community—[he is] the mere trustee and agent for his poorer brethren . . . doing for them better than they would or could do for themselves."

    The ideas above are most characteristic of

    (A) transcendentalism
    (B) socialism
    (C) the doctrine of nullification
    (D) black separatism
    (E) the Gospel of Wealth

GO ON TO THE NEXT PAGE

75. The Platt Amendment of 1901 primarily concerned United States relations with

    (A) Great Britain
    (B) Germany
    (C) China
    (D) Cuba
    (E) Australia

76. Before the Sixteenth Amendment to the Constitution established a federal income tax, the national government collected its greatest revenues from

    (A) customs duties
    (B) a national sales tax
    (C) fines levied in federal court
    (D) rent and lease income from federal properties
    (E) the confiscation of property from convicted felons

77. Harry Truman reversed the momentum of his 1948 reelection campaign when he began using his campaign speeches to criticize

    (A) the "unnecessary" Marshall Plan
    (B) his opponent's "lack of moral decency"
    (C) the "do-nothing" Eightieth Congress
    (D) the "militant" feminist movement
    (E) the "trouble-making" labor unions

78. Which of the following accurately describes the changes undergone by the Student Non-Violent Coordinating Committee (SNCC) and the Congress on Racial Equality (CORE) during the 1960s?

    (A) Over the course of the decade, both groups grew more supportive of American involvement in Vietnam.
    (B) At the start of the decade, both groups were non-violent and integrationist; by the end of the decade they had grown more militant and separatist.
    (C) In 1960, both groups opposed the goals expressed by Martin Luther King, Jr.; in 1970, both groups supported those same goals.
    (D) At the beginning of the decade, both groups focused on numerous political causes; by the end of the decade, each was focused solely on gaining equal rights for women.
    (E) By 1970, both groups had renounced their earlier commitment to the expansion of social welfare programs.

79. Which of the following does NOT correctly pair a Native American tribe and region in which that tribe lived during the 17th century?

    (A) Algonkians, Virginia
    (B) Doegs, Western Virginia
    (C) Pequots, Connecticut Valley
    (D) Pokanokets, Cape Cod
    (E) Sioux, Florida

80. The British established vice-admiralty courts in the colonies primarily to

    (A) prevent the colonists from organizing legislatures
    (B) try Native Americans and French settlers who threatened British colonists
    (C) make it easier to prosecute colonists who violated the Navigation Acts
    (D) protect the rights of free blacks in areas where slavery was permitted
    (E) process Loyalist property claims after the Revolutionary War

81. The ideals stated in the Declaration of Independence are most similar to those expressed in which of the following?

    (A) Machiavelli's *The Prince*
    (B) Plato's *Republic*
    (C) Thomas Hobbes' *Leviathan*
    (D) John Locke's *Two Treatises on Government*
    (E) St. Augustine's *City of God*

GO ON TO THE NEXT PAGE

82. Which of the following best describes the general impact of the War of 1812 on the United States' economy?

   (A) The war permanently altered America's trade alliances, allowing France to supplant England as the country's chief trading partner.
   (B) The disappearance of the English market for tobacco caused an economic collapse that affected the entire South.
   (C) The war quarantined the United States from European technological advances, stalling America's industrial revolution for almost a decade.
   (D) By isolating the United States from Europe, the war had the advantageous effect of promoting economic independence
   (E) War expenses bankrupted the First National Bank, halting the construction of the national railroad and putting thousands out of work.

83. Although the Mormon Church established its first headquarters in Ohio, the church's followers eventually relocated to Utah, primarily because

   (A) the region's isolation offered the church protection from its enemies
   (B) the federal government recruited church members to settle the area
   (C) a prolonged drought left much of Ohio's farmland unusable
   (D) the Shakers, who had already relocated to Utah, invited the Mormons to join their religious community
   (E) Mormon theology required the Mormons to live in complete isolation from the non-Mormon world

GO ON TO THE NEXT PAGE

Deaths in Massachusetts per
100,000 population, by selected
cause (1860 to 1870)

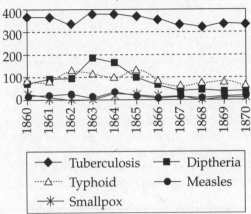

- ◆ Tuberculosis
- ■ Diptheria
- △ Typhoid
- ● Measles
- ✳ Smallpox

Deaths per 100,000, in the sate of Massachsetts	
1860	1,870
1861	1,950
1862	1,950
1863	2,250
1864	2,280
1865	2,100
1866	1,820
1867	1,700
1868	1,860
1869	1,840
1870	1,880

84. Which of the following data, if available, would be LEAST helpful in determining the impact of the Civil War on the death rate in Massachusetts during the period presented above?

(A) The number of wounded veterans who returned to the state
(B) A breakdown of the death rate by race, gender, and profession
(C) Newspaper accounts of the typhoid epidemic of 1863 and 1864
(D) Statistics relating to sanitary conditions in Massachusetts hospitals
(E) The number of medical professionals who enlisted and left the state

85. According to the cartoon, the relocation of the textile industry to the South was facilitated primarily by the region's

(A) availability of slave labor
(B) access to cheap coal
(C) proximity to European trade routes
(D) abundance of skilled fashion designers
(E) favorable weather conditions

86. Union enrollments declined throughout the 1920s for all the following reasons EXCEPT

(A) an increase in the size of the armed forces resulted in fewer potential union members in the work force
(B) pro-business Republican administrations provided less support to union causes
(C) a Red Scare dissuaded potential union members who feared association with left-wing politics
(D) unpopular strikes resulted in bad public relations for unions
(E) businesses offered workers greater benefits, including pension plans and opportunities for profit-sharing

GO ON TO THE NEXT PAGE →

87. Which of the following contributed LEAST to the economic factors that resulted in the Great Depression?

    (A) Technological advances that allowed farmers and manufacturers to overproduce, resulting in large inventories.

    (B) Concentration of wealth in too few hands, guaranteeing that business failures would have widespread ramifications.

    (C) A steadily widening gap between the cost of consumer goods and the buying power of the average consumer.

    (D) Wild speculation by stock investors, producing an unstable and volatile stock market.

    (E) Interventionist economic policies from the federal government, resulting in overly conservative behavior on the part of private investors.

88. Which of the following actions would most likely be taken by the government if it wished to slow the rate of inflation?

    (A) The Treasury Department would increase the amount of currency in circulation.

    (B) The President would order the creation of new jobs within the federal government.

    (C) The Federal Reserve Board would increase the prime interest rate.

    (D) Congress would lower the rate at which businesses are taxed.

    (E) The President's Trade Commissioner would lower export tariffs.

89. In 1932, Herbert Hoover ordered the Army against protesters who had camped in the streets of Washington D.C. throughout the summer. Those protesters were

    (A) farmers demanding that the government buy their surplus crops

    (B) former civilian government employees who had been laid off in the wake of the Depression

    (C) Communist agitators calling for a constitutional convention

    (D) African-Americans demonstrating against civil rights abuses in the South

    (E) World War I veterans demanding early payment of their benefits

90. All of the following exemplify the policy of containment EXCEPT

    (A) the Truman Doctrine

    (B) the Marshall Plan

    (C) the creation of NATO

    (D) the MacArthur-led invasion of North Korea

    (E) the 1948 Berlin airlift

STOP

IF YOU FINISH BEFORE TIME IS CALLED, YOU MAY CHECK YOUR WORK ON THIS TEST ONLY. DO NOT TURN TO ANY OTHER TEST IN THIS BOOK.

HOW TO SCORE THE PRINCETON REVIEW
AMERICAN HISTORY AND SOCIAL STUDIES SUBJECT TEST II

When you take the real exam, the proctors will collect your text booklet and bubble sheet and send your answer sheet to New Jersey where a computer (yes, a big old-fashioned one that has been around since the 1960s) looks at the pattern of filled-in ovals on your answer sheet and gives you a score. We couldn't include even a small computer with this book, so we are providing this more primitive way of scoring your exam.

DETERMINING YOUR SCORE

STEP 1 Using the answers on the next page, determine how many questions you got right and how many you got wrong on the test. Remember, questions that you do not answer don't count as either right answers or wrong answers.

STEP 2 List the number of right answers here.

(A) _____

STEP 3 List the number of wrong answers here. Now divide that number by 4. (Use a calculator if you're feeling particularly lazy.)

(B) _____ ÷ 4 = _____

STEP 4 Subtract the number of wrong answers divided by 4 from the number of correct answers. Round this score to the nearest whole number. This is your raw score.

(C) (A) ____ – (B) _____ = ____

STEP 5 To determine your real score, take the number from Step 4 above and look it up in the left column of the Score Conversion Table on page 135; the corresponding score on the right is your score on the exam.

ANSWERS TO THE PRINCETON REVIEW
AMERICAN HISTORY AND SOCIAL STUDIES SUBJECT TEST II

Question Number	Correct Answer	Right	Wrong	Question Number	Correct Answer	Right	Wrong	Question Number	Correct Answer	Right	Wrong
1	A	___	___	31	E	___	___	61	B	___	___
2	C	___	___	32	C	___	___	62	C	___	___
3	B	___	___	33	D	___	___	63	A	___	___
4	D	___	___	34	E	___	___	64	A	___	___
5	C	___	___	35	A	___	___	65	B	___	___
6	A	___	___	36	D	___	___	66	E	___	___
7	C	___	___	37	B	___	___	67	D	___	___
8	B	___	___	38	E	___	___	68	B	___	___
9	A	___	___	39	C	___	___	69	B	___	___
10	B	___	___	40	E	___	___	70	E	___	___
11	D	___	___	41	B	___	___	71	C	___	___
12	E	___	___	42	B	___	___	72	E	___	___
13	B	___	___	43	A	___	___	73	E	___	___
14	D	___	___	44	C	___	___	74	E	___	___
15	C	___	___	45	D	___	___	75	D	___	___
16	A	___	___	46	B	___	___	76	A	___	___
17	E	___	___	47	B	___	___	77	C	___	___
18	B	___	___	48	C	___	___	78	B	___	___
19	E	___	___	49	A	___	___	79	E	___	___
20	C	___	___	50	A	___	___	80	C	___	___
21	E	___	___	51	E	___	___	81	D	___	___
22	D	___	___	52	C	___	___	82	D	___	___
23	A	___	___	53	A	___	___	83	A	___	___
24	E	___	___	54	D	___	___	84	D	___	___
25	B	___	___	55	A	___	___	85	B	___	___
26	C	___	___	56	D	___	___	86	A	___	___
27	A	___	___	57	C	___	___	87	E	___	___
28	D	___	___	58	B	___	___	88	C	___	___
29	D	___	___	59	D	___	___	89	E	___	___
30	C	___	___	60	A	___	___	90	D	___	___

THE PRINCETON REVIEW AMERICAN HISTORY AND SOCIAL STUDIES SUBJECT TEST SCORE CONVERSION TABLE

Recentered scale as of April 1995

Raw Score	Scaled Score	Raw Score	Scaled Score	Raw Score	Scaled Score
90	800	55	620	20	400
89	800	54	610	19	390
88	800	53	610	18	390
87	800	52	600	17	380
86	800	51	590	16	380
85	800	50	590	15	370
84	800	49	580	14	360
83	790	48	580	13	360
82	790	47	570	12	350
81	780	46	560	11	340
80	780	45	560	10	340
79	780	44	550	9	330
78	770	43	540	8	330
77	760	42	540	7	320
76	750	41	530	6	310
75	740	40	530	5	310
74	740	39	520	4	300
73	730	38	510	3	290
72	730	37	510	2	290
71	720	36	500	1	280
70	710	35	490	0	280
69	710	34	490	−1	270
68	700	33	480	−2	260
67	690	32	480	−3	260
66	690	31	470	−4	250
65	680	30	460	−5	250
64	680	29	460	−6	240
63	670	28	450	−7	230
62	660	27	440	−8	230
61	660	26	440	−9	220
60	650	25	430	−10 through −25	210
59	640	24	430		
58	640	23	420		
57	630	22	410		
56	630	21	410		

PART **III**

The World History
Subject Test

7

Cracking the World History Subject Test

THE TEST

The World History SAT II concentrates on (surprise!) European (Western) civilization. About 60 percent of the questions from the test concern this area of the world, so don't let the title "World History" scare you. You are expected to know very little about the history of the world *per se*. The breakdown of the test is as follows:

ETS numbers the questions from 1 to 95, but you don't have to do them in that order. Answer the questions you know first.

95 questions
1 hour

200 to 800 scoring scale, with guessing penalty

Contents:

Ancient Civilizations	10–15 percent
Middle Ages (750–1450)	10–15 percent
Enlightenment/Renaissance (1450–1750)	15–20 percent
Modern (1750–present)	45–50 percent to 60–70 percent
Cross-chronological	5–10 percent

Regions covered:

Europe	60 percent
The Rest of the World*	40 percent
Middle East	5–10 percent
Africa	5–10 percent
China and Japan	5–10 percent
South Asia	5 percent
Central and S. America	5 percent
Global	3–5 percent

*Many of these questions deal with Europe as it relates to other parts of the world.

Note: In the latest edition of *Taking the SAT II Subject Tests*, the College Board claims that European history only accounts for 50 percent of the World History Subject Test. As of this writing, however, we have found that the test still conforms to our breakdown above. It is possible that the test will change slowly in the future to reflect the College Board's new breakdown.

THE SYSTEM

The idea of studying for a test on Europe and the world in its 3,000 or more years of recorded history can be a little daunting. The best way to study this vast period and to subsequently remember some of the important facts about it on the SAT II is to look at the history in a systematic way. The filter of time shifts through the various episodes of history and, despite the thousands of years that have passed and millions of people who have lived and events that have occurred, only a few incidents and people are deemed worthy enough for you to study as high school students. Unfair and biased, yes; lucky for you as you take this test, yes.

Like any SAT II, the World History Test is a very long, 95-question test, and you need to understand pacing to do your best. So, if you have skipped chapter 2, the pacing section, go back and read it now. Also, if you happen to be studying for both the American History and the World History Tests, you may notice some overlap in the techniques. Feel free to skip over similar sections, but remember, the World History Test does have some significantly different types of questions, so look out for these types as you read this section.

HISTORY AS ERAS, NOT ISOLATED FACTS

Most questions on the test are very specific, but nearly every question is connected to an Era and a Country. As we review European history we'll find that there are only a few events within each period that have remained noteworthy over the passage of time. Thus, if you can recognize the general period (the Era) and the place (the Country) of the question, you will have greatly narrowed your choices for the correct answer. Often, you only need a vague knowledge of what the question is specifically asking in order to answer it. Let's look at an example.

True or False?

Q: During the Middle Ages in Europe, people swore allegiance to their country's flag.

The political power of such monarchies as the Tudors in the late fifteenth century was brought about by

(A) the military strength of the monarch and his ability to keep order
(B) the removal of all church powers from state control
(C) the continental leadership of the Roman Catholic Church
(D) the growth of state-sanctioned religions
(E) the decentralization caused by the feudal system

True or False?

A: False! During the Middle Ages, there were no "countries" as we know them today. Under the system of feudalism, warlords ("nobles") pledged loyalty and military service to a strong lord or king in exchange for land and protection.

Even though you might not know who the Tudors are, you can still answer this question with your general knowledge of the fifteenth century. Think about the period right near the end of the Middle Ages and what would keep a strong monarch in power. We can get rid of (B), (C), (D), and (E) because they would all weaken a monarch in the fifteenth century. Only (A) would help keep a strong monarch in power. Therefore, (A) is the correct answer.

READ — CONNECT TO ERA AND COUNTRY

Your primary approach is to read the question and connect it to its Era and Country.

ELIMINATE ANTI-ERA OR NON-ERA ANSWER CHOICES

Eliminate whatever answer choices cannot be true, based on what you know about that time period and place. You can usually limit your options to a few "maybes" after this step. On the World History SAT II, common sense is a great tool. Don't think that all of the SAT II answer choices are automatically good ones merely because you are staring at them on a printed piece of paper. Some of the choices are ludicrous when you consider the Era and the Country of the questions. Watch out for these and eliminate them.

> Which of the following was a reform established
> following the French Revolution of the eighteenth
> century?
>
> (A) equality for all regardless of race or gender
> (B) the right to decent and affordable housing
> (C) the establishment of a republic
> (D) reduced powers of the military
> (E) the end of feudalistic practices

Think of the Era. What happened during the eighteenth century in France? Choice (A) is out because it implies that French women were granted some type of equal rights, which didn't occur until recently. Choice (B) is incorrect for similar reasons. Choice (D) is incorrect because Napoleon, the great French general, rose to power after the French Revolution. Choice (E) is incorrect because feudalism had been weakening for centuries by the time the French Revolution occurred. So, by eliminating the Anti-Era choices, you find that the correct answer is (C).

LET THE QUESTION BE YOUR GUIDE

The World History SAT II contains a wide variety of question types. So after you have identified the Era and the Country, it is best to approach each specific type of question individually. These question types are outlined in the next section.

LAST RESORT: GUESS AND MOVE ON

If somebody offered you a handful of dollar bills in exchange for all the change in your pocket, would you trade? Of course! It would be easy money. That's why you should always guess if you can eliminate even one answer choice. Who cares if you lose a few quarter-points if you can get a handful of points in return?

Pacing is even more important on this test than on some of the other SAT IIs. Both very long and very short questions are scattered throughout the test. Sometimes the long ones are easy, while the short ones quickly tell you that you have no idea what the answer is. Don't assume that you should skip the long ones and only do the short ones, or the other way around. The essence of pacing is to find out how well you do on each question type. Note how you do on the long, quote-like questions. If you always get them right, always do them. If the short ones throw you, figure out if your mistakes are carelessness or if you personally find a certain type of question generally impossible. Then tailor your test taking accordingly. Never spend too much time on any one question. If you can eliminate even one answer choice, guess and move on.

REVIEW: THE SYSTEM

1. Read the question and connect it to an Era and a Country.

2. Eliminate anti-Era or non-Era answer choices.

3. Let the question be your guide.

4. Last resort: Guess and move on.

THE QUESTIONS

QUOTE QUESTIONS

As many as twenty quote questions may appear on the test, but luckily they are easy to spot and easy to do. In these questions, you are given a quote or a short piece of writing and asked to identify either the speaker, the time period, or the general philosophy of the writer/speaker. These questions are general and the answer choices tend to be very different from each other, so the Era and Country technique works very well. Sometimes two questions refer to one quote, so they're efficient to do. Sometimes several questions refer to a group of quotes; they may be trickier and a little more time-consuming than the standard quote question.

The biggest danger is spending too much time on these questions. When confronted with a quote or short paragraph, if your instinct tells you, "Oh, I'd better read this carefully," it's time to re-train yourself. You want to read quickly and only as much as you need to get a general idea of who is talking about what. The question that follows the quote will always be something on the order of, "Who might have said this?" "This philosophy was popular when?" or "This theory is called what?" And the answers will usually be very distinct from each other, like (A) Gandhi, (B) Franklin D. Roosevelt, or (C) Hitler.

So the most efficient way to approach these questions is to hit them running. **Read the question first** so you know whether you are looking for: a who, a what, or a when. **Then read the quote**, always thinking about what you are looking for. As soon as you grasp what the quote is referring to, jump to the answer choices and find it. If, in the first sentence, you figure out the quote sounds like something a knight would say, go and find that answer. There's no reason to read the whole quote; the SAT II is not so tricky that they would change the meaning in the middle. **If your first impression is not specific enough to get you the answer, go back and finish reading the quote.** All the information to make the right decision is there.

Let's try this approach on an example.

> Have you ever walked into a room in your house and then suddenly forgotten what you came in there for? Reading the quotes on the SAT II World History can give you the same feeling. Until you read the question, you have no idea what you're supposed to get out of the quote. So here's a simple solution— read the question first!

Questions 1–2 refer to the following statement.

"The treaty has no provisions to aid the defeated Central empires towards becoming good neighbors, nothing to help stabilize the new European states, nothing to help reclaim Russia. It does not promote economic cooperation among the Allies nor does it encourage any type of peaceful coexistence. This agreement will undoubtedly lead to worldwide instability."

1. The treaty referred to in the statement above is most likely

   (A) the Congress of Vienna (1815)
   (B) the Treaty of Versailles (1919)
   (C) the Hitler-Stalin Pact (1936)
   (D) the Marshall Plan (1947)
   (E) the Warsaw Pact (1955)

2. The "worldwide instability" mentioned above most likely predicts

   (A) the Crimean War
   (B) the First World War
   (C) the Second World War
   (D) the Cold War
   (E) the Thirty Years War

Looking at the questions, we see that we need to determine when this quote was written. A "quick read" of the quote shows that the war was between the Central states of Europe and the Allies. The treaty is not a fair one, however, so it must be the treaty after World War I that led up to World War II. Therefore, the answer to question 1 is **(B)**, and question 2 is **(C)**. (Even if you are unsure of the name of the World War I treaty, the date, 1919, should give you a clue.)

Sometimes quote questions get a little more complicated by quoting two or more different viewpoints. The goal here is to keep the quotes straight as you answer the question. It may be helpful to jot down what you think about each quote beside it. Don't write much, just one or two words to remind you of it, like "eighteenth century" or "farmer." Try to limit your need to read anything twice; it's a big time-waster.

REVIEW: QUOTE QUESTIONS

1. Read the question first.

2. Read only as much of the quote as necessary. Think Era and Country.

3. Eliminate incorrect answer choices.

4. If more than one choice is left, go back and quickly finish reading the quote.

> "I wanted to avoid violence, I want to avoid violence. Nonviolence is the first article of my faith."
> —Mohandas Gandhi

EXCEPT QUESTIONS

EXCEPT Questions are also very popular on the World History SAT II; there may be up to twenty-five of these questions on the test. LEAST and NOT questions are the ugly cousins of EXCEPT questions, so you can treat them in the same manner.

Except Questions Are True or False Questions in Disguise

The trick to dealing with an EXCEPT Question is to forget about the EXCEPT part and answer it like a True-False Question. Usually, it's the backwards nature of the EXCEPT in the question, not the subject of the question itself, that gets people confused. So, cross out that word and your troubles will be solved. Read the question without the EXCEPT, and then answer "Yes" or "No" to each answer choice. A "Yes" will be a true statement and the "No" will be the false one, or the exception. On an EXCEPT question the right answer will always be the "No." Remember, you are looking for the exception, or the one that is not true for the question itself.

Pop Quiz

Q: Which one of these is not like the others?
- (A) India—Hinduism
- (B) Middle East—Islam
- (C) China—Taoism
- (D) United States—Judaism
- (E) Ancient Rome—Christianity

All of the following countries contributed to the flowering of culture in the Renaissance EXCEPT

(A) Italy	YES. Eliminate.
(B) Germany	NO. It wasn't even around.
(C) France	YES. Eliminate.
(D) Spain	YES. Eliminate.
(E) England	YES. Eliminate.

This is an easy example, but it clearly shows how to use the EXCEPT trick. You will find it much easier to keep track of the question you are trying to answer by using this method.

"One of These Things is Not Like the Others"

Remember the kid's game, "One of these things is not like the others"? Well, that same technique can suit you well on many of the EXCEPT questions on the World History SAT II. Sometimes one answer choice will noticeably stick out from the other answer choices. The one that's not similar to the others is the correct answer, the exception. Match this with the Era and Country technique and you will often find that the exception is the anti-Era choice. It seems that the easiest way for the test-makers to create a "false" answer is to pull something from another time period.

> Blahblah blah eighteenth-century philosophy
> blahblah EXCEPT
>
> (A) religious tolerance
> (B) freedom of thought and expression
> (C) thought about political and social structures
> (D) the communal sharing of land
> (E) value in scientific logic

Eighteenth-century philosophy would place the question in the Enlightenment period in Europe and answer choice (D) noticeably is out of that Era. The idea of communal property in Europe is solidly nineteenth century and it developed as a reaction to the *laissez-faire* economic ideas of the Enlightenment. So, using your Era knowledge, choice (D) is clearly the anti-Era choice and the right answer.

REVIEW: EXCEPT Questions

1. Cross out the EXCEPT—Answer "Yes" or "No."

2. Ask, "Which one of these things is not like the others?"

3. The "No" or the anti-Era/non-Era choice is right.

I, II, III (IV & V) Questions

These are the same questions that you love to hate from the SAT; at least, they are in appearance. Actually, the writers of the SAT II use these questions in two ways. The first way is the way you are used to.

Learn as you go

You approach these questions by learning as you go and using the Process of Elimination (POE). If you know I is wrong, cross out all the answer choices that contain I.

> Which of the following states had centralized
> leadership?
>
> I. Ancient Athens
> II. Eighteenth-century England
> III. Germany in 1939
>
> (A) I only
> (B) II only
> (C) I and II only
> (D) II and III only
> (E) I, II, and III

Start with I: Ancient Athens was a democracy and was decentralized. From this information, we can eliminate (A), (C), and (E) because these choices contain I. Since both (B) and (D) have II, let's look at III to decide which choice is right. Germany in 1939 was ruled by Adolf Hitler under strongly centralized leadership. Therefore, if III is right, the answer must be **(D)**.

Time-sequence questions

The second way that the SAT II writers use the Roman numerals format is to ask you to give an order of events, like the order of the events for the Russian Revolution. These are especially difficult because you must put in chronological order four or five events that you probably remember as a block in time. So, it's best to look toward the *ends*, that is, the beginning event or the final event of the sequence. If you know that choice III occurred first, cross out any ordering that does not have it first. If you happen to know that III was first and IV was last, the odds are that only one answer choice will match this, and you will not have to bother with the ones in the middle. Let's try one of these.

Beginning with the earliest, which of the following represents the correct chronological order of events around the time of the French Revolution?

    I. Declaration of the Rights of Man
    II. The Reign of Terror
    III. The reign of Louis XVI
    IV. The rise of Napoleon

(A) I, II, III, IV
(B) III, I, II, IV
(C) II, I, III, IV
(D) IV, II, I, III
(E) III, I, IV, II

Roman Numeral POE Quiz

Q: Which of the following is true?
    I. The Roman Empire fell in 1972.
    II. Austria's Prince Klemens von Metternich was a conservative.
    III. China is in Asia.
    (A) I only
    (B) II only
    (C) I and II only
    (D) II and III only
    (E) I, II, and III

You should realize that Napoleon came after the French Revolution and that Louis XVI was in power before the Revolution. From this information, you can eliminate (A), (C), (D), and (E). Also, the Reign of Terror came directly after the Declaration of the Rights of Man. Therefore, **(B)** is the correct answer.

REVIEW: ROMAN NUMERAL QUESTIONS

1. Learn as you go by using Process of Elimination.

2. If it's a time-sequence question, look to the ends. Decide what happened first and what happened last.

CHARTS, PICTURES, AND CARTOONS

Expect to find about ten questions on the World History SAT II that refer to either a picture, chart, or political cartoon. You will also see several geography-like questions accompanied by maps. The picture questions tend to be identifications of architectural forms or art. The first rule in dealing with any of these questions is to read the question first. Many of the maps can be confusing and there is no point in studying them if you are not yet sure what the question is. The second step is to identify the region. Often the SAT II writers use these questions to focus on the non-European parts of the world and they are testing whether you know anything about, say, Africa or Latin America. Just as in the Era and Country technique, you want to place yourself in the geographical context of the picture or map of the question.

If these steps do not get you the right answer, use common sense or the information you are given in the question. Ask yourself, "What are they testing with this question?" or "What do I need to know about this region that is different from other regions?" This questioning should get you down to only a couple of choices. Then guess and move on.

Do not get trapped on a chart or picture question. These questions are usually pretty easy, but if one is stumping you, move on. It's a trap to think, "I should be able to get this one!" That steals time away from other questions. Remember, it's foolish to waste time on any one question—keep moving. Let's try some examples.

Roman Numeral POE Quiz

A: Roman numeral I is clearly false so we can get rid of (A), (C), and (E). Is II true? Who cares? Roman numeral III is true, so the answer must be (D), because it is the only answer left that has III in it.

Population in 1981

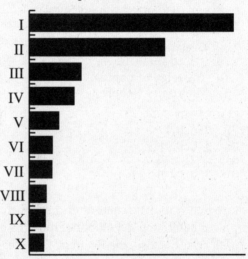

The graph above shows the relative populations of the 10 most populous countries in the world in 1981. Which of the following is country II?

(A) The People's Republic of China
(B) India
(C) The Soviet Union
(D) The United States
(E) Brazil

You may know that China has the largest population in the world, so it can't be country II. Which choice is the next likely to be "highly populated"? If you pick India, **(B)**, you are right. Remember that the former Soviet Union has the largest land mass, but its population is about the same as that of the United States.

Know your geography

For the World History Subject Test, it pays to know your geography. While it clearly helps on map questions, a knowledge of geography can also help on other questions. Often the answer to an EXCEPT question can be found with a little geography knowledge. The EXCEPT may be a country that is geographically far from the other countries listed, or it may be the place that is landlocked while the others have seaports. In the European history review section, pay special attention to the maps in each chapter. Used with the Era and Country technique, geography knowledge will help you score more.

Political cartoons

You will encounter one or two political cartoons on the World History SAT II. They will be like the cartoons on the editorial page of your newspaper, although they may be in a very different style than you are used to. The more modern a cartoon is, the better you will be able to relate to its humor. On the older ones, look for historical clues, so that you can place the Era or Country of the cartoon. If you can connect to the Era of the cartoon, the correct answer will reveal itself to you. If you are unsure of the time period, use common sense to eliminate and then guess.

"I cannot tell a lie: he did it with his little submarine."

The person represented in the cartoon above is most likely

(A) Kaiser Wilhelm II in World War I
(B) Benito Mussolini in World War II
(C) Otto von Bismarck in the Franco-Prussian War
(D) Joseph Stalin in the Cold War
(E) Francisco Franco in the Spanish Civil War

    Connect to the Era of the cartoon—when was submarine warfare important? Both the Franco-Prussian War and the Spanish Civil War were fought on land (just think about them on a map) and the Cold War was a "non-military" diplomatic conflict, so you can eliminate (C), (D), and (E). To distinguish between the remaining two answer choices, it helps to know that Germany had a powerful submarine fleet in World War I. So, the correct choice is **(A)**. The sinking of the *Sussex*, a French passenger ship, was an example of the aggressive submarine warfare of the Germans. When the Germans broke the Sussex pledge and resumed unrestricted submarine warfare, the U.S. entered World War I.

REVIEW: CHARTS, PICTURES, AND CARTOON QUESTIONS

1. Read the question.
2. Identify the region.
3. Use common sense, the information given, and geography knowledge.

Pop Quiz

Q: The Roman Empire in the first century B.C. and the Arab world in the eighth century A.D. extended into how many continents?

FACTOID QUESTIONS — THE NAME GAME

The World History SAT II has, in general, more factoid-based questions with short answer choices than the American History SAT II, which has longer questions and longer answer choices than the World History SAT II. For you, this is both positive and negative. The World History Test questions can be done a little more quickly and there are not as many tricks to interpreting the answer choices, but these factoid questions also tend to be harder and based on more obscure information. If you know the factoid, you are in luck; just answer it and move on. If you are unsure about it, there is still hope.

Play your hunches

Don't psyche yourself out. These questions are easier than you think—even if you have never heard of the question's subject matter! You see, someone has to get these questions right or the SAT II writers couldn't put them on the test. Unlike on the regular SAT and some other standardized tests, here it pays to answer by instinct on the hardest questions. Even on the toughest questions, the answer will probably not be something you've never heard of, so go for what you know. By the same token, you should . . .

Go for the famous person or thing

The answer will more likely be someone or something you've heard of, so even if you think you're stumped, choose the most famous person or thing. Now, if you are sure the most famous person is wrong, eliminate that answer. Then answer the second most famous person. This "educated" guessing takes some practice. As you take practice tests, notice the names that keep cropping up. If you have never heard of one of the correct answers, look that person or event up in an encyclopedia or history text. Here are some examples.

This is about who knows? who knows? who knows?

(A) Aristotle   The famous guy.
(B) Lucretius   Who?
(C) Seneca   Who?
(D) Ovid   Poet, right?
(E) Erasmus   Who?

Blah Something about some great Russian leader blahblahblah

(A) Ivan the Terrible   Heard of him, but not great.
(B) Peter the Great   Must be great, heard of him.
(C) Alexander I   THE Alex the Great was pre-Russia, who's this guy?
(D) Nicholas I   Who?
(E) Nicholas II   Who?

REVIEW: FACTOID QUESTIONS

1. Play the Name Game.

2. Guess and move on.

Remember: The winners of battles write the history, so it should not be surprising that what remains important in your studying is empires, wars, revolutions, and political philosophies (the rationales for the other three). Think of these categories as you read the history review chapter.

8

World History Review

ERA: ANCIENT CIVILIZATIONS

PRE-HISTORY TO 750 A.D.

The beginning

Stonehenge, England: Really Old

True or False?

Q: Most of the major pre-modern civilizations were supported by an industrial economy.

You do not need in-depth knowledge of this Era; just know the basic facts. The first civilizations developed in what we now call the **Middle East**[1] and were dependent on **river irrigation** to develop agriculture. Most of these civilizations had a **stratified social system**, in which priests or royalty were at the top and slaves were at the bottom. The classes in between were rigidly stratified, meaning it was nearly impossible to move from one class to another.

The **Egyptian** civilization developed along the **Nile River**. Remnants of their existence dating back to 3000 B.C. are still visible today. A few things to know about ancient Egyptians: their rulers, called **pharaohs**, directed the construction of the **pyramids**; they had a writing system consisting of pictures, called **hieroglyphics**; they wrote their documents on **papyrus** and they had a great appreciation for the arts and for learning. The Egyptian civilization was destroyed after more than a thousand years of dominance by invaders on horseback, a mode of war then unknown to the Egyptians.

Mesopotamia was the land nestled between the **Tigris** and the **Euphrates** rivers. The **Sumerians** were the first to flourish there and they wrote laws, studied mathematics and astronomy, and used a system of writing known as **cuneiform**. Sumerians traded, using the **barter system**, with Egypt, India, and maybe even as far away as South America.

The next great civilization of Mesopotamia was **Babylon**, named after the people who conquered the Sumerians. One of their rulers, **Hammurabi**, devel-

---

[1]Important names and events will be in bold type throughout the World History Review Chapter.

oped a famous **Code of Law,** which established rules for every aspect of social life. This code, for the first time, extended some legal protection to all the people of the region. The Babylonians also built pyramid-like structures called ziggurats. They fell to the Hittites, "barbarians" from the East.

The **Phoenicians** are another ancient civilization you should know about. They developed on the coast of the Mediterranean Sea and became known for their proficiency in sailing and trading. Phoenicia was more a collection of city-states than a land-based empire, like some of the other ancient civilizations. The Phoenicians are especially noteworthy because they developed the **alphabet** on which Greek, and many of the modern languages, was based.

Other important ancient cultures include the **Hebrews**, who have obviously had a long-lasting impact on Western civilization, and the **Aegeans**, who preceded the Greeks with highly advanced civilizations on the Aegean islands of Crete and Mycenae.

Ancient Greece

As you have heard many times before, much of European culture and civilization is based on the beliefs and accomplishments of the people of ancient Greece. The structure of government employed by the Greeks was especially influential. Some Greek states were ruled by kings, but others were oligarchies (ruled by several members of the elite) or democracies (ruled by the non-slave male population). Still, society was stratified according to class: nobility, merchants, peasants, and slaves.

The two main city-centers in Ancient Greece were **Athens** and **Sparta**; each had very different characteristics. Think of Athens as the democratic (well, partially democratic) politician, and Sparta as the Brigadier General. Athens, a coastal city, amassed significant wealth from trading overseas. It was the place where the cultural elite developed profound philosophies and indulged in what we would today call "the good life," perhaps best represented by their love of wine. It was also a center of the arts, and the birthplace of democracy. Sparta was a much more rigid place (the word "spartan" now means bare) and its people were very warlike. Unlike Athens, Sparta was inland and depended on agriculture, which contributed to a strict social class system, where most people, called helots, led a serf-like existence. For the upper class, the military shaped every aspect of life. From a young age, boys received rigorous military training that stressed equality without individuality.

Greek society contributed overwhelmingly to science, philosophy, art, and literature. Most of the questions you will be asked about Greek civilization on the SAT II will focus on the **arts and culture** from this civilization. The Periclean Age (fifth century B.C., under Pericles) produced the most important cultural contributions, but they remained mostly within, and for, Athens. The **Hellenistic Age** (fourth century B.C.) was dominated by **Alexander the Great**. He expanded the empire so that the contributions of Greece were spread throughout the known world, and the culture of Asia slowly found its way into Greece. Here's a short list of popular Greek works of art and philosophies.

True or False?

A: False! There was no such thing as "industry" until the eighteenth century. The economies of most pre-modern societies were based on either agriculture or trade with other cultures.

Time	Name	Contribution
Pre-Periclean Age	Homer (Epic Poet)	*The Illiad* *The Odyssey*
Periclean Age (5th Century B.C.)	Hippocrates Socrates (Philosopher)	Medicine Rational understanding through questioning and answering
Hellenistic Age (4th Century B.C.)	Plato (Philosopher)	Student of Socrates : "Ideas" are real; philosophers kings.
	Aristotle (Philosopher)	Student of Plato: Logic, linear thinking. Only natural world is real.
Also:	Greek Drama	Comedy and Tragedy
	Architecture	The Parthenon

A Grecian-Style Temple

During the fourth and fifth centuries B.C., there were several wars going on alongside this flourishing of culture, but these are less important on the test. The **Persian Wars**, between Greece and the powerful empire of Persia, ended in a stalemate but caused social and material ruin throughout Greece. Following these wars, Athens adapted its social structure to include a more established **democracy** and **citizenship for many** (Athens still had slaves). Sparta maintained its rigid order, but with difficulty and rebellions from within. The **Peloponnesian War** was a war between Athens and Sparta declared by Pericles of Athens, in which Athens was ultimately defeated. Finally, Greece was conquered, but not destroyed, by **Philip of Macedon**. Because Philip dealt with Greece fairly and sought to appease rather than destroy them, Greek civilization still flourished under Macedonian rule.

Philip's son, **Alexander the Great**, was schooled by the Greek philosopher **Aristotle** and went on to rule the largest empire of the time, spearheaded by his conquest of Persia. Alexander the Great connected much of the known world by a common law and by common trade practices. When Alexander died at age thirty-three, his empire disintegrated, and the Romans began to acquire world power.

Ancient Rome to the Roman Empire

The Roman civilization lasted over 800 years, and this section will review its humble beginnings, its rise, and ultimately, its fall. The Greeks certainly gave the modern world much of its basis for philosophy, art, and culture. But the Romans made practical contributions like **roads**, **bridges**, **aqueducts** (waterways), and a codified legal system. Historically, the provinces of Rome were first established by **Etruscans**. Soon after, Carthage, the arch-enemy city of what was to become Rome, was founded by the Phoenicians.

The class structure of Rome consisted of the **patricians**, or land-owning nobles, **plebeians**, or all other freemen, and slaves. Roman government was organized under a **Republic** with two consuls, annually chosen leaders, who worked in conjunction with a **Senate** (made up of patrician families) and an **Assembly** (open to all plebeians). This structure proved much more stable than the democracies of the Greek polis. Early on, Rome developed civil laws with rules covering individual and property rights. Later, these laws were extended to an international code that Rome applied to its dealings with people abroad.

As Rome began to expand, **Carthage**, a city in North Africa, became its first major enemy. The inevitable wars between the Romans and the Carthaginians were called the **Punic Wars**; there were three of them. The First Punic War was for the control of Sicily, and Rome won. The Second Punic War began with a Carthaginian attack by Hannibal. In his famous military exploit, **Hannibal crossed the Alps**, with elephants, and surprised the Romans in the northern Po Valley. Hannibal continued to enjoy dramatic military success, but after ten years, Rome had resoundingly defeated Carthage, forcing it to surrender its navy and all of its foreign holdings. The Third Punic War, which occurred about fifty years later, was instigated by Rome. Victorious, **Rome burned Carthage to the ground**.

Rome went on to obtain Greece by conquering the **Macedonians**. They also fought the **Gauls** to the north and the Spaniards to the west. So, early Rome was continuously at war, which fueled internal growth and development (roads, aqueducts, etc.) but did not create an environment for cultural achievement. **After obtaining Greece**, Rome developed an interest in the arts, **borrowing and imitating many Greek art forms**.

Still, rapid growth and widening inequities among the classes caused a great deal of civil unrest. During this time, the Senate's power was weakened. In this environment, **Julius Caesar** came to power, first in a three-part union with Pompey and Crassus called the **First Triumvirate**. Caesar was given jurisdiction over southern Gaul and went on to **conquer all of Gaul** and other parts of Europe. But he chose not to conquer Germany, a decision that had a significant impact on later European development. While Gaul (France) underwent "Romanization," Germany did not. Later, Julius Caesar wrested power from Pompey (Crassus had been killed in battle) and crowned himself emperor-for-life. Caesar had popular support among the lower classes, but his disputes with the Senate made his life rather short. He was assassinated by Senators.

Although Sparta defeated Athens in the Peloponnesian War, Sparta did not leave behind an extensive cultural legacy. This was because Sparta placed such a great emphasis on a sparse, military life that its people had little time for art, philosophy or literature. Most of the Ancient Greek culture that has influenced Western Civilization came from Athens and Macedon.

Three reasons why the Roman empire got so big:
1) The Romans had a really good army and they made a big deal out of everything military.
2) Every time the Romans conquered somebody they gained new resources for the next conquest.
3) Rome was good at uniting the people they conquered, which kept the empire together.

Even with Caesar dead, the supporters of a Republic could not maintain control. **Cicero**, a famous orator and powerful Senator, was murdered as the Second Triumvirate emerged with **Octavius** (Julius Caesar's great nephew), **Marc Antony**, and **Lepidus**. Octavius accumulated power in Rome with foreign conquests, while Marc Antony plotted with **Cleopatra** in Egypt. Octavius, with the Senate's permission, conquered Egypt; Marc Antony and Cleopatra committed double-suicide. Their relationship is often portrayed as a "tragic romance." Octavius then assumed the title of **Augustus** as he became emperor.

In the Augustan Age, which lasted about forty years, Rome enjoyed a period of stability and economic prosperity. Augustus called his reign **Pax Romana**—with the idea that there could be peace under Roman domination. Under Augustus' regime, the conquered territories of the Roman Empire were dealt with fairly and their people were often given citizenship rights. After Augustus died, the structure of the emperorship did not change. Under imperial power, the Roman Empire, through additional military conquests, reached its largest geographical proportions.

Pop Quiz

Q: Which one of these is not like the others?
  (A) The Crusades
  (B) Corruption among Church leaders
  (C) Feudalism
  (D) Communism
  (E) The Holy Roman Empire

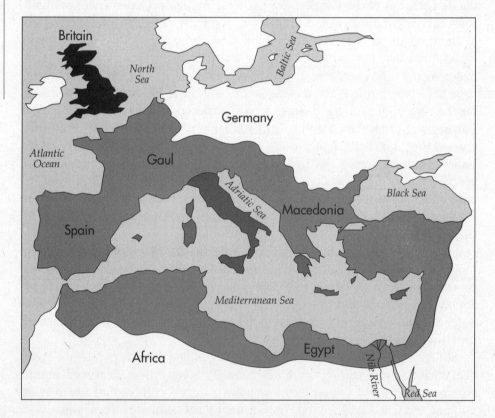

The extent of the Roman Empire at its height.

In this relatively peaceful age, Roman arts and culture flourished, especially in the literature of **Ovid** (*Metamorphoses*) and **Virgil** (*Aeneid*). Glorious buildings and temples were built by the emperors in homage to their gods and often to themselves. **Paganism** was the state religion and Roman citizens were required to give sacrifice to traditional Roman gods. But in an environment of thought and philosophy, many people turned away from the historic **polytheistic** (many gods) religions. Pagan views were rejected by the **monotheistic Jews** (believing in only one god) and also by believers in the new religion of **Christianity**, the followers of the teachings of **Jesus Christ**.

Constantine the Great established an eastern capital for the Roman Empire in **Constantinople**. Probably for political reasons, Constantine adopted **a policy to stop the persecution of Christians** with the **Edict of Milan**. This act of official recognition put the Christian Church in a privileged position. As the Christian Church grew in power, it used its influence to preach an ideal of discipline with a rejection of worldly possessions. A movement called **monasticism** became popular, as monks formed communities in which they led quiet lives of devotion and study.

Following Constantine's death, no controlling leader emerged, so the empire split. The western empire was controlled from Rome and the eastern empire from Constantinople. The end of the Western Roman Empire came shortly after, with the invasion by the "barbaric" **German peoples** of the North. Many of the Germans had been migrating to avoid the **Huns** (led by Attila) and the Germanic tribes spread throughout the western empire.

End of an empire, growth of religion

The eastern empire has come to be known as the **Byzantine Empire**. Within it the Christian Church was preserved. The former greatness and unity of the Roman Empire was somewhat restored under the Byzantine emperor **Justinian** and the region flourished with trade and supported the arts. The Justinian Empire is remembered for its **contributions to law**, its religious art work, especially its **mosaics** (intricate artwork made with small tiles), and its architecture.

During the fourth and fifth centuries A.D., the Church's power grew to fill the vacuum left by the Roman Empire in the West. Within the Byzantine state, the Church grew increasingly independent. While strong emperors, like Justinian, could control Church leaders, the Western Church exercised more independence. The Church would take this position in the Middle Ages.

Pop Quiz

A: Choices (A), (B), (C), and (E) are all associated with the Middle Ages. Communism and other socialist ideologies did not appear until the nineteenth and twentieth centuries.

Religion/Philosophy	Leader/Country	Beliefs
Confucianism	Confucius/China	Social harmony, importance of families
Taoism	Lao-Tzu/China	Harmony with nature, more mystical than Confucianism
Hinduism	no leader/India	Many levels of spirituality and of society; reincarnation
Buddhism	Buddha/India	Meditation, individual enlightenment

In the seventh century, a new faith took hold in the Middle East. This faith, Islam, was monotheistic and **Muslims** believed that **Allah** (God) had transmitted his words to the faithful (in the form of the **Koran**) through his prophet,

Muhammed. Islam's strict codes of belief influenced both religious and political life. Islam spread rapidly through the Middle East and Northern Africa; its growth appeared to threaten Christian institutions. Conflict between Christian and Muslim powers would continue throughout the Middle Ages and Renaissance.

There are a few ancient, non-Western religions or philosophies you will have to know for the SAT II. Quickly review this chart; unless otherwise noted, these religions are not centered on the belief in only one god, like Christianity, Islam, or Judaism.

ERA: THE MIDDLE AGES

750 TO 1300

True or False?

Q: During the Middle Ages, kings did not have absolute power.

Actually the sun did shine on the Middle Ages, which is sometimes called the "Dark Ages," but luckily for you, not for very long. In other words, there's not much you have to remember about the period.

Feudalism

If there is anything you must remember about the Middle Ages, it is about the social and economic system called **feudalism**. Feudalism, a system of organization that emerged from **agriculture-based economies, had a strict hierarchy based on land, wealth, and prestige**. The king of the territory was, of course, at the top. Below him were other nobles who were granted dominion over land in exchange for military service to the king. They were called **vassals** or **sub-vassals**. Most of the people were peasants who actually worked the land.

No "government" or "nation" existed as we know it. Rather, society was organized so that the upper classes protected the land and people, while the lower class worked the land and produced the income from it. Despite this hierarchy, each class was only really responsible to the one directly above it. Peasants answered to their specific lord, not to the king. The system was organized around each vassal's land, the **fief**, and his home or **"manor."** Like the territory, the manor was governed by local customs depending on the character of the lord. The manor housed the lord and his family, the workshops of artisans, a marketplace, and often the land that was tilled. Despite ties to the outside—the manor to the territory and the territory to the empire—each operated more or less as a **self-sufficient unit**.

You need to know a few things about each class. The vassals were obligated to **serve and protect the king** and in exchange received a piece of land to oversee. The noble did not own the land but held it in trust. Laws of inheritance were usually defined by **primogeniture**, meaning the firstborn son of the lord would gain the trust of the fief. This loose system held together because of the **honor code of chivalry**, under which betrayal of one's lord or king was a crime worse than murder. (Of course, betrayals occurred; culprits who were found out did not live long enough to suffer guilt.) **Knights**—noble warriors on horseback—were part of the noble class; most of them were entrusted with land.

Also, know that **peasants and serfs** are not exactly the same thing. Peasants were **free men** who farmed on the fief, but they had rights to use common resources and they could keep a portion of their harvest. Also, those in the peasant class could become skilled artisans, musicians, or hold any other job that might benefit the fief or amuse the lord. Their lot was still hard, but peasants enjoyed some rights. Serfs, on the other hand, were more like **slaves**. They were tied to the land for life and so were their children. In serfdom, everything that the worker produced became the lord's. As hardships grew under an economy based solely on agriculture, more and more peasants were forced into serfdom.

Aside from the king and feudal lords, the only other political powers were the Church and the emperor. The higher **clergy** could be feudal lords themselves, often acquiring lands, extracting **tithes** (payments to the Church), and organizing their own vassals and serfs.

Charlemagne

True or False?

A: True! Even kings had to answer to the pope and to the church. Kings could technically be excommunicated by the church, and there were many disputes between medieval rulers and the clergy. They were also often, disobeyed or manipulated by their vassals.

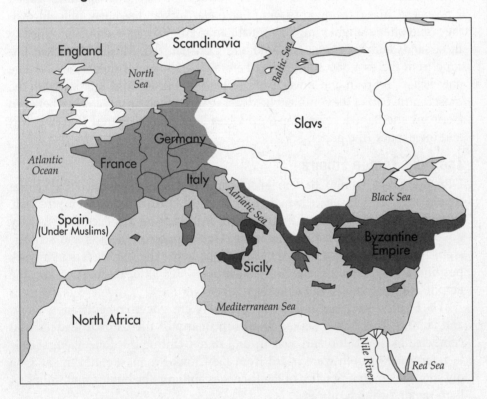

Charlemagne's Empire and Other Medieval Regions

After the Roman Empire broke up and the feudal system emerged, Europe was highly decentralized, meaning that **small territorial units were governed by local kings and lords**. Within these territories, people were governed by local laws and customs rather than imperial rules.

Charlemagne was the first Germanic leader to try to expand and govern what had been the old Western Empire. The pope crowned him emperor and set a precedent by **establishing a relationship between the Church and the state** (really a struggle for power) that would continue through the Middle Ages.

Charlemagne promoted the arts and learning, most of which took place within **monasteries**. Though he was a careful administrator and a powerful military leader, Charlemagne did not act like the supreme emperors that had ruled the Roman Empire. A significant amount of power was vested in the local territories, which were only required to answer to Charlemagne as needed. Most important, **Charlemagne did not levy taxes**. Without an influx of money, few internal improvements could be made in his vast realm. Only Charlemagne could have kept such a disjointed network together as an empire; and after his and his son Louis' death, the vast holdings were divided among his three grandsons according to the **Treaty of Verdun**. The empire began to weaken. The division would become France and Germany, greatly affecting those two regions' cultural and political differences in modern history.

Once Charlemagne's empire was split, the lands became especially vulnerable to attacks. The coastal regions, including England, France, Spain, Ireland, and Russia, were invaded by the **Vikings** of Scandinavia (also called Norsemen). These conquerors were fierce warriors and seamen, pillaging villages and often slaughtering their inhabitants. The Vikings eventually settled in these lands and became assimilated and Christianized. Muslims attacked Europe from the east and south; even before Charlemagne's death they became entrenched in Spain and lower parts of Eastern Europe and Russia. Still, the most central part of the continent held fast against invaders. An alliance between Germany and Italy developed in the dual leadership of the empire (the emperor) and the papacy (the pope).

The Holy Roman Empire

Otto the Great, using Charlemagne's reign as a model, reunited the central region and had himself crowned emperor of the **"Holy Roman Empire."** He expanded the boundaries of the empire, but it was still a collection of loosely governed territories. Like Charlemagne, Otto supported the arts and scholarship. Though he worked with the Church, he kept religious leaders in a weak position and exploited their disorganization. After Otto, the papacy and the empire engaged in a constant struggle for power.

The Church exercised power over everyday life, governing education, work, and culture. This power served to **corrupt many of the Church leaders** who competed like lords for land, wealth, and status. During this time, the first calls to reform the Church were heard from the Cluniac monastic movement. One questionable church practice of the time was **simony**, the buying and selling of high-ranking church offices.

Meanwhile, in the empire's outer reaches, **William the Conqueror** led the Norman (descendants of the Vikings) conquest of England in 1066. Although he introduced feudalism to the region, William served as a powerful king and thus avoided the fragmentation that the system had caused on the continent. In **Spain**, there was a continued struggle between Christian and Muslim groups for power. **Russia**, always remote from the Western world, broke off from the Church of Rome and aligned itself with the **Greek Orthodox Church**, acknowledging Constantinople as its religious capital.

Believe It or Not?

During the fourteenth century, approximately one-fourth of the population of Europe died.

The Crusades

Nearing the second millennium (the year 1000), there was **increased trade** among the feudal fiefs, the central European imperial lands, and other parts of the world. Trade helped to change the rigid social stratification of the manor system as it **required greater specialization rather than self-sufficiency**. It was more profitable for the manor to specialize in one crop and make money by selling it, than to try to satisfy all the needs of the feudal community. Given variation in local climate and soils, a division of labor among the manors seemed much more sensible. As exchanges of goods became more important economically, European nobles and merchants began to vie for trade routes extending towards the east. The growth of trade, along with the religious fervor promoted by the Church, contributed eventually to the Crusades.

Crusades were primarily holy wars, with the Church providing a religious rationale for attacking Muslims, initially in the hope of recapturing the Holy Land (Jerusalem, Palestine). Christians defined Muslims as "unholy" or "pagans" whose slaughter might bring salvation. (For their part, Muslims saw Christians and other non-Muslims as "infidels," which means unfaithful.) Commercially, the **trade routes and commerce** of the Muslims appealed to European merchants, the lands of the Muslims looked good to knights and vassals in search of **larger kingdoms**, and the **riches** of the Muslim world looked good to the Church. The First Crusade was very successful for the Europeans because the Muslim empire, under the Seljuk Turks, was in a relatively peaceful, yet divided, state. **The Crusaders took Jerusalem**. As hoped, this opened up new contacts with the East and trade to and from Europe flourished.

The Second and Third Crusades are intertwined; they began when **Muslims attacked and recaptured Jerusalem**. The Europeans were led by Emperor Frederick Barbarossa of Germany, King Philip Augustus of France, and King Richard I of England. Despite an overwhelming effort and flow of money into the campaign, the Europeans did not win back Palestine. Still, they retrieved one port city on the Mediterranean that allowed a continued trade route and a passage to Jerusalem on holy pilgrimage. The Crusades, which began just before the twelfth century, ended toward the close of the thirteenth century.

The height of the Middle Ages

Given the new importance of trade, **towns with wealthy merchants** arose in place of or alongside the once all-powerful manors. Within the towns, the "middle-class" merchants or **burghers** became politically powerful. Like their manorial predecessors, the towns had a great deal of independence within the empire. But towns were intrinsically more interdependent than the manors of the feudal system, which paved the way toward the formation of nations. One effect of interdependence was a weakened social structure and more movement and flexibility among the classes.

The **twelfth and thirteenth centuries** are viewed as the height of the Middle Ages. The contact with the Muslim world helped spur new thoughts and theology, broadening the perspective of the heretofore insular Europeans. **"Reason"** evolved as the principle tool by which to investigate religious faith. This gave rise to **heresies**, which are religious beliefs or practices that do not conform with

Believe it!

The bubonic plague, known as the Black Death, spread throughout Europe in the mid-fourteenth century and infected a large percentage of the population. The disease spread easily because European cities at that time were extremely unsanitary. It took Europe until the end of the fourteenth century to fully recover from the devastation.

the traditional Church doctrine. Ironically, many heretics wanted merely to return to the simpler ways of early Christianity; they **rejected the worldliness and richness of the Church**.

The openness of thought led to the founding of the first **universities** where men studied philosophy, law, and medicine, and learned from the advances of Muslim cultures. In science, the ideas of **Aristotle**, Ptolemy and other Greeks reemerged alongside those of Jewish and Muslim scholars. The growth of schools and learning was called **scholasticism** and it was primarily based on **Greek philosophy**. Two branches existed within scholasticism: the **realists**, who followed the ideas of Plato, and the **nominalists**, who followed Aristotle. These names can be confusing since the actual theory sounds like the opposite of the name. Platonists believe that "thoughts" and "essences" are real even if we cannot sense or touch them, whereas Aristotelians believed that reality existed in particular objects and denied that the human mind could conceive of anything beyond that rational world. **Thomas Aquinas** was a famous realist of this period who wrote *Summa Theologica*, outlining his view of contemporary Christian thought. In addition to scholasticism, a philosophy of **mysticism** developed which proposed that humans had a small bit of the divine in them and that revelation was possible through a mystic communication with God. Though the Church did not condone this philosophy, elements of mysticism are evident in writings of the time.

Also, a **court life** took root among the noble classes. It placed an emphasis on poetry and music. Women gained a more respected place within the court and were allowed to pursue creative interests. An important musical form of the time was the **Gregorian chant**. Most of these scholarly and artistic pursuits were related to religious studies, but some developed as secular (non-religious) endeavors.

Chartres, France: A Cathedral With Both Romanesque and Gothic Elements

Among the greatest artistic achievements of the Middle Ages were the **cathedrals**. In the early Middle Ages, churches were built in a bulky **Romanesque** style. Later, with architectural advancements, the **Gothic** style developed. Gothic cathedrals were built with the idea of getting the worshippers closer to God. To achieve this, architects used **flying buttresses** that gave support for tall windows and vaulted ceilings. The cathedral became not only an art form in itself, but an **arena for art**. The Church sponsored artists to adorn the inside of cathedrals with paintings. Music became an intrinsic part of ceremonies, and religious dramas, often called **miracle plays**, were performed within the church.

France: A Cathedral's Flying Buttresses

These outpourings of art and philosophy led to some doubts about the supremacy of the Catholic Church. But at the beginning of the thirteenth century, the Church was led by a strong pope, Innocent III, who issued strict decrees on Church doctrine. The pervasiveness of the Church and its ultimate power is sometimes referred to as the **Universal Church, or the Church Militant**. Under Innocent III, **persecution of heretics and Jews** became widespread and a fourth, ultimately unsuccessful, Crusade was attempted. This crusade was particularly motivated by greed, as the Crusaders conquered—and sacked—the already Christian Constantinople, declaring a "Latin Empire" there. A few years later, Pope Gregory IX established the **Inquisition**, a formalized questioning and persecution of heretics. Punishment for "non-believers" ranged from excommunication to exile to execution.

The rise of nations

In the rise to nationhood, different parts of Europe took different paths during the thirteenth century. Germany's reigning family died out without a suitable successor to the emperorship and the region entered a period known as an **interregnum** (a time between kings). **Thus Germany and its ally, Italy, became**

decentralized into a group of strong, independent townships and kingdoms. In this atmosphere, merchants and tradesmen became even more powerful. In northern Germany, an association of merchants called the **Hanseatic League** led the region's progress in international trade and commerce.

France, on the other hand, became a **centralized monarchy** under the rule of Philip Augustus. Later, under Philip IV, the **Estates General** was established as a political body of representatives from different provinces. Wealthy townspeople as well as the traditional clergymen and nobles comprised this body, which advised the King on issues of taxation and financial policy.

England created its own unique form of government. Since the time of William the Conqueror, England had had a tradition of a strong monarchy. Under the monarchy of King John, powerful English nobles rebelled and forced him to sign the **Magna Carta**. This document reinstated the feudal rights of the nobles, but also extended the rule of law to other people in the country, namely the growing burgher class. This laid the foundation for the Parliament. Initially, an assembly was established with nobles who were to represent the views of different parts of England in law-making, advisement to the King, and taxation issues. After a trial period, the **Parliament** was established. Later, two branches were constructed: the **House of Lords** (nobles and clergy) and the **House of Commons** (knights and wealthy burghers). The House of Lords presided over legal issues and the advisement of the King, and the House of Commons dealt with issues of trade and taxation.

France and England battled each other intermittently during the **Hundred Years' War** over claims to the French crown. (The war—more appropriately, wars—actually lasted 116 years.) France declared war on the pretext that England had neglected feudal duties to some of its lords, but the conflict was more likely over the trade capabilities of a specific province. With greater sums of money and the support of the Pope, France took the lead at first. But England came back with dramatic victories as they used a new war technology, the **longbow**. Still, the war dragged on. Near the end of the war, the French, at the end of their rope, were inspired by **Joan of Arc**, a peasant who had visions that God had chosen her to save France. So, with newly revived spirits, and because England was actually worse off than it seemed, France marched to victory.

Eastern Europe and **Russia** at this time were very different from the west. The Greek Orthodox Christians of this area spent much time and effort defending themselves from the colonization of various western invaders. While successful in this endeavor, Russia was also attacked from the east and fell to the **Tartars under Genghis Khan**. This cultural rift further split eastern from western Europe as the area remained under Tartar rule for two centuries.

ERA: THE RENAISSANCE

1300 TO 1600

The period of 1300 to 1600 is often seen as a **bridge between the Middle Ages and the Modern Age** and it is characterized **by increased international contacts through exploration and trade**, the **rise of nationhood**, and the cultural and intellectual flowering of the **Renaissance**.

Political and social upheaval

The early stages of this Era were marked by political and social upheavals, like the **Hundred Years' War** and **peasant uprisings**, which contributed to the weakening of medieval traditions in all classes of society. The clergy, though many among them were devout, became an increasingly secular (non-religious) group, interested in money, power, and the occasional cultural pursuit. In general, the importance of the clergy and its ability to command respect decreased in this period. The noble class also changed, as the nature of warfare and chivalry changed. The introduction of gunpowder and other weapons of destruction helped to undermine the whole honor system. Mercenary soldiers (soldiers-for-hire) took the place of landowning knights, and the noble class turned to trade, industry, and money-making.

Also, the ideal of **virtú** came to replace the honor code of the Middle Ages. Virtú was a badge of culture, of dedication to the arts and sciences, and was a source of "intellectual bonding" among men of the noble class. The burgher class continued to grow and prosper in the areas of trade and politics. As the primary money-making class, the burghers wanted a say in their town's governance. Artisans flourished because there was a high demand for craft and beauty due to the ideal of virtú and the influx of money and artistic influences from the Far East. The peasant class, needless to say, did not enjoy this prosperity. Famine and disease were part of everyday life. Peasant revolts were common as the farmers' social conditions worsened and taxation by the nobles and burghers increased.

Two specific events also contributed to the social turbulence of the time: the **Black Death**, later identified as the bubonic plague, and the **invention of the printing press**. The Black Death first struck Europe about 1350, and this contagious disease killed nearly a quarter of the existing population. Its rapid spread occurred in part because of the chronic malnutrition of the peasant classes and because of unsanitary living conditions. The disease's widespread destruction contributed to a conviction that life was uncertain and fleeting. In this atmosphere, people's focus shifted away from "otherworldly" matters like the Church and its vague life-after-death salvation and towards more human-centered and temporal pleasures of the flesh.

Second, and of more lasting importance, **Johannes Gutenberg** invented the Gutenberg printing press with movable type, and printed the first mass-produced Bible. Once the Bible was printed, Gutenberg and others realized how easy it would be to print and widely distribute just about anything. As a result literacy rates increased immensely. Now, both traditional teachings and controversial ideas could be widely read and spread throughout the literate world.

Arts and sciences of the Renaissance

During this time, the prevailing ideology of European civilization shifted from the Church-dominated theology of the Middle Ages to the philosophy of **humanism**. Humanism places emphasis on the potential for the individual to achieve greatness, whether in the artistic, scholarly, political, or spiritual realm. Humanism led to a general rebirth in scholarly thinking, which was accompanied by increasing rejection of the absolute power of the Church.

Although **Renaissance means "rebirth,"** European civilization had not been completely shut off in the Middle Ages. Still, the arts gained nearly unprec-

During the Middle Ages, before the invention of the printing press, most people didn't know how to read because there was nothing to read. Reading material existed only in the form of manuscripts, which literally means "things written by hand." Most of the reading and writing was done by monks in monasteries, and it was mostly of a religious nature.

edented support in this Era, fueled by the booming economy and the international exchange of ideas fostered by trade. **Northern Italy**, the crossroads of the modern world of trade, was the center of Renaissance art and culture in the fourteenth and fifteenth centuries. Free of any centralized government, the city-states of Milan, Florence, and Venice rose to individual importance under the patronage of powerful merchant families. **The Medici family** of Florence, for instance, were renowned for their support of the arts.

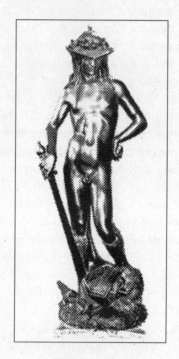

Donatello's David, 1425

Italians of this period contributed enormously to literature, painting, sculpture, and intellectual writing. Renaissance paintings celebrated the beauty of the human body. Figures were more natural and realistic than the exaggerated, flat ones of medieval paintings. These works used a technique called perspective, meaning that some things were painted in the foreground and some things were painted in the background. In the chart below are listed several great artists of the time.

Name	Description of Work
Donatello	Sculptor of *David*, reintroducing the art of the realistic (and naked) human form.
Boticelli	Painter of the *Birth of Venus*.
Leonardo da Vinci	The "Renaissance Man," versatile in art, science, and engineering; painted *Mona Lisa* and *The Last Supper*.
Michelangelo	Some call him the greatest painter and sculptor of the time; decorated the Sistine Chapel; also sculpted a *David*.

Michelangelo's *David*, Florence, Italy: One of Many Reproductions

In the midst of this artistic flourishing, Italy was awash in political intrigue. This, in part, inspired Niccolo **Machiavelli** to write one of the most influential political works of all time, *The Prince*. He wrote—some say satirically—that a monarchy should be distinct from the Church and that a leader should act purely in self-interest rather than on the basis of vague moral tenets. He may have been describing the reality of Italian statecraft, rather than advocating it. Nevertheless, many modern ideas of leadership and statecraft stem from this work, but the term **Machiavellian** often has a negative connotation. A "Machiavellian" ruler is one who is ruthlessly selfish, scheming, and manipulative.

In the fifteenth and sixteenth centuries, the ideas of the Italian Renaissance migrated north and cultural achievements blossomed in the so-called **Low Countries** (today, known as the Netherlands and Belgium) and England. **Erasmus**, one of the most well-known learned men of the time, counseled kings and popes. He wrote *In Praise of Folly* which satirized what he thought were the most foolish political moves to date. **Sir Thomas More** of England was a contemporary of Erasmus who wrote a book called *Utopia*, which described an ideal society where everyone shared the wealth, had a place to live, and had food to eat. More and Erasmus were **Christian humanists**, meaning that they believed in the potential for good in humankind and that they sought moral guidelines for people as they pursued their personal goals.

Later scholars were not as charitable to the virtue of men. **Montaigne**, a French essayist, and **William Shakespeare**, the English playwright and poet, were skeptical about human nature. Both focused on everyday problems, such as death and the difficult moral questions people face. Shakespeare's work, of course, has endured, in part because the writer so deftly combined the variety of human character and life. His work showed a life of alternating episodes of joyful confidence, dark pessimism, and tragic comedy.

"A prudent ruler ought not to keep faith when by so doing it would be against his interest, and when the reasons which made him bind himself no longer exist. If men were all good, the precept would not be a good one; but as they are bad, and would not observe their faith with you, so you are not bound to keep faith with them."
—Niccolo Machiavelli in *The Prince*

The Renaissance also brought a "rebirth" in the study of the **natural sciences**. The age of exploration was fueled by advances in navigation technology and **astronomy**. **Copernicus** ignited a scientific revolution when he theorized that the universe was sun-centered (heliocentric) rather than Earth-centered. Johannes **Kepler** and **Galileo** went on to gather scientific information that supported Copernicus in the late sixteenth and early seventeenth centuries. Other scientists, like **Leonardo da Vinci**, became interested in medicine and anatomy, the study of the human body.

ERA: THE AGE OF DISCOVERY

1270 TO 1550

True or False?

Q: The indigenous people of the American continents benefited greatly from their contact with European explorers.

The **Age of Exploration and the Renaissance are concurrent**, and the environment of the High Middle Ages contributed to the blossoming of each. Exploration was fueled by the desire to increase trade connections and to make money. The Crusades of the Middle Ages had whetted the appetite of European nobles for far-eastern goods. **Marco Polo** was the first European to develop a long-standing relationship with Asia, as he traveled and lived in the Orient in the late thirteenth century.

Geographic exploration was aided by improved technology in shipbuilding, navigation, and cartography (map-making). In addition to the prospect of new trade routes, explorers and their sponsors were also motivated by the glory of conquering new worlds and a mission to convert others to Christianity. The following is a chart of explorers who opened the new world to Europe.

Name	Act of Exploration
Amerigo Vespucci	Mapped Atlantic coast of S. America and convinced many that these lands were not India
Vasco da Gama	Sailed to India around the Cape of Good Hope, Africa
Balboa	First European to "sight" the Pacific Ocean First to circumnavigate the globe
Cortés	A conquistador who conquered the Aztecs
Pizarro	A conquistador who conquered the Incas of Peru

Exploration and the importance of trade caused the **centers of power to shift in Europe**. Germany was no longer the strong Empire it had been; instead, **countries with borders on the Atlantic Ocean (England, France, Spain, and Portugal)** became powerful due to increased trade. Portugal was especially influential because the country was strategically placed near the coast of Africa. It had long-standing trade relations with Muslim nations, and its royal family supported exploration led by Prince Henry the Navigator. These seafaring nations competed with each other by rapidly acquiring colonies and conquering new lands. All these events contributed to the growth of nationalism and strong monarchies. Merchants wanted protection for their trade routes and, at first, the costly and risky explorations could only be accomplished with the backing of a strong and wealthy state.

The Church acquiesced to state interests by revising its strict ban on what are now standard business practices like lending money and charging interest on loans. A new business structure emerged: **the joint-stock company**, an organization created to pool the resources of many merchants, thereby reducing the costs and risks of colonization. These "corporations" secured royal charters for colonies, like the Jamestown colony in Virginia, and funded them for business purposes. The **Muscovy Company of England** was the most powerful "corporation" of its time, monopolizing trade routes to Russia.

Increased trade led to an early theory of economics for the nations of Europe. In the Middle Ages, every kingdom or fief tried to subsist solely on the products of its own land. With new avenues of trade and new stores of wealth, this system was no longer desirable. Thus, **mercantilism** took its place. Under this theory, a country would actively seek to trade, but would try not to import (take into the country) more than it exported (sold to other countries); that is, it would attempt to avoid a "trade deficit." Such deficits reflected dependency on other countries, hence weakness. Of course, one country's surplus (exports more than imports) requires another country's deficit (imports more than exports). To resolve this dilemma, European nations were feverish to colonize. Colonies gave the mother country resources (not considered "true" imports), while creating new markets for exports.

While exploration is often seen as an unfettered good, the indigenous American peoples clearly suffered as their lands were stolen from them and their people were killed by disease and warfare. Europeans ransacked the highly civilized cultures of North and South America in search of gold, silver, and such **new resources as maize and tobacco**. Exploration also led to the **creation of the African slave trade** because "labor-intensive" crops like tobacco, coffee, and sugar could be cultivated in the Americas.

ERA: THE REFORMATION

1500 TO 1650

Corruption and confusion

Forces within the Catholic Church had been in conflict since the late Middle Ages. Remember that the Greek Orthodox Church split from the Roman Church around the dawn of the second millennium. In the twelfth century, the French kings demanded that the papacy be established in Avignon, near France, instead of Rome, in what was known as the **Babylonian captivity**. When the papacy was returned to Rome, the French appointed one of their own, creating **The Great**

Schism. For thirty years, the two popes both claimed to be the true leader of Christendom. Such politics served to confuse and undermine allegiances to the Catholic Church.

The **Reformation** was a movement that called for reform of the Catholic Church, usually with the pious intent of returning to the simple teachings of scripture. The scholarly works and ideology of the Renaissance cast doubt upon the once unquestioned institutions of the Roman Catholic Church. And despite the rise of strong monarchies that weakened the status of the clergy, the Church still owned vast tracts of land and other resources. While the Church's wealth and land holdings had been acceptable in the Middle Ages, now, in the sixteenth and seventeenth centuries, it caused anger and grief, especially among the noble and peasant classes who felt "robbed" of these resources. This resentment and mistrust of the Church, fueled by abuses of power such as simony, the sale of high Church offices, was known as **anti-clericalism**.

Martin Luther

Martin Luther, a German friar, unwittingly tapped into this ire as he challenged the sanctity of many Church practices. His first protests concerned the **sale of indulgences**, which were payments to the Church that would supposedly reduce the punishment for sins in the afterlife. That in itself would have been OK by Luther, but some clergy were selling the indulgences with the idea that sins could be completely washed away with the payments. Luther saw such practices as blasphemous, supplanting spirituality with crass materialism. As was traditional in a theological dispute, Luther posted his arguments against this practice, his **"Ninety-five Theses,"** at the local church. His treatise commanded an immediate following among disenchanted parishioners.

Luther began preaching against the rigid organization of the Church, believing that each individual must forge a relationship with God. This challenged the privileges of the clergy; if people could speak directly to God, who needed the Church? Luther further inflamed the clergy by arguing that salvation was not dependent on obeying Church rituals or receiving sacraments, but on faith alone. He even challenged the pope, reasoning that no mortal man could have the final say on the interpretation of holy scripture. Although he was excommunicated, Luther continued to preach to his ever-growing following.

Religious wars ultimately swept through Germany; northern German forces were primarily Lutheran, while southern peoples remained Catholic. **The Peace of Augsburg** in the middle of the sixteenth century recognized both the Lutheran and Catholic religions in Germany.

Protestants

Spurred by Luther's success, other anti-Catholic religious sects took root and spread outside of Germany. These new Christian religions came to be known collectively as **Protestantism** (because they "protested" the established Church).

John Calvin, from France, led another powerful Protestant group by preaching an ideology of predestination. **Calvinist** doctrine stated that God had predetermined an ultimate destiny for all people, most of whom God had already damned. Only the few, the Elect, would be saved, he preached. The city of Geneva in Switzerland invited Calvin to construct a Protestant theocracy in their city, which had a central location and was near France. Consequently, Calvinist teachings became more widely known, and were as influential to successive Protestant Reformations as were the doctrines of Luther.

The reformation in England was motivated by political as well as religious reasons. **King Henry VIII** did not have a son as heir to his throne and sought to abandon his wife, Catherine of Aragon, because of it. When the pope denied the annulment (an official disregard that the marriage ever occurred), Henry VIII renounced Rome and declared himself the head of religious affairs in England. He presided over what was called the Church of England, often called the **Anglican Church**. Henry VIII went on to marry five more wives and to father a son. Henry might not have believed it if someone had told him that his daughter, Elizabeth, would become one of the most powerful English rulers of all time.

Counter-Reformation

The Catholic Church was not used to being so successfully challenged and at first responded ineffectively to the new religious trends. Slowly, it began to institute reforms, since many nations remained devout to the religion. This movement was called the **Counter-Reformation** and its primary goal was to **contain the spread of Protestantism**. Spain, a dedicated Catholic country, led many of the reforms. One reform was to ban the sale of indulgences by "pardoners." Another was to confer more authority on bishops and parishes. Weekly mass became obligatory, and the supreme authority of the pope was reaffirmed. In this period, a former Spanish soldier and intellectual, **Ignatius Loyola**, founded the Society of Jesuits, which was influential in restoring faith in the teaching of Jesus as interpreted by the Catholic Church. The Jesuits practiced self-control and moderation, believing that prayer and good works led to salvation. The pious example of the Jesuits led to a stricter training system and higher expectations of morality for the clergy. Because of their oratorical and political skills, many Jesuits were appointed by kings to high palace offices.

The **Council of Trent**, a meeting of church officials, presided over the counter-reform period for about twenty years, dictating and defining the Catholic interpretation of religious doctrine. Without bowing to Protestant demands, the Council clarified its position on important religious questions, like the nature of salvation. Also, in this period, the **Inquisition's** tactics of trying and punishing heretics reemerged.

Art in the Reformation

The focus of this period was obviously religious, and much of the artwork of this time simply drew from the work of the Renaissance. Still, a few "greats" stand out. **El Greco**, a painter active in Spain, created dark and emotional pieces that reflected the religious themes of the Spanish Counter-Reformation. Also from Spain, **Miguel de Cervantes** wrote *Don Quixote,* which at once satirizes and idealizes the human condition. Finally, the great Dutch painters, **Rembrandt** being the most famous, worked at this time. A Protestant, Rembrandt painted both secular and religious subjects. His paintings are known for conveying the humanity of his subjects. In some paintings, his subjects appear virtually to emanate light.

During a period known as the Great Schism (1378–1417), there were actually two popes in Europe. One lived in Rome and the other in the French city of Avignon. People had to choose which pope they wanted to believe was the true ruler of the Catholic Church.

ERA: ABSOLUTE MONARCHIES

1500 TO 1650

At this time, most nations were led by monarchies, royal families, or **sovereigns** who felt that their right to govern was ordained by God. Under this idea of **divine right**, it was essential for royalty to maintain pure bloodlines to God, so intermarriage among royal families of different nations was common. Thus, the monarchies also gained international influence as the ties of marriage and inheritance led to far-flung empires. **Absolutism** was the concentration of the power of a nation in the hands of one absolute leader.

Monarchies contributed to the idea of strong national loyalties, which led to many conflicts, internally and externally. The wars of this time fall into three categories: religious fights between Protestants and Catholics, internal civil wars between a monarch and disgruntled nobles, and battles stemming from the trade disputes of rival nations. In the beginning of this Era, **Spain** was the world's strongest nation, with a powerful naval fleet and an extensive empire. Yet the balance of power would shift, and the rival nations of **England** and **France** would eventually emerge as great powers. Briefly outlined below are the troubles of the major players of the time: Spain, England, France, Germany, and Russia.

> Pay attention to all the maps in this book. It's very helpful to know your geography on the World History SAT II.

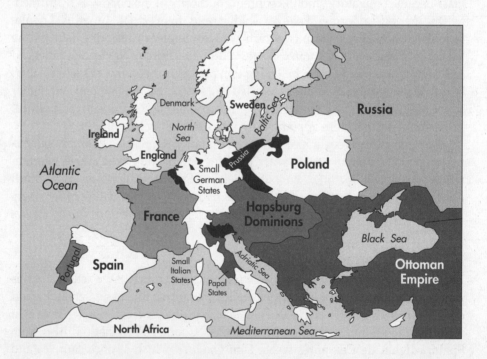

Absolute Monarchies

Spain

King Ferdinand and Queen Isabella initiated the glory days of Spain by supporting exploration and then reaping the benefits of the gold and other resources plundered from the new colonies. To protect their trade routes and their colonies, the Spanish built a formidable naval fleet, and they ruled the seas for several decades.

The international importance of Spain grew under **Charles V**, who inherited a large empire. He held lands in parts of France (Burgundy), the Netherlands, Austria and Germany. These possessions, plus the new colonies in the Americas, brought wars as well as riches. Spain fought France over control of Italy, and the Ottoman Turks over power in the Mediterranean. In Germany, Charles defended Catholicism over the encroachment of Protestantism. He eventually abdicated, giving his brother, Ferdinand I, control over Austria and the Holy Roman throne of Germany. To his son **Philip II**, he conferred the throne of Spain and jurisdiction over Burgundy, Sicily and the Netherlands.

Under Philip, the Spanish empire crumbled. The Dutch (of the Netherlands) revolted and won independence from Spain. Spanish forces fighting for Catholicism in France fared poorly, and the English defeated and devastated the Spanish Armada as it tried to attack the British Isles. Once independent of Spanish rule, **the Dutch** were particularly successful traders and merchants, colonizing lands and developing trade in both the Far East and the Americas.

England

The **Tudors** were one of the first strong royal families of England who ruled with relative peace and prosperity. Henry VIII was a Tudor and, after a brief period under his son Edward VI, his policies were continued by his daughter, **Queen Elizabeth**. The **Elizabethan Age** fostered commercial expansion and encouraged exploration and colonization in the New World, especially after the English fleet had helped destroy the Spanish Armada. The arts also flourished at this time, with great English writers like Shakespeare and Ben Johnson.

The **Stuart** royal family gained power following Elizabeth's reign, and helped to unleash political and religious conflicts. One dispute between the monarchy, King James I and then King Charles I, and the nobles of Parliament was over **taxation**. Another conflict emerged between the **Puritans**, who followed Calvinist teachings, and the Anglican followers of the King, who were more conservative, essentially Catholics without a pope. Eventually, the forces of Parliament joined with the Puritans to oppose the monarchy. Led by **Oliver Cromwell**, a Puritan, the Parliamentary army deposed King Charles I and executed him (which was shocking, since monarchs were supposedly handpicked by God). After overthrowing the king, Cromwell governed as **Protector** of the state, but encountered resistance from merchants and nobles who resented his strict Puritan ideology. On Cromwell's death, Charles I's two sons, Charles II and James II, ruled England in turn, but James's Catholic sympathies riled the still-suspicious Parliament, which forced him to abdicate. In what was known as the **Glorious Revolution**, William and Mary of the Netherlands were asked to rule England with the stipulation that they agree to a Declaration of Rights that limited the powers of the monarchy. This act gave Parliament greater control of England, with the monarchy in a cooperative rather than a leading role. The event signaled a long period of internal peace in England. The unique British political structure influenced social theorists of the eighteenth century, the era of Enlightenment.

France

Unlike England, France was ruled by a series of strong and able monarchs during a time known as the **Bourbon Dynasty**, and the Estates-General (representing clergy, nobles, and peasants and merchants) was not nearly as powerful as the English Parliament. **Cardinal Richelieu**, a Catholic, played an important role as minister to the Bourbons. His primary political goal was to strengthen the French crown. So, while clashes erupted among Catholics and Protestants (known as **Huguenots**) in France, Richelieu did not seek to destroy the Protestants, but compromised with them and even helped them to attack the Catholic Hapsburgs of Germany. (Richelieu had joined forces with Dutch Calvinists and Swedish Lutherans to preserve the power of German royalty.) A **new bureaucratic class** was established under Richelieu, the *noblesse de la robe*. The bureaucracy Richelieu and then his successor, Cardinal Mazarin, established prepared France to hold the strong position it would achieve in Europe under Louis XIV.

Germany

Germany, remember, did not have a strong monarchy or centralized leadership; it was a collection of independent states. The **Hapsburg** family presided over what they considered the Holy Roman Empire, but the emperor's position was weak, especially compared to the monarchs of other nations. The **Thirty Years' War** began when the Protestant territories challenged the authority of the Catholic emperor, even though he was only a figurehead. This war effectively ended the **Peace of Augsburg**. Religious conflicts fueled the already tense relationships among the provinces and encouraged the intervention of other nations in the conflict, like France under Richelieu. This regional conflict between German Protestants and Catholics grew into a war between all of the European powers, though actual fighting stayed within the German empire. After thirty years of this kind of highly concentrated battle, many parts of Germany were left depopulated and devastated.

Russia

Russia still retained a feudal social order. The first **czar** (or tsar, from the Latin caesar) came to power upon the **overthrow of Mongol rule**. Russia never experienced a "Renaissance" period, remaining instead a feudalistic society under the rule of absolute monarchy. **Ivan the Terrible** set a precedent by expanding the Russian empire eastward by force and by ruthlessly suppressing any opposition to him. All trade was conducted through him, so no merchant class had a chance to develop.

Remember, you don't need to memorize every fact in this book or any other book. That would drive anyone crazy. Gather as many facts as you can, but more importantly, make sure that you have a good feel for what happened in the different Eras and the different countries.

ERA: THE ENLIGHTENMENT OR THE AGE OF REASON

1600 TO 1770

While the Renaissance is considered a rebirth and a return to ancient intellectual pursuits, the **Enlightenment** is seen as the first stage of the truly Modern Age. The ideas and achievements of the intellectuals and scientists of the Enlightenment are considered radically new and not just embellishments on the works of the past. (In the grand scheme of things, this is probably an exaggeration.)

The Scientific Revolution

Science has existed, of course, since people first made fire, but most of the work ancient scientists did would be called philosophy today. Aristotle thought and theorized about nature, but he didn't really do anything akin to what we consider science in the Modern Age. During the Enlightenment, the **scientific method**, in which a scientist uses **experimentation** based on a hypothesis, was developed. With precise scientific instruments, like the microscope and the telescope, one scientist could test again what another scientist had originally tested. Many scientific inquiries were conducted with **practical goals** in mind, such as the creation of labor-saving inventions or the development of power sources from water or wind. People tried to standardize weights and measures. Scientific inquiry extended beyond national borders and discoveries were internationally shared.

Copernicus's work in astronomy during the late Renaissance challenged established belief so much that it led to a flurry of scientific inquiry in the field. **Galileo** was the strongest proponent of the heliocentric (sun-centered) view of the solar system, for which he was punished, but not killed, by the Church. The concept that the universe was not centered around the Earth (or man) totally disrupted the view of the universe for many Europeans. Yet, this idea served to inspire deep thought and inquiry about the natural and philosophical world.

Once the old ideas had been shaken up, anything was possible. In this atmosphere, **René Descartes** founded a philosophy based on **human reason**, arguing that rational thought, without the constraints of theological preconditions, was the best method of inquiry. He wrote, "*Cogito ergo sum*," (I think, therefore I am) and argued that systematic doubt was a precondition to real knowledge. **Francis Bacon** focused on the practical aspects of scientific inquiry, arguing that science was not pursued for "science's sake," but as a way to improve the human condition. Bacon's ideas greatly influenced the scientific development of **technology** and usable inventions.

Sir Isaac Newton was a mathematician, physicist, and philosopher who postulated **theories of gravity** (that is, why objects fall, and why people are not constantly crushed by objects falling from outer space). Newton and many other Enlightenment scientists were religious and tried to reconcile their Christian beliefs with their scientific discoveries. Thus, Newton used the metaphor of **God as a great clockmaker**—God created the world, but then stepped back, allowing it to run and evolve by its own internal mechanism, i.e., natural laws. Many scientists were skeptical of God's existence, but even today, the "clockmaker" rationale is used to maintain both faith in God and faith in scientific reason.

Political and social thought

Though scientific thought was international, the center of the Enlightenment for social and political thought was **France**. *Philosophes* were not really philosophers, but social critics who based everything on the merits of reason. There were **deists** (those who believed in a rational, Newtonian God) and **atheists** (those who did not believe in God) within this group, but they were all opposed to vague spiritual and mystic religious beliefs and doctrines. **Voltaire** was a famous philosopher who espoused the **ideal of toleration**. Since absolute truths now seemed implausible, it seemed wrong to persecute "heretical" ideas.

Political science emerged during this period, as philosophers grappled with the nature of social structures and questioned the religious view of a divine birthright of kings. The idea of a **social contract** emerged, the belief that governments are formed not by divine decree, but to meet the social and economic needs of the governed. Partially based on the assumption that individuals existed before governments did, these political scientists felt that, in some ways, the individual took precedence over the state and was endowed with universal "natural rights."

Three important political theorists of this time would influence the revolutions of the next Era. **Thomas Hobbes**, who wrote *Leviathan*, thought that, because people are by nature evil, the state must be controlled by a wise, but absolute monarch. Hobbes used the social contract theory to demonstrate why a king had a responsibility to his subjects. **John Locke** had a kinder opinion of mankind and felt that people were born free and had certain inalienable rights. Governments, Locke felt, should represent the interests of the people. (You may have guessed correctly that Locke's theories were influential in the founding of the United States Constitution.) **Jean-Jacques Rousseau** took the social contract theory to its furthest extreme, arguing that all men were equal and that society should be organized according to **"the General Will"** of the people. In a rational society, therefore, each individual "subjects himself" to this General Will, which serves as the sovereign, or ruling lawmaker. Under this philosophy, the individual is not only protected by the community, but is free, because it is the essence of freedom to "obey a law which we prescribe for ourselves."

Enlightened despots

The new political ideas had an effect on the leadership of the monarchs, even if it was for political reasons rather than truly charitable views on the rights of their people. For example, the ideals of tolerance, justice, and improvement of people's lots in life became guidelines for the governing of monarchs. The term **"enlightened despot"** applies to a ruler who governs with some consideration of his or her responsibility to the people of the nation. Even in those countries where the despots were not enlightened, this period was marked by political stability.

France had an untyrannical, if not quite enlightened monarch. The **Peace of Westphalia**, drawn up at the end of the Thirty Years' War, was an acknowledgment that the German empire was no longer a central power in Europe, and it

Pop Quiz

A: Choices (A), (B), (C), and (D) are all scientists and philosophers associated with the Enlightenment. Ptolemy is a medieval astronomer who believed that the world was the center of the universe, and that the sun and the stars revolved around it.

made France, under the leadership of **Louis XIV**, one of the true European powers. Louis XIV's long reign exemplified the grandiose whims of an absolute monarchy. Calling himself "the Sun King" and "the Most Christian King," he patronized the arts as long as they contributed to the glorification of France and its culture, which became much admired and emulated. Louis XIV wanted conquered lands to increase the cultural status of France, but his many territorial invasions and wars proved costly and ineffective. Undoubtedly, his folly inspired the political theorists and philosophers of France.

After the Peace of Westphalia, the independence of small German states was affirmed, and **Prussia** became the strongest of these provinces. **Frederick the Great** followed the example of his father Frederick Wilhelm I and ruled his land with efficiency and justice. Frederick the Great distinguished himself as the most enlightened of the great leaders of Europe with his notions of religious tolerance and with genuine efforts to improve the status of the serfs. He gave equal status to Protestants and Catholics, and encouraged immigration into Prussia. Dramatic improvements were made in the technology of agriculture, and thus in the lives of peasants. Frederick the Great also stimulated internal production of luxury goods, like porcelain and silk, and opened up new avenues of trade for Prussia.

Peter the Great of Russia also tried to improve the lot of his subjects; he was convinced that he could only do so by **westernizing Russia**. Peter the Great made some internal improvements and founded St. Petersburg as his model for a great Western city. But he also brought an obsession with wealth and luxury to the czars who would succeed him. Under Catherine the Great, more enlightened policies of education and western culture were implemented. Still, Russia suffered because its czars allowed repressive serfdom to continue, and prohibited the growth of a merchant class.

ERA: THE AGE OF REVOLUTIONS

1775 TO 1815

The time frame for the Age of Revolutions should be easy to remember because the **American Revolution** occurred just before the **French Revolution** and the **Latin American Revolution**. Other than that date of 1776, which is branded into the heads of most American students, you won't have to know anything about the American Revolution for the World History SAT II. Still, it doesn't hurt to remember that it was between the American colonies and the British Empire, with the French helping out the colonists.

The French Revolution

You will have to know about the French Revolution, which is much more complicated than the American Revolution. First, it had a greater impact on all of Europe. The French Revolution was radical and violent. It upset and changed the entire structure of the country's life and governance. Before the revolution, the country was led by a monarch and a governing body, the **Estates General**, that was meant to represent the interests of the people. This representative body was made up of three estates or classes. The First Estate was the clergy, the Second Estate was the nobility, and the **Third Estate** was everybody else, namely, the middle class and the peasantry. In reality, the Estates General hadn't met for decades and its composition was inherently unfair. Over 80 percent of the population was in the Third Estate, yet this class had a vote equal in weight to the votes of the much smaller nobility and clergy groups. In addition, the clergy and nobility would often vote the same way and in opposition to the Third Estate, so the majority of the population could be easily overruled.

Several factors contributed to the revolution. First, the **tax structure** was grossly unfair, as nobles and the clergy were exempt from paying taxes, which meant that the entire tax burden fell upon the Third Estate. This problem was made worse by the fact that the country was in economic distress. Louis XIV had depleted the national treasury on costly wars and on supporting the American colonists in their war. Second, the ideas **of the Enlightenment** had spread throughout the middle class and the peasantry, stimulating the hope for a country with equal rights for all.

King Louis XVI, like his grandfather Louis XV, tried to institute tax reforms in order to avoid a revolt. Louis XVI called a meeting of the Estates General, but the Second Estate managed to escape taxation again. Furious, the Third Estate refused to vote, so the actions of the body were brought to a halt. The Third Estate, led mostly by lawyers and powerful businessmen, declared itself to be the **National Assembly** and claimed to represent all France. Meanwhile, the peasants had revolted because bad harvests had led to a food shortage. Because the King's army was so busy trying to quell the **riots of the peasants**, it did not depose the National Assembly. Amid this chaos, peasants **stormed the Bastille**, a prison that was thought to hold political prisoners. Though only a few prisoners were actually freed, this triumph over the government is considered the seminal event of the revolution.

Through these separate political events, the middle class and the peasants joined together to oust the privileged classes. Under the slogan, **"Liberty, Equality, Fraternity"** they established a centralized government, passed laws to equalize the tax system, and opened government positions to all qualified citizens. The National Assembly also eliminated serfdom and the feudal rights of the aristocracy, passed **the Declaration of the Rights of Man** (like the Bill of Rights), and confiscated the wealth and land of the church. Despite these accomplishments, the National Assembly was **pressured by foreign powers** (monarchs who did not like the events happening in France), and there was **dissension in the Third Estate**, especially among pious Catholic peasants who did not agree with the treatment of the Church. Soon the revolution became more radical and bloody as a few hard-core revolutionaries decided to "save" the revolution from itself by whatever means available, including terror.

The **Reign of Terror** was the revolution's bloodiest hour. **Robespierre** and the **Jacobins**, the leaders during this time, were strict and unyielding believers in the ideals of equality and the utopia that they thought the revolution would bring. Anyone who could not be converted to their way of thinking would be **guillotined** (not exactly the freedom of thought or speech that the revolutionaries espoused). Louis XVI and Marie Antoinette were executed, along with many others, even fellow revolutionaries who held views different from Robespierre. The revolutionaries even started their own calendar to mark time from Bastille day rather than use the dates from the traditional Christian calendar.

Many feared the wrath of Robespierre, preferring stability and order to the high ideals of the Jacobins. Robespierre himself was put to death at the guillotine. After the Reign of Terror, the **Directory**, a group of five men elected by the propertied classes, was created to restore a measure of calm in revolutionary France. It lasted until destroyed by a *coup d'etat* (overthrow), which brought to power a man who would have an immense impact on history: Napoleon.

Napoleon Bonaparte

Napoleon is a strange historical phenomenon. Although he was an absolute dictator, he had not come from the noble classes and he considered himself a revolutionary. Nonetheless, Napoleon's infamy is based on his **military success** and **his desire to conquer all of Europe**.

> "My principle is: France first...."
> —Napoleon Bonaparte

After military successes against Austria and England, Napoleon returned to France, **overthrew the Directory**, and had his action **reaffirmed by a popular vote**. Domestically, Napoleon initiated many reforms in agriculture, infrastructure, and education. He also normalized relations with the church and restored a degree of tolerance and stability. But Napoleon's real concern was continued conquest and the spread of "France's glory" throughout Europe and the New World. After Napoleon's troops conquered **Austria, Prussia, Spain, and Portugal**, he crowned himself **emperor**, fancying himself the new Charlemagne.

But Napoleon's reign was short-lived. France lacked the resources to control a far-flung empire: Napoleon had set up **ineffectual leaders** (his relatives) in the satellite states and **nationalistic uprisings** undermined his power. Spain, for example, resisted domination fiercely with guerilla warfare and the help of England. Then Napoleon made the **grave military mistake of attacking Russia**, in the winter, with short supplies and disloyal troops. Napoleon's resounding defeat fueled revolts in other captive nations and the former emperor was forced into exile.

The leaders of the countries that had overthrown Napoleon met in Vienna to decide what to do to restore order (and their own power) in Europe. The principal members of the coalition against Napoleon were **Prince von Metternich of Austria, Alexander I of Russia**, and the **English Duke of Wellington**. At first, disagreements among them prevented much progress. Hearing this, Napoleon decided to return from exile and make an attempt to regain power. At **Waterloo**, the allies joined together against the common threat of Napoleon and he was defeated decisively and sent to permanent exile on the island of St. Helena.

The allies' meeting resumed and their eventual agreements were called the **Congress of Vienna (1815)**. It was decided that a **balance of power** should be maintained among the existing continental powers in order to avoid the rise of another Napoleon. France was dealt with fairly; its borders were cut back to their pre-Napoleonic dimensions, but it was not punished militarily or economically. In general, the Congress of Vienna restored stability by reaffirming monarchical rule, but it ignored many of the ideals put forth by French Revolutionaries.

Latin American revolutions

In Latin America, the colonies were inspired by the success of the American Revolution and by the ideas of the Enlightenment and the French Revolution. The Latin American colonies hoped to gain independence from European rule for themselves. In addition, they fiercely opposed the tax system that the imperial governments forced upon them.

One of the first revolts took place in **Haiti**, a French island colony with large plantations and widespread slavery. **Pierre Toussaint L'Ouverture** led a violent, lengthy, but ultimately successful slave revolt there. Napoleon's forces imprisoned Toussaint but could not stop the revolt.

South America and **Mexico** each fought against Spanish rule. Two brilliant generals led the successful overthrow of colonial rule in South America: **Simon Bolivar**, who gained control over Venezuela and Colombia, and **José de San Martín**, who liberated Chile and Argentina. The forces of these two generals met in Peru, where Spanish forces were finally defeated. **Brazil** was granted independence by the Portuguese royal family without bloodshed and established a native Brazilian monarchy.

ERA: THE RISE OF MODERN STATES

THE NINETEENTH CENTURY: 1815 TO 1900

During this century, many political, social, and economic forces molded European society even more profoundly than the so-called Age of Revolutions. The **industrial revolution** and **new political ideologies** imposed radical changes on societies all over the world.

The Industrial Revolution

"The power of population is indefinitely greater than the power in earth to produce subsistence for man."
—Thomas Malthus, *Essay on the Principles of Population*

Prior to the late eighteenth century, Europe was overwhelmingly rural. In fact, the term "manufacturing" described the work of the individual craftsman, not a factory. In **England**, near the turn of that century, industrialization began in the **textile industry**. Instead of one person performing all tasks in the cloth-making process, a "factory system" developed where one person would spin the thread, another would dye it, and a third would weave it into cloth. This **division of labor** is one cornerstone of an industrialized system. The organization of these small **cottage industries** would later be the model for larger factories.

The move to industrialization was aided by the Scientific Revolution. The late eighteenth century was marked by an increased **faith in science and the rewards of scientific progress**. This attitude contributed to the acceptance of industrialization. Specific inventions, like the **steam engine**, would create energy sources vital to the new industries. The **use of coal** to improve the iron-smelting process was also invaluable to the rise of industrialization. All these innovations made it easier and cheaper to produce cotton textiles by means of **mass production**.

The rise of textile factories led to an **increased population in the cities** and the development of a new middle class and a new working class. The **middle class** made money from the fruits of industrialization as investors, inventors, and merchants. These people were not from privileged classes; they often worked up from the bottom to achieve their relative fortunes.

The **working class** consisted of people who left the farms of the countryside to work in the new factories. Often peasants were forced off farms, as landowners "enclosed" or removed common lands that peasants had used for grazing their livestock. Working conditions in the factories were horrible: eighteen-hour shifts, dangerous machinery, and miserably low wages. Women and children were employed because they could be paid less and could more easily thread the machines with their small hands. Some traditional craftsmen rebelled against industrialization because their work was being outsold by mass-produced goods. One famous group, the **Luddites** of England, destroyed textile machinery. Yet, unlike the feudal system, the factory system did offer some hope of advancement to the working class. Throughout the nineteenth century, industrialism would loosen the rigid separation of the classes.

Invasion of the isms: Nationalism, liberalism, and other ideologies

In the early part of the nineteenth century, the European world was stable internationally. Internally, however, problems and dissension arose. Several "progressive" ideologies challenged the conservative forces of the nobility and the clergy. **Conservatives** hoped to keep the status quo with ruling monarchies and strong noble classes, and for a time were able to squelch nationalistic and liberal voices.

Nationalism, a mutual respect among countrymen and the promotion of pride in a common language, heritage, and other customs, had been emerging since the Middle Ages. This challenged monarchy because kingdoms were often amalgamations of many different nationalities. (Kingdoms' attempts to dominate regions were similar to the former Soviet Union's attempt to rule many different nationalities, some of which have recently gained independent status.)

Liberalism is based on the ideas of the Enlightenment and represents granting equal political and economic freedom to all. Any increased power or knowledge among the people threatened the status quo of a monarch's rule. Within the ideology of liberalism, the merits of the industrial revolution were praised and described in terms of the "Enlightenment of Man." The right to own property was seen as universal (again, a challenge to the nobles and the clergy). **Capitalism** (private ownership of the means of production and distribution, and private retention of the profits) was seen as a noble endeavor which would lead to the betterment of each man involved.

Many proponents of early liberalism and capitalism might seem conservative today, but apply the term "liberalism" within its proper Era. **Adam Smith**, who wrote *The Wealth of Nations*, argued that government should not interfere with a nation's economy or with each man's individual self-interest. This idea, known as **laissez-faire**, has since influenced the economic doctrines of most of the world. Smith believed that if everyone worked for his own individual good, a nation's economy would be balanced and all would prosper, as if by an "invisible hand." The writings of Smith had many supporters, but the works also inspired dissent. The intellectual movements of **Socialism**, **Marxism**, **Anarchism**, and then **New Liberalism** all oppose some aspect of the theories of nationalism and industrial capitalism.

Time Period	Movement	Political Theorist	Theory
Late eighteenth to early nineteenth century	Liberalism	Adam Smith, Thomas Malthus	Laissez Faire; Imminent overpopulation of the world can only be checked by famine and letting the poorer classes starve.
		Herbert Spencer	Social Darwinsim "survival of the fittest."
Mid-to-late nineteenth century	New Liberalism	John Stewart Mill	Freedom of speech and thought: clashing opinions will yield the best solutions. Wanted to extend the vote to the poor and to women.
	Socialism		Collective ownership of the means to produce and distribute the nation's wealth; sharing national resources. Supported by the working classes.
	Marxism	Karl Marx	Class struggle as the foundation for communism, the fullest development of socialism. State, as a tool of owner class, will "wither away."
	Utopian Socialism	Robert Owen, Charles Fourier	Self-contained communities based on sharing and equality of all members; sometimes sexually unrestricted.
	Anarchism	Pierre-Joseph Proudhon	Government and all other concentrations of wealth and power are coercive and therefore illegitimate. Society should be organized as a union of collectives.

"Let the ruling classes tremble at a Communist Revolution. The proletarians have nothing to lose but their chains. They have a world to win. Workingmen of all countries, unite!"
—From *The Communist Manifesto* by Karl Marx

Karl Marx's theories were as influential as Smith's, though their beliefs were diametrically opposed. Marx, who wrote *The Communist Manifesto* and *Das Kapital*, believed that history was a series of class struggles between the **owners of capital**, or ruling class, and the **proletariat**, or working class. He argued that although the worker had contributed most of the value of the product he made, he received only enough compensation (wages) to stay alive and continue to make more wealth for the owner. Marx advocated a revolt of the workers to take control of the means of making capital (the machines and factories). Then they would decide what should be made, and would divide the wealth—the items produced—equally among themselves. One important thing to remember: Marx was not Russian and he never envisioned any communist revolution in rural Russia. He was German and his writings were a reaction to what he saw in Germany's industrialized state. Marx expected a revolution to take place in an industrialized nation.

Political developments

The **balance of power** instituted by the Congress of Vienna forestalled major wars from occurring among the European powers, and the ideology of conservatism led to the suppression of revolutionary ideas internally. Yet, the nations of Europe could not help but respond to the changing demographics unleashed by the industrial revolution, mainly the growth of the middle class.

Great Britian was the wealthiest and most powerful nation in the world at this time, aided by its industrial status and its resourceful colonies. Internally, **Great Britain** responded to pressure from the middle class by **changing the voting laws** to more fairly represent the growing population of wealthy men in the cities with the Reform Act of 1832, and by **abolishing slavery in the colonies** in 1833. Towards the middle of the century, the lower classes, in a movement called Chartism, demanded universal manhood suffrage, which was granted in the 1880s.

France, on the other hand, was not very stable, and its leaders less skillful in appeasing the quick-to-riot masses. The history of nineteenth-century France is a **series of revolts** followed by short periods of peace. Some of these periods are outlined below. You will not be expected to know much about France's ever-changing internal politics, just to know they were ever-changing.

France's nineteenth-century politics

Louis XVIII	The Congress of Vienna restored him to the throne.
Charles X	Succeeded Louis XVIII, very conservative, deposed in July revolution of 1830.
Louis Phillippe	More liberal than Charles X, relatively stable for twenty years, deposed in the Revolution of 1848.
Napoleon III	Elected "emperor" of France and foreign lands in 1851. Though a dictator, had wide popular support. Fell from power upon France's defeat in the Franco-Prussian War, 1870.
The Third Republic	A consitutional and democratic government that ruled from 1870 to 1940. Conservative compared to the radical Commune of Paris, which it defeated in 1871.

Because of political unrest, France did not develop many industries. Though Paris was a cultural center, the majority of the country remained rural. This **lack of industry** would affect the political stature of France in the late nineteenth and the twentieth centuries.

The nations that comprised **Germany and the Austrian Empire** (also known as the Hapsburg Empire) hadn't been united since the decline of Charlemagne's Empire in the Middle Ages. In the nineteenth century, **nationalistic sentiments** emerged in the region. **Prince von Metternich** of Austria, a conservative, was very influential in repressing these forces. Inspired by France's revolution in 1848, German nationalists attempted to set up a parliamentary government but failed.

German unification was achieved under **Otto von Bismarck**, a Prussian general who was driven more by a desire for Prussia to overcome the Hapsburg powers than by nationalistic sentiments. The Austro-Prussian War thus became the fight to control Germany, and Prussia won in a quick and dramatic fashion. Bismarck then conspired to engage France in a war, so that he could further consolidate German power. The resulting Franco-Prussian War he also won quickly and upon this victory, Bismarck declared the unification of the German empire. He supported King William I of Prussia as the new German emperor and oversaw the creation of the **Reichstag**, a legislative body representing the middle and lower classes. After unification, **Germany quickly industrialized** and became a strong economic and political power. In contrast to the laissez-faire approach of Great Britian and the United States, Germany's government largely controlled the industrialization of the country and aided in the creation of large-scale markets throughout its empire.

Italy, like Germany, had been a decentralized collection of states for centuries, but the country tried to achieve national unity during this period. The process of **unification in Italy** was directed by Prime Minister **Camillo Cavour** who favored diplomacy over war and insurrection. Though it took many decades of maneuvering, complete Italian unification was achieved in the 1870s. Northern Italy became industrialized during this time, but southern Italy, for the most part, remained rural.

Russia had gained some prestige in Europe after the Congress of Vienna, but its people still lived under medieval serfdom. **The Decembrist Revolt**, a coup (overthrow) following the death of Alexander in 1825, was an attempt by the army to force the czar to adopt a constitution, but it failed. Nicholas I came to power and sought to stamp out revolutionary ideas through secret police terror. His attack on liberal and revolutionary currents thus occurred just as many other countries were moving in the opposite direction. Not only did Russian politics stagnate, but so did its science and industry. The resounding defeat of Russia in the **Crimean War** showed the backwardness of the country and came to symbolize the need for change. In an attempt to modernize Russia, the new czar **Alexander II** declared the **emancipation of the serfs**, which proved to be only a limited victory for the peasants since they were still poor. (The emancipation of the serfs in Russia came just a few years before the emancipation of the slaves in the United States.) Industrialization proceeded slowly; Russia always seemed to lag behind the rest of Europe. Most significantly, a **Trans-Siberian** railroad to link the eastern and western parts of Russia was begun, but not completed until 1905. Political and economic dissatisfaction continued to burden Russia throughout the late nineteenth century.

Towards the end of the nineteenth century, nearly every European power had embraced some form of nationalism. **Imperialism**, the act of conquering and presiding over colonies, went hand-in-hand with establishing national pride. **England** held the most colonies (fifty-five), with France at a distant second (twenty-nine). Germany, Italy, Russia, and even the United States held at least a few colonies. Imperialism spread **western influence** to all parts of the globe, affecting education, culture, science, and politics in the colonized lands. Imperialism also spread resentment throughout the "non-western" countries. These hostile feelings soon led to wars and revolts as the colonized areas fought to overcome the western imperialistic powers.

ERA: WORLD WAR I

1900 TO 1920

At the turn of the twentieth century, the "old world" of absolute monarchs and privileged nobles continually clashed with "new world" ideas of nationalism, industrialism, and new political ideologies. In this Era, wars and revolutions caused an irrevocable break between these worlds.

Internal political unrest

Industrialization of the European countries was changing the fabric of people's lives. For many, the spirit of nationalism took on the aspect of a new religion; to die for your country seemed a worthy death. At the same time, anarchism gained adherents, people who thought that the only hope for an equal society was to get rid of the governments, if not simply to kill all the monarchs.

Events in Russia at this time clearly exemplify the tensions between industrialism, imperialism, and social unrest that were present in most European countries. The fact that Russia remained an absolute monarchy and was attempting to industrialize explains part of the tension. Also, like the rest of Europe, Russia was trying to expand its territories and gain influence in China through colonization. (The **Boxer Rebellion** for Chinese independence and against all foreign influence had just been squelched by the combined might of America and several European nations.) Because Japan was also trying to colonize China, the **Russo-Japanese War** started. The Japanese navy crushed the Russian navy in a short-lived war. Japan's victory only fueled the social discontent in Russia.

Russian socialists were classified as **Bolsheviks** (the "majority" party) and **Mensheviks** (the "minority" party). The Bolsheviks incited many of the famous revolts that led to the Russian government's takeover by communism. The **Russian Revolution of 1905** began when a peaceful demonstration of socialists was ruthlessly suppressed by the czar's troops, an action called **"Bloody Sunday."** In the months that followed, workers struck, peasants revolted, and soldiers mutinied until the czar promised to create a constitutional monarchy with an elected national assembly. Still, the powers of this new assembly, the **Duma**, were greatly restricted by the czar.

International alliances lead to war

The growing spirit of nationalism also led to tensions among the great powers of Europe. Since the Franco-Prussian War, **France and Germany** had acknowledged each other as **enemies**, with much of their disputes over the historically divided region of Alsace-Lorraine (a dispute dating back to Charlemagne's Treaty of Verdun! The conflict had begun in 1851, when Germany seized Alsace-Lorraine from France.). In order to bolster their own positions, France and Germany each devised a series of **diplomatic alliances** with other powerful nations. Several different configurations emerged over the years, but by 1907, the **Triple Alliance of Germany-Austria-Italy** and the **Triple Entente of France-England-Russia** were established. These two sets of allies would pit themselves against each other in the First World War.

The **Balkans**, which were then part of Austria, were rebelling against the Hapsburg empire for national independence. In 1914, the **Archduke Franz Ferdinand of Austria was assassinated by a Serbian nationalist**. Immediately, the alliance system pulled the **major European powers into war**. Austria declared war against Serbia, believing that the nationalists could be easily crushed. Germany sent troops to support Austria but also to protect its own interests. Russia backed Serbia; France backed Russia and also feared for its own borders once Germany had mobilized. England jumped in and so did Italy, both against Germany (even though Italy had been Germany's ally). So began the most international of wars up to that time.

Most Europeans were supportive of the war, believing that the fighting would be quick and that it would bring glory to each nation. That conviction proved terribly wrong. Because of **new weapons technology** and strategic maneuvers like **trench warfare**, this war was exceedingly long, brutal, and costly in terms of human lives and money. The sides were evenly matched, so the war mainly consisted of battles in which thousands and thousands of men ("cannon-fodder," they were called) were slaughtered. It was a **stalemate until 1917**, when the **Russian Revolution began and the United States entered the war**, instigated by pro-English sentiments and aggressive **submarine warfare** from the Germans. The Russian Revolution took an exhausted Russia out of the picture as the new Bolshevik government signed an armistice with Germany, the Treaty of Brest-Litovsk.

The United States' entry opened a **floodgate of well-needed supplies** and manpower to the forces of England and France. Germany's forces were near the breaking point. The war ended soon after and peace talks began, culminating in the Treaty of Versailles.

Immediately following the war's end, a revolt occurred in Germany. The emperor abdicated his throne and fled, while moderate Socialists assumed control. The new government, the **Weimar Republic**, ruled until 1933.

Treaty of Versailles

Though the fault for World War I lay mostly in the system of alliances and misguided nationalism, the war had brought unprecedented suffering to the countries of Europe. The victors wanted **someone to blame and someone to pay—Germany**. The Paris Peace Conference was called to arrange a settlement: Germany wasn't invited. The talks were directed by the **"Big Four": President Woodrow Wilson of the U.S.; Prime Minister David Lloyd George of England; Premier Georges Clemenceau of France; and Premier Vittorio Orlando of Italy.**

Wilson was the voice of moderation, hoping that this would be an opportunity to establish international laws and accepted standards of fairness. His **Fourteen Points** addressed these issues and called for the creation of a joint council of nations called the **League of Nations**. Other leaders, like Clemenceau, were out for German blood, and desperate to control their borders. They wanted to **cripple Germany economically** so that it could never again rise to power. The resulting **Treaty of Versailles** was a compromise of these extremes, but Germany got stuck with the tab: it lost its colonies and the Alsace-Lorraine region; its armed forces were dismantled; it had to pay about $30 billion (called **war reparations**) to the victors; and it had to concede that the war was all its fault.

While the treaty did call for the creation of a League of Nations, this project received only mild support from England and France. Moreover, Germany, Russia, and the United States (despite Wilson, the U.S. Congress refused to join) were not members of the League.

The peace would be uneasy for several years and several conferences were held among the major European powers in the next decade. Two significant treaties helped keep the peace: the **Locarno Treaty**, which implemented a more realistic reparations payment plan for Germany (the **Dawes Plan**) and defused tensions at the French-German borders, and the **Kellogg-Briand Pact**, in which the major European powers agreed to use diplomacy rather than war to settle their political differences. In the long run, these measures helped achieve international stability for a time, but they did not avert war.

Pop Quiz
A: Russia

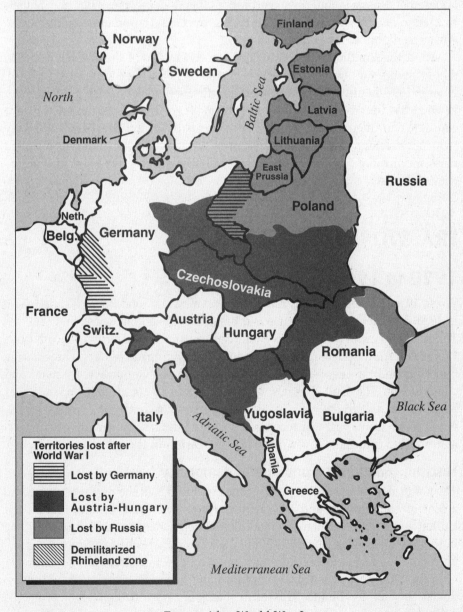

Europe After World War I

The Russian Revolution of 1917

The reforms that followed the Revolution of 1905 brought some peace to Russia. But the **hardships of World War I** (famine, war casualties, and weak leadership) inspired peasants and workers to renew their call for revolution and social change. Strikes and protests against the czar broke out in early 1917, and **czar Nicholas II was forced to abdicate**. (Later, the Bolsheviks killed the czar and his family.)

A relatively moderate **Provisional Government** was set up to share power with more radical local councils, or **Soviets**, which represented the interests of workers, peasants, and soldiers. This situation was unstable because the interests of the Provisional Government and the Soviets were never reconciled. The Provisional Government wanted to continue the war against Germany in the hopes that Russia could then become a liberal democracy. But the Soviets wanted to end the war quickly and they supported a communist authoritarian government, not a democratic one.

Amid this conflict, **V.I. Lenin**, the Marxist leader of the Bolshevik party, mobilized the support of the workers and soldiers for the communist platform. Later in 1917, **Lenin and his followers overthrew the Provisional Government**, in what has become known as the **Russian Revolution** (some refer to it as a coup). Lenin then ended the war with Germany in the **Brest-Litovsk treaty** (which was later nullified upon Germany's Western defeat). Under his vision of mass socialization, Lenin rigidly set about **nationalizing** the assets and industries of Russia.

ERA: WORLD WAR II

1920 TO 1945

World War I had been called "the war to end all wars," and it was inconceivable in 1920 that another world war could break out so soon after the first. Yet, the Treaty of Versailles and ideals of nationalism contributed heavily to the post-World War I atmosphere of discontent among the European powers. Three starkly opposing political ideologies would emerge: **liberal democracy, fascism, and communism**. The United States, whose response to these developments was **isolationism**, would end up playing an important role in the Era. And economic pressures of costly post-war reconstruction and burdensome reparations on Germany would contribute to a **worldwide depression in the 1930s**.

Fascism, communism, and liberal democracy

The political ideology of Western Europe and the U.S. at the time was shaped by **a fear of communism and a weariness from war**. Great Britain, France, the United States, and Germany were all liberal democracies at this time, but none of them had strong leadership. While the United States had experienced prosperity in the 1920s, most of Europe remained desperate for basic necessities.

Italy, riding a wave of anti-communist and nationalist sentiments, became a fascist state under **Benito Mussolini**. **Fascism** is an ideology that promotes nationalism, glory, and honor under an iron dictatorship, and the word fascism

Pop Quiz

Q: What event led to the onset of World War II?

alludes to the former glory of the Roman Empire. Mussolini's charisma and rousing patriotism seduced many people desperate for leadership and strength in the war-torn country. The negative connotation of the word fascist is well-deserved. Mussolini came to power via gang warfare tactics and, once in power, ruthlessly suppressed any political opposition to his regime.

After the Revolution, **Russia** joined Germany as the other "bad boy of Europe." Lenin's philosophy was advertised to the other countries of the world, declaring that communism would only work if there were a worldwide revolt of the workers. This led to talk of a "communist plot," which caused fear and hysteria among the other European nations and the United States. As a result, the Union of Soviet Socialist Republics (U.S.S.R.), as it became known, was **isolated economically and politically** from the rest of the world. (This actually helped the U.S.S.R. avoid the Great Depression.)

Meanwhile, the Soviets concentrated on their own domestic problems. Lenin first instituted the **New Economic Policy**, which had such capitalistic aspects as allowing farmers to sell portions of their grain. This plan was successful for agriculture, but Lenin did not live long enough to encourage its expansion into other parts of the Soviet economy. When Lenin died, **Joseph Stalin** came to power and, as General Secretary of the Communist party, imposed an economic policy of ruthless **agricultural collectivization** and construction of large, nationalized factories. The program was carried out in a series of **Five Year Plans**. Stalin believed that by combining all the farms, agricultural production would be made more efficient and productive, and that once the peasants weren't needed in the fields, they would willingly go to work in the new factories. Many peasants resisted—and often paid with their freedom or lives.

Notwithstanding his ruthlessness, Stalin's plan did finally industrialize the U.S.S.R. and improve economic conditions for the multitudes. Still, to retain firm control of the Communist Party (and of life in general in the Soviet Union), Stalin used terror tactics that he borrowed from the czar, such as a secret police force, bogus trials, and assassinations. He set up **labor camps**, or prisons, to punish any who opposed him. Stalin's rule is now called the **Great Terror**; up to twenty million people may have been killed by his government.

Hitler's rise to power

The **Weimar Republic of Germany** was greatly disliked by the German people because of its association with defeat, both in the war and at the various treaty-signings. Also, **inflation** was rampant in Germany, caused by both the large war debt and the worldwide depression. **Adolf Hitler** rose to power in this atmosphere. Like Mussolini's Fascism, Hitler's **Nazism** inspired rabid nationalism and dreams of the renewed greatness of a long-lost empire.

But Hitler's philosophies were more insidious than Mussolini's. Hitler believed in social Darwinism and the superiority of one race over others. He felt that the **Aryan race** (characterized by tall, white, blond, blue-eyed people, even though Hitler himself was rather small and dark) was the most superior, and that it was being corrupted by "inferior" races, especially the **Jews**. He thought that the Jews should be eliminated and the German people should take over Europe. The Germans, Hitler argued, needed the extra living space and resources to fully develop as a race.

Pop Quiz

A: In 1939, Germany invaded Poland. In response, England, France, and Poland declared war on Germany.

The Nazi party (which is short for the National Socialist German Workers party) began to gain political power in the 1920s with Hitler as its "guide," or Führer. At first, the Nazi party gained votes democratically and participated in the Reichstag, Germany's parliament. But when the country found itself caught in the throes of the Great Depression (early 1930s), Hitler gained his most forceful political clout. Many who disagreed with Hitler's philosophy still backed him since they felt he was the country's only hope. **In 1933, Hitler was named Chancellor** and, when the president of the Weimar Republic died, Hitler was solely in control. Under his domination, German society was as rigidly controlled as the Soviet Union's, with as much if not more terror. The Nazi regime did reinvigorate the economy thanks to Hitler's massive arms build-up. The making of weapons and the training of soldiers and police soon rectified the unemployment problem. Meanwhile, Hitler began to round up primarily Jews, but also Gypsies, homosexuals and other "outsiders," sending them to **concentration camps**.

World War II

Though the nations of the world could easily see the burgeoning aggression of the Nazi and Fascist regimes, the other European nations sought **appeasement rather than war**, while the **United States favored isolation** from the events. The primary spokesman for diplomacy over war was **Prime Minister Neville Chamberlain of Great Britain**.

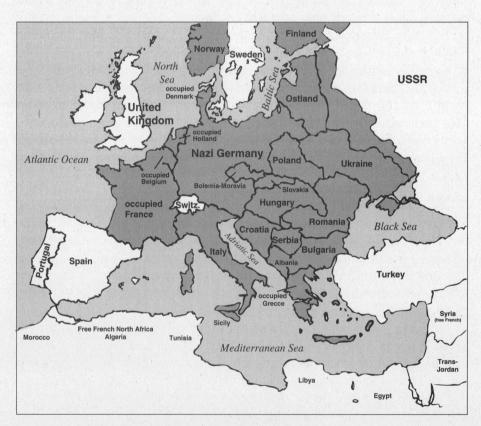

Nazi Germany's Occupation 1943

In 1936, Hitler began his military onslaught by **occupying the Rhineland**, a strip of French territory that bordered on Germany. He joined in an alliance with Italy to create the **Axis Powers**; later Japan would enter into this alliance. Mussolini had also begun military expansion by invading Ethiopia. In 1938, Germany annexed Austria and threatened to invade Czechoslovakia. **The Munich Conference of 1938**, which included Hitler, Mussolini, and Chamberlain, was called to avert the invasion (called the **Sudetenland crisis**), but Hitler's march was only stayed for about a year. In 1939, **Hitler invaded Czechoslovakia** and signed the secret Nazi-Soviet Pact: Stalin and Hitler, though ideological enemies, agreed that Germany would not invade the U.S.S.R. if the U.S.S.R. stayed out of Germany's military affairs. So Stalin got a measure of security and Hitler got a clear path by which to take Poland. **Hitler invaded Poland** shortly thereafter and **Great Britain**, realizing that all diplomacy had failed, **declared war on Germany**, with France reluctantly following suit.

Hitler's forces were devastating. Using a new form of mechanized warfare, they employed motorized tanks, planes, and trucks, rather than just moving men and equipment on foot. This tactic was known as *blitzkreig*, or lightning war, because it destroyed everything in its path with unprecedented speed. Within a year the **Axis powers controlled most of continental Europe**. Great Britain, under the determined leadership of new Prime Minister **Winston Churchill**, faced Germany alone. **Hitler tried to air bomb Great Britain into submission**, but Britain survived, aided by U.S. supplies and the new technology of radar, which helped the British air force locate German planes. Also, Hitler decided to nullify the Nazi-Soviet Pact and invade the U.S.S.R. in the winter (as Napoleon did a century earlier). The movement of men and supplies into Russia pulled some of the pressure off Great Britain.

In the Pacific arena, **Japan** was invading other Asian countries. Like Nazis, Japan's leaders believed themselves racially superior to those they dominated. **By 1941, Japan had invaded Korea, Manchuria**, and other significant parts of **China**, and was threatening action in **Indochina**. For trade reasons, the United States viewed this action as hostile. But the ultimate hostility came on December 7, 1941, when the Japanese bombed Pearl Harbor. This action would greatly affect the outcome of the war as it forced the **United States to enter into the war against Japan and Germany**.

After the U.S. entry into the war, Germany proceeded with one of its most heinous policies, namely the **final solution to the Jewish problem**. The "solution" was the systematic mass murder of millions of people through the use of gas chambers and other methods of mass slaughter. These actions are now remembered as the **Holocaust**.

By 1941, the **Allied powers** included Great Britain, France, the Soviet Union and the United States. The Axis powers were Germany, Italy, and Japan. It took several years before the U.S. and Great Britain could launch a land attack against Germany, but once the Allied forces successfully invaded **Normandy**, Hitler's days were numbered. The U.S.S.R. had withstood the German onslaught and the Allied forces closed in on Hitler's troops from the eastern and the western fronts until they reached Berlin. It is believed that Hitler committed suicide and the war in Europe came to an end.

Napoleon Bonaparte and Adolph Hitler were both men of small stature (they were short). Both men thought they could take over all of Europe (Napoleon in the nineteenth century and Hitler in the twentieth century). Both men made the same mistake: invading Russia.

But the war in the Pacific dragged on. The Japanese were particularly dedicated to their cause and often fought hopeless battles to the death. Casualties on both sides were very high. A land war victory over Japan, it was thought, would have claimed an enormous number of casualties, so the United States used an atomic bomb to force the Japanese into submission. On August 6, 1945, the **U.S. exploded an atomic bomb over Hiroshima**, and a few days later, dropped another bomb on **Nagasaki**. Japan surrendered.

ERA: POST-WAR EUROPE

1945 TO 1990

Cold War Europe

Countries that signed the Warsaw Pact after World War II:
Soviet Union
East Germany
Poland
Czechoslovakia
Hungary
Romania
Bulgaria
Albania

The Cold War

Prior to 1991, when the Soviet Union disbanded, many people in their teens and twenties found it hard to imagine that the U.S.S.R. and the United States had ever been allies. That's because **Cold War tensions** between these two **superpowers** shaped foreign policy decisions for nearly fifty years. During the Cold War, the U.S. and the U.S.S.R. never declared war on each other, but they wrestled for power through **intervention** into the affairs of other nations, using diplomatic, economic, subversive, and military means.

Woodrow Wilson's dream of an international body to legislate diplomatic differences emerged after World War II as the **United Nations**. This body has been more successful than the League of Nations, but was—and still is—undermined by the nationalistic concerns of its members.

The first arena for U.S.-Soviet tensions was the **rebuilding of Europe** after the war. Germany was partitioned into eastern and western sectors and the U.S.S.R. wanted to take the neighboring countries (Poland, Czechoslovakia, Hungary, Romania, and Bulgaria) into its "sphere of influence." Winston Churchill called the western borders of these nations the **"iron curtain,"** and Europe was clearly divided into **communist (Eastern Bloc)** and anti-communist (most of western Europe) regions.

United States President Harry S Truman began a policy of **"containment"** with the **Truman Doctrine**. He felt that U.S. support of anti-communist western European nations would help "contain" the spread of communism in these areas. The **Marshall Plan** built on this idea by offering economic assistance to the war-torn nations of Europe. Eastern Bloc nations and the Soviet Union refused the assistance and, in retaliation, blockaded West Berlin from the U.S. supplies. (The city of Berlin was in East Germany.) The U.S., England, and France overcame the blockade by bringing the supplies in by air, a measure referred to as the **Berlin Airlift**. Next, the Western European nations allied in a common defense treaty, the North Atlantic Treaty Organization **(NATO)**, in case of a Soviet attack. The Eastern Bloc countries, viewing the formation of NATO as a pretext for western invasion, allied with the U.S.S.R. in a similar treaty, the **Warsaw Pact**.

The Cold War extended to **Asia**, brought on by the **Communist Revolution in China**. In the 1950s, both the Soviet and Chinese governments put political pressure on the countries of Southeast Asia. The U.S. responded by suppling military assistance to any pro-American governments in the area. The **Korean War** was a civil war ignited by the North Korean (pro-Soviet) invasion of South Korea. The United States and a smattering of United Nations forces helped defend South Korea. Later in the 1960s, a somewhat similar political situation would escalate into the **Vietnam War**.

The Cold War also fueled the build-up of war technologies in the **nuclear arms race** and the creation of space technology known as the **Space Race**. This scientific one-upmanship would continue until the late 1960s and early 1970s when disarmament talks between the U.S. and U.S.S.R. were initiated. The decision for the superpowers to use moderation and discussion rather than silent aggression in this period was called **détente**. It came about after a couple of serious military conflicts involving the superpowers. First, the **Cuban Missile Crisis** occurred. In this scary affair, the U.S.S.R. placed offensive missile bases on the shores of communist Cuba after **the U.S. financed an invasion of Cuba at the Bay of Pigs**. And second, the United States waged war in **Vietnam** to stem the growth of communism in Asia. Also, the Chinese government and the U.S.S.R. no longer enjoyed friendly diplomatic relations, in an event known as the **Sino-Soviet** split, so the U.S.S.R. became more willing to negotiate with the United States. These events helped bring the reality of potential worldwide nuclear annihilation into focus for the leaders of the United States and the U.S.S.R.. The **nuclear disarmament** treaties of the 1970s are called the Strategic Arms Limitation Talks, or **SALT I** and **SALT II**.

Pop Quiz

Q: Which one of these is not like the others?
 (A) Warsaw Pact
 (B) Vietnam War
 (C) Space Race
 (D) Fascism
 (E) Cuban Missile Crisis

The early 1980s[2] brought a small window of renewed, though still "cold," hostility between the U.S. and the U.S.S.R., under Ronald Reagan and Leonid Brezhnev. When Mikhail Gorbachev came to power in the U.S.S.R., he instituted policies of "openness" (*glasnost*) and urged a "restructuring" (*perestroika*) of the Soviet economy. Gorbachev himself would eventually be replaced since his reforms led to the disintegration of the Communist Party and the Soviet Union itself in 1991. Communist governments in the other Eastern Bloc countries also disbanded. **German reunification** is considered a triumphant result of these events, while the ferocious wars among the Balkan states exemplify the potential for tragedy in this area of social unrest.

The Middle East

Pop Quiz

A: Choices (A), (B), (C), and (E) are all associated with the Cold War. While fascism was the driving ideology leading up to World War II, communism was the major force during the Cold War.

In the 1970s, the nations of the Middle East gained significant political power because this area is **rich in oil**, a necessity in modern industrial societies. The countries of this region formed a monopoly, **OPEC**, to better control the availability, and thus the price, of world oil reserves. Because of the wealth of the area's resources, the United States and the former Soviet Union have exerted **cold war influence** in this region. The region has also been historically volatile due to religious **conflicts**; Jews, Muslims, and Christians all have religious ties to the region. Arab and Israeli forces have engaged in military conflicts intermittently throughout the 1970s, 1980s, and 1990s. Other noteworthy conflicts include the **invasion of Afghanistan** by the Soviet Union in 1979 and the **Iranian hostage crisis** in which American hostages were held by religious zealots for more than a year.

Social tensions

In America, the 1960s were a time of radical political demonstration and social unrest. Though the **civil rights movement** was unique to the U.S., student protests took place throughout Europe. Many protests, like **Prague Spring**, dealt with intellectual repression in Soviet Bloc nations. There were also **protests about nuclear proliferation in Europe**, as Europeans felt increasingly resentful about their land being a missile-base for U.S.-Soviet tensions. The fear of nuclear arms was connected to a concern for the well-being of the earth; the **environmental movement** gained steam in the 1970s. The **feminist movement** also gained acceptance at this time as women fought for equal economic and social opportunities.

In response to these pressures and the perceived pressure of communism, the liberal democracies of America and Europe, sometimes referred to as **welfare states**, undertook many social reforms, such as passing environmental protection and anti-discrimination laws. These reforms were in addition to the earlier social insurance reforms like health care, unemployment insurance, and expanded educational opportunities to their citizens.

---

[2]Don't worry about events of the late 1970s and the 1980s for this SAT II. No more than a couple of questions will deal with this time period. That's because historians haven't had a chance to figure out what was really important in the Era, and so they don't know what to expect high school students to know.

WHAT YOU HAVE TO KNOW ABOUT SELECTED REGIONS IN THE MODERN AGE

The world history test is mostly about European history. Questions concerning the regions of Africa, China, India, Japan, the Middle East, and Latin America are few and far between. Most of the questions about these non-European regions are related to Europe and have been discussed accordingly in the Eras above. For instance, there might be a question about Japan's involvement in World War II or a question about the Latin American wars of independence from colonial rule. Still, a few questions usually pertain to the indigenous history of these regions. Following is a lean list of important events in each of these regions. This short treatment of the histories of these regions does not imply that they have a less complicated or less rich heritage than Europe; it only reflects the weight of importance the College Board gives these regions on the World History SAT II.

Africa

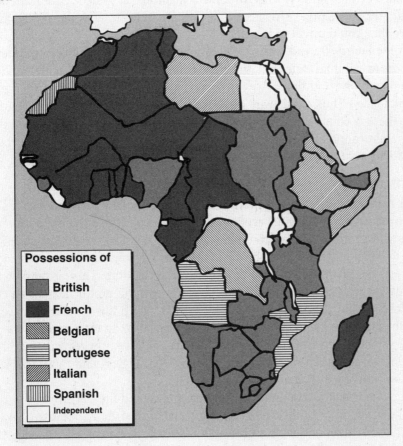

Dates Of African Independence

South Africa—1910
Ghana—1957
Zaire—1960
Nigeria—1960
Rwanda—1962
Kenya—1963
Zimbabwe—1980

Possessions of

- British
- French
- Belgian
- Portugese
- Italian
- Spanish
- Independent

European Colonies in Africa, 1914

Since the Age of Discovery, Africa's resources have been thoroughly abused by European countries. Its people were kidnapped and sold into **slavery** to supply much of the manpower used in the colonization of the Americas. Also, the landscape of the continent (**deserts, jungles, savannahs**) makes it difficult for the African countries to become self-sufficient in large scale, industrialized agriculture.

In the nineteenth century, Africa was colonized by European powers, primarily by Great Britain and France. The continent of Africa is a mix of **different cultures and religions**, but the colonial powers usually did not respect the divergent cultural roots of the tribes when they established colonial states. In addition to controlling the political and economic institutions, the colonists sought to educate the African natives, "savages" to them, in more western ways of thinking. Missionaries sought to convert Africans to Christianity, without respect for the cultures and religions that the tribes historically held. Today, this kind of colonial dominance is called **cultural imperialism**.

The area now known as **South Africa** was inhabited by both British and Dutch settlers. South Africa is rich in gold and diamonds, and, in the **Boer War**, Dutch settlers called **Afrikaners** tried to wrest the land from British control. Though the British won, the Afrikaners had an increasing impact on the political structure of the country. The Afrikaners instituted a system called **apartheid** which stripped native Africans of all political powers and sharply restricted where they could travel or live.

In the late 1950s and early 1960s, many African colonies **became independent from colonial** rule, but the new countries still existed with unnatural divisions among traditional African tribes. (The divisions were intensified under colonial rule.) Thus, **civil wars** have been waged throughout much of Africa. Also, the new countries are hurt by unsophisticated or inappropriate technology in agriculture and the general lack of coherent industrialization. Because of these conditions, many African countries today suffer from famine and poverty.

Latin America

Latin America has a **western heritage** since its countries were among the first colonized by Europe. But its economic and political development has diverged sharply from the European continent. After the Latin American countries won their independence, most established authoritarian rule. The primary economic base was the **plantation system** of large-scale agriculture. This farming method usually requires a large, low-paid work force, and the products are **cash crops** like tobacco and cotton, rather than foodstuffs. With this system in place, the wealthy landowners had no incentive to industrialize. In most countries a two-class system emerged—the very poor and the very wealthy. Brazil and Argentina developed trade routes with Europe and the Far East, and thus fared better economically than others.

The political and economic histories of Mexico and the Caribbean show that they fared worse than their neighboring countries, partially because of American colonial intervention. U.S. President **Theodore Roosevelt** was especially paternalistic toward Latin America because he felt it was within the U.S. sphere of influence. He oversaw the construction of the **Panama Canal**, which aided international merchant ships. The canal was politically ticklish because it was "owned" by the United States because that country constructed it, even though it was obviously built in Panama.

Latin American Nations

In the late twentieth century, the regions of Latin America have remained relatively unstable, characterized by political revolutions and economic strife. Some countries were influenced by communism, most notably **Cuba under Fidel Castro**. Some nations have endured under military dictators. And a few countries have emerged as democracies.

China

The modern history of China begins with the Tang and Sung dynasties, which ruled over **strong centralized governments**. Despite the rule of absolute monarchies, much of the government of China was run by a **highly educated civil service**. These bureaucrats were scholars of Confucianism—a conservative philosophy of societal relations and personal conduct—and were placed in their well-respected ranks by an examination process. **Industry, invention, and trade** characterized this society at the time of Europe's Middle Ages. The Chinese had developed the technology for the printing press and gunpowder and used advanced techniques in agriculture and the production of silk. **Mongol invaders** took control of China in the twelfth and thirteenth centuries.

When Chinese rule fell to the Ming and Manchu dynasties, China became very **conservative and isolated**. The emperors essentially outlawed commerce and trade. By the nineteenth century, China was under heavy pressure to trade internationally. The **British East India Company** began trading with the Chi-

If a question asks about an important leader in world history whom you're not familiar with, chances are the answer has to do with something very important that this person did. Remember, ETS doesn't test obscure facts.

nese on a limited scale. The British were heavily dependent on the Chinese for tea, but experienced a trade imbalance, because the Chinese did not, in return, covet any British products. So the British "created" a market by smuggling opium, made in India, to China. The Chinese government was vehemently opposed to this, but British continued the illegal trading which led to the **Opium War**, in which British forces easily defeated the Chinese. This war resulted in several British-controlled ports in China; international trade then began on a wide scale. Most of this trade did not benefit the Chinese because the companies were foreign-owned. A **Chinese nationalist movement** began and, in an effort to "take back" the country from foreign interests, the **Boxer Rebellion** erupted in 1900. A coalition of foreign countries suppressed the revolt.

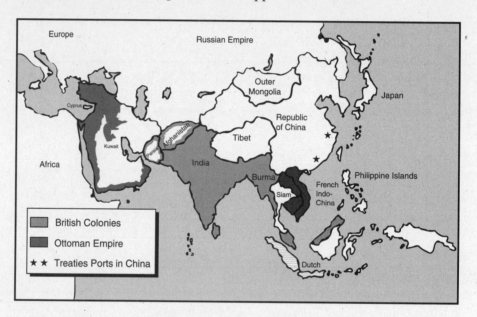

European Colonies in Asia, 1914

In the early twentieth century, another reform movement was led by Sun Yat-sen, and these protests started what would lead to several decades of civil war in China. **Chiang Kai-shek** was a noted nationalist and **Mao Tse-tung** was a powerful communist. China became a communist state under Mao in 1949. Through the 1950s and 1960s, Mao led several movements to encourage agricultural reform and discourage bureaucratization, often at the expense of the cities and intellectuals. The most violent of these movements was the Great Proletarian **Cultural Revolution**.

Japan
Unlike China, an enormous land mass packed with different ethnic groups and cultures, Japan is a **small and culturally unified nation**. For this reason perhaps, Japan did not become overrun by foreign interests, but developed its own **merchant class**. When the last member of the traditional military elite, the **Shoguns**, died, Japan established, in the Meiji Restoration, an emperor who was committed to modernizing the country. Japan became one of the only Asian nations to industrialize in the nineteenth century. **Industrialization and trade** bolstered

Japan's economy and its nationalistic sentiments. In the early twentieth century Japan expanded its territory through aggressive actions. After conquering many of its neighbors, Japan joined in an **alliance with Hitler** in World War II and proceeded to bomb the United States at Pearl Harbor. After Japan's defeat in the war, the nation allied itself with American and European interests and formed a **constitutional democracy**.

India

India had traditionally been **politically fragmented** and its society has been rigidly classified according to the **religious caste system** suggested by **Hinduism**. Thus, India was unprepared to defend itself against the mercantile interests of the British trading companies in the eighteenth century. Through colonial domination, the **British East India Trading Company** came to own or control most of India. After the Indian Mutiny of 1857, the British government assumed control of the colony, but nationalistic fervor was rising. In 1885, the **Indian National Congress** was established. The movement for Indian independence was mobilized under a spiritual leader, **Mohandas Gandhi**, who gained massive support using **passive, non-violent resistance**. Instead of fighting with weapons, Gandhi's followers staged peaceful demonstrations and used boycotts and strikes to gain attention. (Gandhi's teachings partly inspired the civil disobedience of the U.S. civil rights movement led by Dr. Martin Luther King, Jr.) India was granted independence after World War II. Once an independent nation, India split over **religious differences between the Muslims and the Hindus**. A separate region of India gained independence as Muslim **Pakistan**, and most of the rest of India remained Hindu. Hindu-Muslim conflicts, however, have continued to flare into the 1990s.

Islamic society and the Middle East

Since Middle Eastern history was closely tied to the development of Western Europe, much of the important information about this region that you should know for the subject test is incorporated into the Eras above, most notably the Post-War Europe section.

Through the later Middle Ages, the Middle East was controlled by the **Ottoman Empire**. Though the **Turks** had military might and a large land area under their control, the Ottoman Empire stagnated because the **rulers neglected science, industry, and commerce**. The Ottoman Empire was something of a hollow shell, impressive on the outside but without substance on the inside.

So, in the eighteenth and nineteenth centuries, the Middle East presented yet another opportunity for **European colonial expansion**. France controlled Tunisia, Algeria, and Morocco; the Russians were influential in Persia (Iran); and through **the Anglo-Ottoman free-trade treaty of 1838**, Britain controlled the commerce of most of Asia Minor. **Egypt** remained independent under the strong leadership of Mohammed Ali until Britain gained the rights to the **Suez Canal**, a waterway link vital to trade. The Suez Canal linked Europeans from the Mediterranean Sea to the rest of the Islamic and Asian worlds. In the early twentieth century, some Islamic nations, like Turkey, led by the **Young Turks**, fought for independence while others were granted independence through diplomatic means.

Strategy Review

1. Read the question; connect it to an Era and a Country.
2. Eliminate Anti-Era or Non-Era answer choices.
3. Let the question be your guide.
4. Last resort: Guess and move on.

REVIEW OF THE ERAS

Now that you've reviewed world history, quiz yourself to find out how much you remember. Next to each Era, write down a few things you remember about it.

ANCIENT CIVILIZATIONS

_____
_____
_____
_____
_____

MIDDLE AGES

_____
_____
_____
_____
_____

THE RENAISSANCE

_____
_____
_____
_____
_____

THE AGE OF DISCOVERY

_____
_____
_____
_____
_____

THE REFORMATION

_____

_____

_____

_____

_____

ABSOLUTE MONARCHIES

_____

_____

_____

_____

_____

THE ENLIGHTENMENT OR THE AGE OF REASON

_____

_____

_____

_____

_____

THE AGE OF REVOLUTIONS

_____

_____

_____

_____

_____

THE RISE OF MODERN STATES

_____
_____
_____
_____
_____
_____

WORLD WAR I

_____
_____
_____
_____
_____
_____

WORLD WAR II

_____
_____
_____
_____
_____
_____

POST-WAR EUROPE

_____
_____
_____
_____
_____
_____

SELECTED NON-WESTERN REGIONS OF THE WORLD

AFRICA

_____
_____
_____
_____
_____

LATIN AMERICA

_____
_____
_____
_____
_____

CHINA

_____
_____
_____
_____
_____

JAPAN

_____
_____
_____
_____
_____

INDIA

_____

_____

_____

_____

_____

ISLAMIC SOCIETY AND THE MIDDLE EAST

_____

_____

_____

_____

_____

9

The Princeton Review
World History
Subject Test

The Princeton Review World History Subject Test

The test that follows is a simulated World History Subject Test.
  In order to get a good estimate of your score, you should take this exam under test conditions.

◆ Give yourself an hour to do the test when you are not going to be bothered by anyone. Unplug the phone and tell your parents to tell your friends that you are not home.

◆ Clear away a space to work in. You want no distractions.

◆ Have someone else time you. It's too easy to fudge the time when you are keeping track of it yourself.

◆ Tear out the answer sheet provided in the back of the book. This way, you will get the feel for filling in all those lovely ovals.

◆ Don't worry about the instructions; just pick the correct answer.

◆ Instructions for grading the exam are on page 228.

GOOD LUCK!

WORLD HISTORY
SUBJECT TEST

WORLD HISTORY SUBJECT TEST

Directions: Each of the questions or incomplete statements below is followed by five suggested answers or completions. Select one that is best in each case and then fill in the corresponding oval on the answer sheet.

1. The assassination of Archduke Franz Ferdinand is regarded by most historians as the immediate cause of the

   (A) Crimean War
   (B) Franco-Prussian War
   (C) Russo-Japanese War
   (D) First World War
   (E) Second World War

2. The Ottoman conquest of Constantinople in 1453 coincides with which of the following events in Europe?

   (A) The Lutheran Reformation
   (B) The invention of the printing press
   (C) The creation of the League of Nations
   (D) The Muslim invasion of Spain
   (E) The fall of the Carolingian empire

	NUCLEAR EXPLOSIONS 1957–1961			
	US	USSR	UK	France
1957	32	13	7	
1958	77	26	5	
1959	0	0	0	
1960	0	0	0	3
1961	10	32	0	2

3. The table above indicates that between 1957 and 1961

   (A) the United States, the Soviet Union and the United Kingdom prohibited the French from detonating any nuclear devices
   (B) the United States and the Soviet Union escalated the Cold War
   (C) the United Kingdom and France cooperated to create a European nuclear arsenal
   (D) the United States, the United Kingdom, France and the Soviet Union had all developed a nuclear capability
   (E) the United States' production of nuclear weapons declined.

Questions 4–5 refer to the passage below.

"An accountable peasantry subject to other men; much use of the service tenement (i.e., the fief) rather than salary, which was inconceivable; the dominance of a military class; agreements concerning obedience and protection which bound man to man and, in the military class, assumed the distinctive form called vassalage, the breakdown of central authority."

4. The passage above most likely describes conditions in

   (A) imperial Rome
   (B) thirteenth-century France
   (C) fifteenth-century Florence
   (D) nineteenth-century Britain
   (E) twentieth-century Japan

5. According to the passage, the holder of a fief

   (A) must provide military service to his lord
   (B) is most likely a peasant
   (C) exercises power throughout his lord's territory
   (D) must pay rent on his land to his lord
   (E) cannot be a member of the clergy

GO ON TO THE NEXT PAGE

Photo by Julian Ham

6. The building pictured above was most likely constructed in

(A) ancient Greece
(B) feudal Japan
(C) medieval France
(D) Renaissance Florence
(E) post-industrial Germany

7. All of the following held colonies outside of Europe during the seventeenth century EXCEPT

(A) Germany
(B) France
(C) the Netherlands
(D) England
(E) Portugal

8. "The power of population is indefinitely greater than the power in earth to produce subsistence for man. Population, when unchecked, increases in a geometrical ratio. Subsistence only increases in an arithmetical ratio."

The statement above was drawn from the writings of

(A) Friedrich Engels
(B) Adam Smith
(C) John Maynard Keynes
(D) Charles Darwin
(E) Thomas Malthus

9. Which of the following is a system of thought based on the ideas of St. Augustine and Aristotle?

(A) scholasticism
(B) neo-Platonism
(C) capitalism
(D) socialism
(E) determinism

Photo by Julian Ham

10. The painting above would most likely be found in

(A) a Gothic cathedral
(B) a Buddhist monastery
(C) an Egyptian temple
(D) a Renaissance palazzo
(E) an English colonial meeting house

11. European crusaders of the twelfth century visited all of the following cities EXCEPT

(A) Antioch
(B) Constantinople
(C) Limasol
(D) Baghdad
(E) Acre

GO ON TO THE NEXT PAGE →

12. Which of the following Russian leaders was most responsible for adopting Western European customs in the Russian empire?

    (A) Ivan the Terrible
    (B) Peter the Great
    (C) Catherine the Great
    (D) Nicholas II
    (E) Rasputin

Question 13 refers to the following table

SELECTED COUNTRIES in 1978	
Ethiopia	120
Haiti	260
Egypt	390
Taiwan	1400
Israel	3500
Saudi Arabia	7690

13. The numbers in the table above represent

    (A) population in thousands
    (B) net exports in millions of U.S. dollars
    (C) per capita income in U.S. dollars
    (D) national debt in millions of U.S. dollars
    (E) per capita calorie consumption

14. Which of the following based his political philosophy on the ideas of nationalism?

    (A) V. I. Lenin
    (B) Adolf Hitler
    (C) Charlemagne
    (D) Julius Caesar
    (E) Suleiman the Magnificent

15. All of the following led to the Russian Revolution of 1917 EXCEPT

    (A) Russian defeats during the First World War
    (B) dissent and disobedience in the Russian Army
    (C) mistreatment of the peasants
    (D) poor working conditions in newly industrialized areas of Russia
    (E) the promulgation of Wilson's Fourteen Points

16. Which of the following most likely accounts for the growth in human population between 3000 B.C. and A.D. 200?

    (A) The invention of spoken language
    (B) The development of plant and animal domestication
    (C) The use of more efficient methods of warfare
    (D) The decline of species that competed with humans for food
    (E) An increase in the availability of wild game

17. "Men are born and remain free and equal in rights; social distinctions may be based only upon general usefulness."

    The statement above most likely comes from

    (A) the Declaration of Independence
    (B) the Declaration of the Rights of Man
    (C) the Magna Carta
    (D) the Emancipation Proclamation
    (E) *The Pilgrim's Progress*

18. Confucianism is characterized by all of the following beliefs EXCEPT

    (A) nobility is acquired though virtue, not birth
    (B) people should treat others as they themselves would be treated
    (C) everyone should carry out his social duties with devotion
    (D) government must have the confidence of the people
    (E) devotion to one's family is not as important as devotion to oneself

GO ON TO THE NEXT PAGE

Questions 19–20 refer to the following passage.

"In conformity, therefore, to the clear doctrine of the Scripture, we assert, that by an eternal and unmistakable counsel, God has once and for all determined, both whom he would admit to salvation, and whom he would condemn to destruction."

19. The passage above exemplifies the ideas of

    (A) secular humanism
    (B) predestination
    (C) historical determinism
    (D) classical liberalism
    (E) Taoism

20. The passage above is taken from the writings of

    (A) Erasmus of Rotterdam
    (B) John Calvin
    (C) Karl Marx
    (D) John Stuart Mill
    (E) Lao Tse

Reprinted with permission of The American Museum of Natural History.

21. An archaeologist examining the mask pictured above would be able to prove that the object

    (A) had a religious significance to its creator
    (B) is thirty centimeters high
    (C) was made with metal tools
    (D) resembles other objects found in South America
    (E) is constructed of tropical hard wood

GO ON TO THE NEXT PAGE →

22. "Is it better to be loved than feared or feared than loved? It may be answered that one should wish to be both, but it is much safer to be feared than loved when one of the two must be chosen. Men on the whole are ungrateful, fickle, false, cowards, covetous."

    The passage above is taken from

    (A) Machiavelli's *The Prince*
    (B) Plato's *Republic*
    (C) Paine's *Common Sense*
    (D) Hobbes' *Leviathan*
    (E) Hitler's *Mein Kampf*

23. All of the following are predominantly Islamic states EXCEPT

    (A) Pakistan
    (B) India
    (C) Morocco
    (D) Yemen
    (E) Malaysia

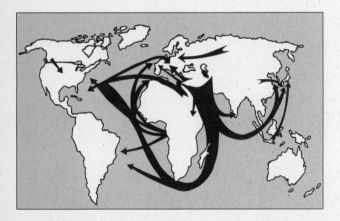

24. The map above most likely illustrates

    (A) the distribution of oil from major sources
    (B) patterns of immigration
    (C) the age of exploration
    (D) the sale of ancient artifacts
    (E) the movement of Allied troops during the First World War

25. "What a piece of work is man, how noble in reason, how infinite in faculties, in form and moving, how express and admirable in action, how like an angel in apprehension, how like a god! The beauty of the world! The paragon of animals!"

    The passage above was written by

    (A) Erasmus of Rotterdam
    (B) Omar Khayyám
    (C) William Shakespeare
    (D) Charles Darwin
    (E) Petrarch

26. Nicholas Copernicus, Rene Descartes and Martin Luther were alike in that they each

    (A) developed important scientific theories
    (B) agreed upon man's place in the universe
    (C) practiced a religion different from that of their fellow countrymen
    (D) founded universities
    (E) promulgated ideas that opposed those of the Roman Catholic church

27. Paintings of the High Renaissance are characterized by all of the following EXCEPT

    (A) the depiction of religious subjects
    (B) the use of perspective
    (C) the idealization of the human form
    (D) an exact imitation of nature
    (E) an accurate depiction of human anatomy

28. Which of the following statements about the countries of sub-Saharan Africa is LEAST accurate?

    (A) Their people have a lower per capita income than do Europeans.
    (B) Many were colonized by Europeans during the nineteenth and twentieth centuries.
    (C) Most have gained their independence from colonial powers since the Second World War.
    (D) They share a common culture, language and religion.
    (E) Their economies depend more on natural resources than on manufacturing.

GO ON TO THE NEXT PAGE →

29. The belief that heretical or unaccepted views should not be subjected to government persecution would most likely be expressed by

    (A) Thomas Hobbes
    (B) Voltaire
    (C) Plato
    (D) Pope Innocent III
    (E) John Calvin

30. "Behold then the true form and worth of foreign trade, which is, the great revenue of the king, the honour of the kingdom, the noble profession of the merchant, the school of our arts, the supply of our wants, the employment of our poor, the improvements of our lands, the nursery of our mariners, the wars of the kingdoms, the means of our treasure, the sinews of our wars, the terror of our enemies."

    The economic theory described above is best termed

    (A) mercantilism
    (B) feudalism
    (C) utopian socialism
    (D) free-market capitalism
    (E) Marxism

31. By 1884, all of the following countries had industrial economies EXCEPT

    (A) Britain
    (B) France
    (C) Germany
    (D) Russia
    (E) Italy

32. The political system of seventeenth-century Japan was most similar to that of

    (A) Athens in 500 B.C.
    (B) eleventh-century France
    (C) seventeenth-century England
    (D) nineteenth-century China
    (E) eighteenth-century North America

33. An immediate cause of the French Revolution was

    (A) the excess spending of the monarchy coupled with the refusal of nobles to pay taxes
    (B) the smuggling of arms from Russia to the French peasantry
    (C) Napoleon's defeat at Waterloo
    (D) the popularity of the ideas of Thomas Hobbes among the French middle class
    (E) the desire of the population for a stronger monarchy

34. Galileo's "Dialogue Concerning the Two System's" contradicted the scientific conclusions arrived at by

    (A) Zeno
    (B) Aristotle
    (C) Hippocrates
    (D) Ptolemy
    (E) Epicurus

GO ON TO THE NEXT PAGE

<u>Questions 35–39</u> refer to the following map. For each question, select the appropriate location on the map.

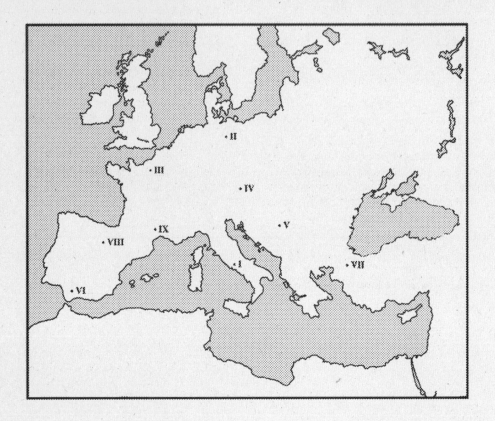

35. The site at which Martin Luther posted his 95 theses

    (A) I
    (B) II
    (C) III
    (D) IV
    (E) V

36. The site from which Columbus departed on his first voyage west in 1492

    (A) I
    (B) II
    (C) III
    (D) VI
    (E) VII

37. The site at which Charlemagne was declared Emperor of Rome

    (A) I
    (B) II
    (C) V
    (D) VI
    (E) VII

38. The site of the capital of the Eastern Roman (Byzantine) Empire

    (A) I.
    (B) III
    (C) IV
    (D) VI
    (E) VII

39. The site at which medieval scholasticism found its greatest proponents

    (A) II
    (B) III
    (C) IV
    (D) VIII
    (E) IX

GO ON TO THE NEXT PAGE

Questions 40–41 refer to the following passage.

"It is not from the benevolence of the butcher, the brewer or baker, that we expect our dinner, but from their regard to their own self-interest."

40. The statement above was written by

   (A) John Locke
   (B) Thomas Hobbes
   (C) Charles Darwin
   (D) Adam Smith
   (E) Thomas Jefferson

41. The idea expressed in the statement above is part of which of the following systems of thought?

   (A) social Darwinism
   (B) Keyneseian economics
   (C) laissez-faire capitalism
   (D) Lutheranism
   (E) scholasticism

42. The Middle Kingdom of ancient Egypt (2050–1750 B.C.) was characterized by all of the following EXCEPT

   (A) a hierarchical system of government
   (B) a pictographic writing system
   (C) the existence of a military elite
   (D) a wide distribution of wealth
   (E) the development of useful irrigation systems

43. The processes of empire-building under China's Wen and Europe's Charlemagne had which of the following in common?

   (A) Both allowed conquered peoples to practice their traditional religions.
   (B) Both brought diverse cultures under the control of a single ruler.
   (C) Neither had strong backing from the dominant religious establishment.
   (D) Neither emperor resorted to violence in order to achieve his goals.
   (E) Each emperor imposed his own language on the peoples he conquered.

44. Which of the following conflicts arose in part over religious differences?

   (A) The Thirty Years' War
   (B) The First World War
   (C) The War of the Roses
   (D) The Hundred Years' War
   (E) The Seven Years' War

45. Which of the following was not a country under the control of Napoleon Bonaparte?

   (A) Spain
   (B) Italy
   (C) England
   (D) Poland
   (E) Lithuania

46. Between 1815 and 1914, the population of Europe increased from 100 million to 460 million, despite the departure of 40 million emigrants. Which of the following was NOT a reason for the population increase?

   (A) Improvements in public health and hygiene
   (B) The absence of any major wars
   (C) The development of more productive agricultural methods
   (D) The popularity of religious beliefs that encouraged childbearing
   (E) An increased standard of living in industrialized nations

47. England's early victories in the Hundred Years' War were due in part to

   (A) the religious convictions shared by English soldiers
   (B) the efficient use of the longbow
   (C) the introduction of the stirrup in cavalry warfare
   (D) the dissatisfaction of French peasants with their king
   (E) the support of the papacy

GO ON TO THE NEXT PAGE

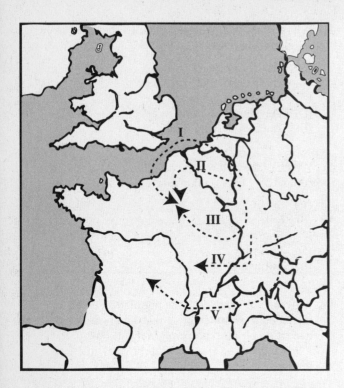

48. In the map above, which of the following represents the route taken by the German army when invading France during the First World War?

    (A) I
    (B) II
    (C) III
    (D) IV
    (E) V

49. By 1800, Britain had colonies in all of the following areas EXCEPT

    (A) North America
    (B) Indonesia
    (C) India
    (D) the Caribbean
    (E) Australia

Questions 50–51 refer to the following passage.

"History is composed of cycles. Although technological advances change the scope with which worldwide conflicts ensue, future events are somewhat predictable from similar events in the past. And yet with all this knowledge, with all this opportunity to better mankind, self-serving politicians ignore the root causes of events and forge blindly on."

50. The author of the passage above would best be described as a

    (A) determinist
    (B) capitalist
    (C) nihilist
    (D) fatalist
    (E) monarchist

51. Which of the following is an example of the cycles described in the passage above?

    (A) The popularity of Greek culture in the later Roman Empire
    (B) The destruction of Pompeii and Hiroshima
    (C) The eastern campaigns of Napoleon and Hitler
    (D) Japanese and American involvement in Southeast Asia
    (E) French policy towards Germany in 1919 and towards Algeria in the 1950s

52. Between the Middle Ages and the Renaissance, the center of European trade moved from

    (A) central Europe to the Atlantic coast
    (B) western to eastern Europe
    (C) the Mediterranean to the Atlantic
    (D) northern Europe to the Mediterranean
    (E) the Atlantic coast to the Mediterranean

GO ON TO THE NEXT PAGE

53. All of the following are reasons why Europeans did not colonize Africa until the nineteenth century EXCEPT

    (A) the African coastline had few natural harbors
    (B) The climate of coastal Africa fostered many diseases dangerous to Europeans
    (C) strong African kingdoms successfully repelled foreign incursion
    (D) Europe lacked the navigational technology to reach sub-Saharan Africa
    (E) African terrain did not lend itself to cash-crop agriculture based on the European model

Photo by Julian Ham

54. The statue shown above reflects which of the following artistic influences?

    (A) Ancient Roman and French Gothic
    (B) Celtic and Viking
    (C) Sung-dynasty Chinese
    (D) Spanish Baroque
    (E) Ottoman and Byzantine

55. All of the following are reasons for the rapid decolonization of Africa that has occurred since 1945 EXCEPT

    (A) the growth of African nationalism
    (B) a decline in Europe's imperial ambitions
    (C) the influence of the United Nations
    (D) the spread of conflict during the Second World War to the North African coast
    (E) direct United States intervention

56. One result of the Congress of Vienna was

    (A) the creation of a Polish state
    (B) the expansion of French territory
    (C) the unification of Italy
    (D) the establishment of Swiss neutrality
    (E) the imposition of war reparations on Germany

57. All of the following have contributed to the political instability of Latin American nations EXCEPT

    (A) the ethnic diversity of their populations
    (B) the disruptive influence of Asian governments
    (C) their reliance on the military to keep order
    (D) the intervention of multinational corporations
    (E) the population's relative lack of political experience

58. Babylonian civilization was characterized by all of the following EXCEPT

    (A) a codified legal system
    (B) an understanding of arithmetic and geometry
    (C) an economy based on hunting and gathering
    (D) an ability to track the course of planets
    (E) a written language

GO ON TO THE NEXT PAGE

Questions 59–60 refer to the following passage.

"The West has been through the trials brought about through excessive nationalism and yet sits idly by while millions of people are ruthlessly oppressed in search of the elusive quality of independence. When will the West learn that it must share its wisdom with these communities that are willing to sacrifice lives for the ability to govern themselves. The West should, and even must, take the lead in enforcing the peace."

59. The passage above is advocating a course of action best described as

   (A) isolationist
   (B) interventionist
   (C) colonialist
   (D) nationalistic
   (E) Realpolitik

60. Which of the following best exemplifies a failure to act according to the principles described above?

   (A) the United States during the disturbances in Central Africa in the 1960s
   (B) the Soviet Union during the Vietnam War from the 1950s through 1970s
   (C) the United states during the Yom Kippur War in 1973
   (D) France during the War of the Spanish Succession
   (E) France and England during the First World War

61. All of the following are characteristics of West Germany after the Second World War EXCEPT:

   (A) a free market economy
   (B) membership in the North Atlantic Treaty Organization
   (C) a stable, democratic government
   (D) a de-emphasis on socialism and public welfare
   (E) the growth of industry

62. By the seventeenth century, which of the following was still unknown to European scientists?

   (A) The structure of human anatomy
   (B) The laws of gravity
   (C) The relationship between germs and disease
   (D) The methods and functions of calculus
   (E) The science of optics

63. Which of the following is true of Buddhism?

   (A) Peace and enlightenment are sought through meditation.
   (B) Confucianism is the basis of its belief system.
   (C) True believers pay tribute to Buddhist priests in exchange for the absolution of sins.
   (D) It has its origins in Chinese philosophy.
   (E) Buddhist believe that faith alone justifies their beliefs.

64. The decision of Tsar Nicholas II to allow a national assembly in Russia in 1905 led to

   (A) the emancipation of the serfs
   (B) the establishment of a vigorous democratic tradition
   (C) the appeasement of Orthodox Church leaders
   (D) the creation of long-term plans for government reform
   (E) the introduction of limited representative government

65. The region along the border shared by India and China can best be described as

   (A) arid
   (B) tropical
   (C) swampy
   (D) flat
   (E) mountainous

66. The discovery of the Rosetta Stone led to which of the following?

   (A) The ability of archaeologists to read and understand Egyptian hieroglyphics
   (B) The discovery that Egyptian culture predated that of Babylon
   (C) The development of a theory of a universal language
   (D) An understanding of the Babylonian political system
   (E) Innovations in Italian Renaissance architecture

GO ON TO THE NEXT PAGE

Reprinted with permission of The American Museum of Natural History.

67. The structure pictured above was most likely built by the

    (A) Egyptians
    (B) Romans
    (C) Mayans
    (D) Incas
    (E) Hebrews

68. Immediately following the First World War, France enjoyed economic prosperity largely due to

    (A) its strong and stable constitutional monarchy
    (B) the war reparations paid by Germany
    (C) the stability of French trade during the Great Depression
    (D) the growth of trade-unionism among French workers
    (E) an economic alliance with the Soviet Union

69. The English Reformation arose as a result of

    (A) the English belief that Roman Catholicism was undemocratic
    (B) the King's desire to establish royal control over church affairs
    (C) a long-standing feud between English Catholics and German Lutherans
    (D) the execution of Charles I by Puritan leaders
    (E) England's desire to reintroduce Latin to the liturgy

70. During the Sung dynasty (AD 960–1279) Chinese bureaucrats were chosen on the basis of

    (A) birthright
    (B) examinations
    (C) popular acclaim
    (D) success in combat
    (E) family wealth

71. The departure of Chiang Kai-shek from mainland China in 1949 led to

    (A) the establishment of two contending Chinese states
    (B) a relaxation of Cold War tensions
    (C) Soviet withdrawal from mainland China
    (D) the end of Communist rule in China
    (E) the unconditional surrender of Japan to the Allies

72. The Boer War of 1899–1902 led to the formation of

    (A) the Transvaal Republic and the Orange Free State
    (B) Lesotho, Botswana and Swaziland
    (C) an egalitarian British colony in South Africa
    (D) an independent state dominated by former colonists
    (E) the Organization of African Unity

73. All of the following were policies of Frederick the Great of Prussia EXCEPT

    (A) agricultural reform
    (B) religious tolerance
    (C) mercantilism
    (D) German unification
    (E) militarism

74. Mikhail Bakunin and Pierre-Joseph Proudhon were both

    (A) free-market capitalists
    (B) liberal democrats
    (C) anarchists
    (D) Christian socialists
    (E) Marxist-Leninists

GO ON TO THE NEXT PAGE

Questions 75–76 refer to the following passage.

"Attention: all people in markets and villages of all provinces in China—now, owing to the fact that Catholics and Protestants have vilified our gods and sages, have deceived our emperors and ministers above, and oppressed the Chinese people below, both our gods and our people are angry at them, yet we have to keep silent. This forces us to practice the I-ho magic boxing so as to protect our country . . . in order to save our people from miserable suffering."

75. The passage above was most likely written in

(A) 1815
(B) 1853
(C) 1900
(D) 1938
(E) 1949

76. The revolt encouraged by the author of the passage above

(A) was suppressed by a coalition of Western nations
(B) led to the Japanese invasion of Manchuria
(C) was a direct response to the United states "opening" of Japan
(D) brought an end to the Opium War
(E) led to the installation of a Chinese Communist government

77. The Franco-Prussian War (1870–1871) resulted in

(A) a failure to achieve German unification
(B) the German annexation of Alsace-Lorraine
(C) Italian unification
(D) Otto von Bismarck's elevation to emperor
(E) the defeat of Napoleon Bonaparte

78. During the Second World War, the Axis powers held territory in all of the following countries EXCEPT

(A) Poland
(B) Ethiopia
(C) China
(D) Portugal
(E) France

79. Historians are LEAST likely to agree about which of the following?

(A) The population of France in 1930
(B) The membership of the North Atlantic Treaty Organization
(C) The date of the Allied summit at Yalta
(D) The causes of the Cold War
(E) Political boundaries in contemporary Europe

80. The investiture controversy of the Middle Ages was

(A) a disagreement between the Pope and secular rulers over the appointment of bishops
(B) a widespread heresy that Innocent III sought to eliminate by launching a crusade
(C) a quarrel between Florentine political factions
(D) a scandal involving King John that led to the church interdict over England
(E) a dispute over the orthodoxy of granting land to monasteries

GO ON TO THE NEXT PAGE

81. During the Spanish Civil War, Francisco Franco's Nationalist forces were assisted by

   (A) France and England
   (B) Germany and France
   (C) Portugal and the United States
   (D) Germany and Italy
   (E) the United States and the Soviet Union

82. All of the following were important reasons for the flourishing of art and literature in twelfth-century Europe EXCEPT

   (A) improvements in clerical education
   (B) the desire of popes and kings to assert their power over one another
   (C) contact with the sophisticated societies of the Islamic world
   (D) a steady revival of the European economy
   (E) the widespread availability of ancient Greek literature

83. "To understand the modern world, we must first understand the sixteenth and seventeenth century. However, an understanding of these centuries is dependent upon our knowledge of the secular political philosophies. These philosophers are solely responsible for what we call the modern age."

   Which of the following would most likely be included among the philosophers mentioned above?

   (A) Jean-Jacques Rousseau
   (B) Thomas Hobbes
   (C) Martin Luther
   (D) Thomas Aquinas
   (E) Marie Curie

Questions 84–85 refer to the statement below.

"Without the shedding of any blood I returned from Munich bearing peace with honor."

84. The statement above was made by

   (A) Winston Churchill
   (B) Woodrow Wilson
   (C) Adolf Hitler
   (D) Neville Chamberlain
   (E) Franklin D. Roosevelt

85. The policy exemplified by the statement above is called

   (A) appeasement
   (B) pacifism
   (C) isolationism
   (D) interventionism
   (E) gun-boat diplomacy

86. Which of the following events precipitated the outbreak of the Second World War?

   (A) Germany's annexation of the Sudetenland
   (B) Japan's bombing of Pearl Harbor
   (C) Germany's invasion of Poland
   (D) Germany's "blitzkrieg" bombing of London
   (E) Italy's alliance with Germany and Japan

87. The Nazi-Soviet Pact led to which of the following?

   (A) The division of Poland and the Baltic states between Hitler and Stalin
   (B) The outbreak of the Russian Revolution
   (C) The Communist Party purges of the 1930s
   (D) The appointment of Hitler to the office of Chancellor
   (E) The destruction of Stalingrad

GO ON TO THE NEXT PAGE

88. Place the following German regimes in the proper chronological order:

    I.   The Weimar Republic
    II. The Federal Republic of Germany
    III. The Third Reich

    (A) I, II, III
    (B) II, III, I
    (C) III, I, II
    (D) I, III, II
    (E) II, I, III

89. All of the following were results of the Glorious Revolution of 1688 in Great Britain EXCEPT

    (A) the exile of King James II
    (B) an increase in religious tolerance
    (C) the unification of the British Isles
    (D) the outbreak of a long civil war
    (E) the establishment of a limited parliamentary monarchy

90. In 1240, the Mongols held territory in all of the following EXCEPT

    (A) Poland
    (B) France
    (C) China
    (D) Persia
    (E) Korea

91. The Marshall Plan was significant because it

    (A) involved the United States in the rehabilitation of post-World War II Europe
    (B) contradicted the Cold War doctrine of President Truman
    (C) enabled the Allies to win the Second World War earlier than expected
    (D) compelled the Soviet Union to withdraw from East Germany
    (E) was the first time the United States intervened in European affairs

92. "I assert that no movement can last without stable leaders and that imperialism can enable communist revolutions to happen in non-industrial countries."

    The statement above best summarizes the political views of

    (A) Karl Marx
    (B) Peter the Great
    (C) Nicholas II
    (D) Joseph Stalin
    (E) Dean Acheson

93. Both Bismarck and Cavour began their respective unification movements

    (A) with the support of the Vatican
    (B) by petitioning the United States for assistance
    (C) while fighting against Napoleon Bonaparte
    (D) by extending the borders of their home countries
    (E) by invading France

94. Herbert Spencer contributed to the development of Charles Darwin's theories by

    (A) applying Darwin's ideas to human behavior
    (B) supplying genetic evidence to prove Darwin correct
    (C) using Darwin's theories to prove the continuity of several species
    (D) proving the impracticality of Darwin's original theoretical work
    (E) tracing all existing species to a single ancestor

95. India's caste system, Japan's samurai class, and France's Three Estates all embody the principles of

    (A) social Darwinism
    (B) Marxism
    (C) social stratification
    (D) dynasticism
    (E) egalitarianism

STOP

IF YOU FINISH BEFORE TIME IS CALLED, YOU MAY CHECK YOUR WORK ON THIS TEST ONLY.
DO NOT TURN TO ANY OTHER TEST IN THIS BOOK.

HOW TO SCORE THE PRINCETON REVIEW
WORLD HISTORY SUBJECT TEST

When you take the real exam, the proctors will collect your text booklet and bubble sheet and send your answer sheet to New Jersey where a computer (yes, a big old-fashioned one that has been around since the 1960s) looks at the pattern of filled-in ovals on your answer sheet and gives you a score. We couldn't include even a small computer with this book, so we are providing this more primitive way of scoring your exam.

DETERMINING YOUR SCORE

STEP 1 Using the answers on the next page, determine how many questions you got right and how many you got wrong on the test. Remember, questions that you do not answer don't count as either right answers or wrong answers.

STEP 2 List the number of right answers here

(A) _____

STEP 3 List the number of wrong answers here. Now divide that number by 4. (Use a calculator if you're feeling particularly lazy.)

(B) _____ ÷ 4 = _____

STEP 4 Subtract the number of wrong answers divided by 4 from the number of correct answers. Round this score to the nearest whole number. This is your raw score.

(C) (A) _____ – (B) _____ = _____

STEP 5 To determine your real score, take the number from Step 4 above and look it up in the left column of the Score Conversion Table on page 229; the corresponding score on the right is your score on the exam.

ANSWERS TO THE PRINCETON REVIEW
WORLD HISTORY SUBJECT TEST

Question Number	Correct Answer	Right	Wrong	Question Number	Correct Answer	Right	Wrong	Question Number	Correct Answer	Right	Wrong
1	D	___	___	33	A	___	___	65	E	___	___
2	B	___	___	34	D	___	___	66	A	___	___
3	D	___	___	35	B	___	___	67	C	___	___
4	B	___	___	36	D	___	___	68	B	___	___
5	A	___	___	37	A	___	___	69	B	___	___
6	C	___	___	38	E	___	___	70	B	___	___
7	A	___	___	39	B	___	___	71	A	___	___
8	B	___	___	40	D	___	___	72	D	___	___
9	A	___	___	41	C	___	___	73	D	___	___
10	D	___	___	42	D	___	___	74	C	___	___
11	D	___	___	43	B	___	___	75	C	___	___
12	B	___	___	44	A	___	___	76	A	___	___
13	C	___	___	45	C	___	___	77	B	___	___
14	B	___	___	46	D	___	___	78	D	___	___
15	E	___	___	47	B	___	___	79	D	___	___
16	B	___	___	48	B	___	___	80	A	___	___
17	B	___	___	49	E	___	___	81	D	___	___
18	E	___	___	50	A	___	___	82	E	___	___
19	B	___	___	51	C	___	___	83	B	___	___
20	B	___	___	52	A	___	___	84	D	___	___
21	A	___	___	53	D	___	___	85	A	___	___
22	A	___	___	54	A	___	___	86	C	___	___
23	B	___	___	55	E	___	___	87	A	___	___
24	A	___	___	56	D	___	___	88	D	___	___
25	C	___	___	57	B	___	___	89	D	___	___
26	E	___	___	58	C	___	___	90	B	___	___
27	D	___	___	59	B	___	___	91	A	___	___
28	D	___	___	60	A	___	___	92	D	___	___
29	B	___	___	61	D	___	___	93	D	___	___
30	A	___	___	62	C	___	___	94	A	___	___
31	D	___	___	63	A	___	___	95	C	___	___
32	B	___	___	64	E	___	___				

THE PRINCETON REVIEW WORLD HISTORY SUBJECT TEST
TEST SCORE CONVERSION TABLE
Recentered scale as of April 1995

Raw Score	Scaled Score	Raw Score	Scaled Score	Raw Score	Scaled Score
95	800	60	650	25	430
94	800	59	640	24	430
93	800	58	640	23	420
92	800	57	630	22	410
91	800	56	630	21	410
90	800	55	620	20	400
89	800	54	610	19	390
88	800	53	610	18	390
87	800	52	600	17	380
86	800	51	590	16	380
85	800	50	590	15	370
84	800	49	580	14	360
83	790	48	580	13	360
82	790	47	570	12	350
81	780	46	560	11	340
80	780	45	560	10	340
79	780	44	550	9	330
78	770	43	540	8	330
77	760	42	540	7	320
76	750	41	530	6	310
75	740	40	530	5	310
74	740	39	520	4	300
73	730	38	510	3	290
72	730	37	510	2	290
71	720	36	500	1	280
70	710	35	490	0	280
69	710	34	490	−1	270
68	700	33	480	−2	260
67	690	32	480	−3	260
66	690	31	470	−4	250
65	680	30	460	−5	250
64	680	29	460	−6	240
63	670	28	450	−7	230
62	660	27	440	−8	230
61	660	26	440	−9	220
				−10 through −25	210

Index

L

Laissez-faire 60, 158
large-scale agriculture 38
Latin American Revolution 153
Leader of the Common Man 50
League of Nations 68, 162
Lee, General Robert E. *56*
Legislature 42
Lend-Lease Act 73
Lenin, V.I. 164
Lepidus 132
Lewis and Clark Expedition 45
Liberalism 157
Liberia 49
Lincoln, Abraham 54
Lincoln-Douglas debates 54
Lincoln's Plan vs. the Radical Republicans 57
Literary Muckrakers 64
Literature 48
Locarno Treaty 163
Locke, John 152
Lodge, Henry Cabot 68
lost generation 70
Louis XIV 153
Louisiana Purchase 44
L'Ouverture, Toussaint 44
Loyola, Ignatius 147
Lusitania 67
Luther, Martin 146

M

MacArthur, Douglas 74
Machiavelli 143
Madison, James 42, 46
Magna Carta 140
Malcolm X 80
Manifest Destiny 52, 58
Mann, Horace 49
Marc Antony 132
March on Washington 80
Marshall Court 47
Marshall Plan 75, 169
Marx, Karl 158
Maximum rate laws 61
Mayflower Compact 38
McCarthyism 77
McKinley and Imperialism 63
McKinley tariff 62
McKinley, William 59, 62
Meat Inspection Act 65
Mercantile Laws 39
Mercantilism 39
Mexican-American War 53
Mining 58
Missouri Compromise 48
Monopoly 60
Monroe Doctrine 47
Monroe, James 47

Montaigne 143
Montgomery Bus Boycott 78
Mormons 49
Muckrakers 64–65
Munich Conference of 1938 167
Mussolini, Benito 73, 164
Mutual Assured Destruction 75

N

NAACP 64, 80
Nagasaki 74, 168
Nation of Islam 80
National Conservation Commission 65
National Republicans 49
National Urban League 64
Nationalism 157
Native Americans 58
NATO 75, 169
Naturalist writers 48
Navigation Acts 39
Nazism 73
Netherlands 39
Neutrality Acts 73
Neutrality, at First 73
New Deal 70–72, 71–72, 75
New England 38
New Territories—New Compromises 53
Newton, Isaac 151
Nineteenth Amendment 64
Nixon, Richard 81–82
"No taxation without representation." 40
Nonintercourse Act 46
North vs. South vs. West 52
Northern Securities Case 65
Nullification crisis *50*
Nuremberg tribunal 74

O

Octavius 132
OPEC 82, 170
Open Door Policy 63
Opium War 174
Organized Labor 61
Otto the Great 136
Ovid 132

P

Paine, Thomas 41
Palmer Raids 69
Panama Canal 65
Panic of 1837 51
Panic of 1893 62
Parks, Rosa 78
Parliament 140
Party Politics Revisited 49
Peace Corps 78
Peace Negotiations 67
"Peace without victors" 67

ABOUT THE AUTHOR

Grace Roegner Freedman has been teaching and developing course materials for The Princeton Review for many years. In addition to developing test-prep courses for the American History and European History Achievement Tests, she has written materials for the SAT and LSAT test-prep courses. Grace attended New College of the University of South Florida as an undergraduate and is currently working on a Ph.D. in Political Science at Columbia University in New York City. She lives in Brooklyn with her husband, Michael Freedman, and their son, Jacob.

NOTES

The Princeton Review
Diagnostic Test Form ○ Side 1

1.
YOUR NAME: _____
(Print)　　　　　　　Last　　　　　　　First　　　　　　　M.I.

SIGNATURE: _____　　　DATE: ___/___/___

HOME ADDRESS: _____
(Print)　　　　　　　Number and Street

_____
City　　　　　　　State　　　　　　　Zip Code

PHONE NO.: _____
(Print)

IMPORTANT: Please fill in these boxes exactly as shown on the back cover of your test book.

5. YOUR NAME
First 4 letters of last name | FIRST INIT | MID INIT

(bubbles A–Z for each column)

2. TEST FORM
_____

3. TEST CODE

4. REGISTRATION NUMBER

6. DATE OF BIRTH

MONTH	DAY	YEAR
○ JAN		
○ FEB		
○ MAR		
○ APR		
○ MAY		
○ JUN		
○ JUL		
○ AUG		
○ SEP		
○ OCT		
○ NOV		
○ DEC		

7. SEX
○ MALE
○ FEMALE

SCANTRON® FORM NO. F-592-KIN
© SCANTRON CORPORATION 1989　3289-C553-5
ALL RIGHTS RESERVED.

Begin with number 1 for each new section of the test. Leave blank any extra answer spaces.

SECTION 1

1 Ⓐ Ⓑ Ⓒ Ⓓ Ⓔ　26 Ⓐ Ⓑ Ⓒ Ⓓ Ⓔ　51 Ⓐ Ⓑ Ⓒ Ⓓ Ⓔ　76 Ⓐ Ⓑ Ⓒ Ⓓ Ⓔ
2 Ⓐ Ⓑ Ⓒ Ⓓ Ⓔ　27 Ⓐ Ⓑ Ⓒ Ⓓ Ⓔ　52 Ⓐ Ⓑ Ⓒ Ⓓ Ⓔ　77 Ⓐ Ⓑ Ⓒ Ⓓ Ⓔ
3 Ⓐ Ⓑ Ⓒ Ⓓ Ⓔ　28 Ⓐ Ⓑ Ⓒ Ⓓ Ⓔ　53 Ⓐ Ⓑ Ⓒ Ⓓ Ⓔ　78 Ⓐ Ⓑ Ⓒ Ⓓ Ⓔ
4 Ⓐ Ⓑ Ⓒ Ⓓ Ⓔ　29 Ⓐ Ⓑ Ⓒ Ⓓ Ⓔ　54 Ⓐ Ⓑ Ⓒ Ⓓ Ⓔ　79 Ⓐ Ⓑ Ⓒ Ⓓ Ⓔ
5 Ⓐ Ⓑ Ⓒ Ⓓ Ⓔ　30 Ⓐ Ⓑ Ⓒ Ⓓ Ⓔ　55 Ⓐ Ⓑ Ⓒ Ⓓ Ⓔ　80 Ⓐ Ⓑ Ⓒ Ⓓ Ⓔ
6 Ⓐ Ⓑ Ⓒ Ⓓ Ⓔ　31 Ⓐ Ⓑ Ⓒ Ⓓ Ⓔ　56 Ⓐ Ⓑ Ⓒ Ⓓ Ⓔ　81 Ⓐ Ⓑ Ⓒ Ⓓ Ⓔ
7 Ⓐ Ⓑ Ⓒ Ⓓ Ⓔ　32 Ⓐ Ⓑ Ⓒ Ⓓ Ⓔ　57 Ⓐ Ⓑ Ⓒ Ⓓ Ⓔ　82 Ⓐ Ⓑ Ⓒ Ⓓ Ⓔ
8 Ⓐ Ⓑ Ⓒ Ⓓ Ⓔ　33 Ⓐ Ⓑ Ⓒ Ⓓ Ⓔ　58 Ⓐ Ⓑ Ⓒ Ⓓ Ⓔ　83 Ⓐ Ⓑ Ⓒ Ⓓ Ⓔ
9 Ⓐ Ⓑ Ⓒ Ⓓ Ⓔ　34 Ⓐ Ⓑ Ⓒ Ⓓ Ⓔ　59 Ⓐ Ⓑ Ⓒ Ⓓ Ⓔ　84 Ⓐ Ⓑ Ⓒ Ⓓ Ⓔ
10 Ⓐ Ⓑ Ⓒ Ⓓ Ⓔ　35 Ⓐ Ⓑ Ⓒ Ⓓ Ⓔ　60 Ⓐ Ⓑ Ⓒ Ⓓ Ⓔ　85 Ⓐ Ⓑ Ⓒ Ⓓ Ⓔ
11 Ⓐ Ⓑ Ⓒ Ⓓ Ⓔ　36 Ⓐ Ⓑ Ⓒ Ⓓ Ⓔ　61 Ⓐ Ⓑ Ⓒ Ⓓ Ⓔ　86 Ⓐ Ⓑ Ⓒ Ⓓ Ⓔ
12 Ⓐ Ⓑ Ⓒ Ⓓ Ⓔ　37 Ⓐ Ⓑ Ⓒ Ⓓ Ⓔ　62 Ⓐ Ⓑ Ⓒ Ⓓ Ⓔ　87 Ⓐ Ⓑ Ⓒ Ⓓ Ⓔ
13 Ⓐ Ⓑ Ⓒ Ⓓ Ⓔ　38 Ⓐ Ⓑ Ⓒ Ⓓ Ⓔ　63 Ⓐ Ⓑ Ⓒ Ⓓ Ⓔ　88 Ⓐ Ⓑ Ⓒ Ⓓ Ⓔ
14 Ⓐ Ⓑ Ⓒ Ⓓ Ⓔ　39 Ⓐ Ⓑ Ⓒ Ⓓ Ⓔ　64 Ⓐ Ⓑ Ⓒ Ⓓ Ⓔ　89 Ⓐ Ⓑ Ⓒ Ⓓ Ⓔ
15 Ⓐ Ⓑ Ⓒ Ⓓ Ⓔ　40 Ⓐ Ⓑ Ⓒ Ⓓ Ⓔ　65 Ⓐ Ⓑ Ⓒ Ⓓ Ⓔ　90 Ⓐ Ⓑ Ⓒ Ⓓ Ⓔ
16 Ⓐ Ⓑ Ⓒ Ⓓ Ⓔ　41 Ⓐ Ⓑ Ⓒ Ⓓ Ⓔ　66 Ⓐ Ⓑ Ⓒ Ⓓ Ⓔ　91 Ⓐ Ⓑ Ⓒ Ⓓ Ⓔ
17 Ⓐ Ⓑ Ⓒ Ⓓ Ⓔ　42 Ⓐ Ⓑ Ⓒ Ⓓ Ⓔ　67 Ⓐ Ⓑ Ⓒ Ⓓ Ⓔ　92 Ⓐ Ⓑ Ⓒ Ⓓ Ⓔ
18 Ⓐ Ⓑ Ⓒ Ⓓ Ⓔ　43 Ⓐ Ⓑ Ⓒ Ⓓ Ⓔ　68 Ⓐ Ⓑ Ⓒ Ⓓ Ⓔ　93 Ⓐ Ⓑ Ⓒ Ⓓ Ⓔ
19 Ⓐ Ⓑ Ⓒ Ⓓ Ⓔ　44 Ⓐ Ⓑ Ⓒ Ⓓ Ⓔ　69 Ⓐ Ⓑ Ⓒ Ⓓ Ⓔ　94 Ⓐ Ⓑ Ⓒ Ⓓ Ⓔ
20 Ⓐ Ⓑ Ⓒ Ⓓ Ⓔ　45 Ⓐ Ⓑ Ⓒ Ⓓ Ⓔ　70 Ⓐ Ⓑ Ⓒ Ⓓ Ⓔ　95 Ⓐ Ⓑ Ⓒ Ⓓ Ⓔ
21 Ⓐ Ⓑ Ⓒ Ⓓ Ⓔ　46 Ⓐ Ⓑ Ⓒ Ⓓ Ⓔ　71 Ⓐ Ⓑ Ⓒ Ⓓ Ⓔ　96 Ⓐ Ⓑ Ⓒ Ⓓ Ⓔ
22 Ⓐ Ⓑ Ⓒ Ⓓ Ⓔ　47 Ⓐ Ⓑ Ⓒ Ⓓ Ⓔ　72 Ⓐ Ⓑ Ⓒ Ⓓ Ⓔ　97 Ⓐ Ⓑ Ⓒ Ⓓ Ⓔ
23 Ⓐ Ⓑ Ⓒ Ⓓ Ⓔ　48 Ⓐ Ⓑ Ⓒ Ⓓ Ⓔ　73 Ⓐ Ⓑ Ⓒ Ⓓ Ⓔ　98 Ⓐ Ⓑ Ⓒ Ⓓ Ⓔ
24 Ⓐ Ⓑ Ⓒ Ⓓ Ⓔ　49 Ⓐ Ⓑ Ⓒ Ⓓ Ⓔ　74 Ⓐ Ⓑ Ⓒ Ⓓ Ⓔ　99 Ⓐ Ⓑ Ⓒ Ⓓ Ⓔ
25 Ⓐ Ⓑ Ⓒ Ⓓ Ⓔ　50 Ⓐ Ⓑ Ⓒ Ⓓ Ⓔ　75 Ⓐ Ⓑ Ⓒ Ⓓ Ⓔ　100 Ⓐ Ⓑ Ⓒ Ⓓ Ⓔ

The Princeton Review Diagnostic Test Form ○ Side 2

Completely darken bubbles with a No. 2 pencil. If you make a mistake, be sure to erase mark completely. Erase all stray marks.

Begin with number 1 for each new section of the test. Leave blank any extra answer spaces.

SECTION 2

1	A	B	C	D	E	26	A	B	C	D	E	51	A	B	C	D	E	76	A	B	C	D	E
2	A	B	C	D	E	27	A	B	C	D	E	52	A	B	C	D	E	77	A	B	C	D	E
3	A	B	C	D	E	28	A	B	C	D	E	53	A	B	C	D	E	78	A	B	C	D	E
4	A	B	C	D	E	29	A	B	C	D	E	54	A	B	C	D	E	79	A	B	C	D	E
5	A	B	C	D	E	30	A	B	C	D	E	55	A	B	C	D	E	80	A	B	C	D	E
6	A	B	C	D	E	31	A	B	C	D	E	56	A	B	C	D	E	81	A	B	C	D	E
7	A	B	C	D	E	32	A	B	C	D	E	57	A	B	C	D	E	82	A	B	C	D	E
8	A	B	C	D	E	33	A	B	C	D	E	58	A	B	C	D	E	83	A	B	C	D	E
9	A	B	C	D	E	34	A	B	C	D	E	59	A	B	C	D	E	84	A	B	C	D	E
10	A	B	C	D	E	35	A	B	C	D	E	60	A	B	C	D	E	85	A	B	C	D	E
11	A	B	C	D	E	36	A	B	C	D	E	61	A	B	C	D	E	86	A	B	C	D	E
12	A	B	C	D	E	37	A	B	C	D	E	62	A	B	C	D	E	87	A	B	C	D	E
13	A	B	C	D	E	38	A	B	C	D	E	63	A	B	C	D	E	88	A	B	C	D	E
14	A	B	C	D	E	39	A	B	C	D	E	64	A	B	C	D	E	89	A	B	C	D	E
15	A	B	C	D	E	40	A	B	C	D	E	65	A	B	C	D	E	90	A	B	C	D	E
16	A	B	C	D	E	41	A	B	C	D	E	66	A	B	C	D	E	91	A	B	C	D	E
17	A	B	C	D	E	42	A	B	C	D	E	67	A	B	C	D	E	92	A	B	C	D	E
18	A	B	C	D	E	43	A	B	C	D	E	68	A	B	C	D	E	93	A	B	C	D	E
19	A	B	C	D	E	44	A	B	C	D	E	69	A	B	C	D	E	94	A	B	C	D	E
20	A	B	C	D	E	45	A	B	C	D	E	70	A	B	C	D	E	95	A	B	C	D	E
21	A	B	C	D	E	46	A	B	C	D	E	71	A	B	C	D	E	96	A	B	C	D	E
22	A	B	C	D	E	47	A	B	C	D	E	72	A	B	C	D	E	97	A	B	C	D	E
23	A	B	C	D	E	48	A	B	C	D	E	73	A	B	C	D	E	98	A	B	C	D	E
24	A	B	C	D	E	49	A	B	C	D	E	74	A	B	C	D	E	99	A	B	C	D	E
25	A	B	C	D	E	50	A	B	C	D	E	75	A	B	C	D	E	100	A	B	C	D	E

SECTION 3

1	A	B	C	D	E	26	A	B	C	D	E	51	A	B	C	D	E	76	A	B	C	D	E
2	A	B	C	D	E	27	A	B	C	D	E	52	A	B	C	D	E	77	A	B	C	D	E
3	A	B	C	D	E	28	A	B	C	D	E	53	A	B	C	D	E	78	A	B	C	D	E
4	A	B	C	D	E	29	A	B	C	D	E	54	A	B	C	D	E	79	A	B	C	D	E
5	A	B	C	D	E	30	A	B	C	D	E	55	A	B	C	D	E	80	A	B	C	D	E
6	A	B	C	D	E	31	A	B	C	D	E	56	A	B	C	D	E	81	A	B	C	D	E
7	A	B	C	D	E	32	A	B	C	D	E	57	A	B	C	D	E	82	A	B	C	D	E
8	A	B	C	D	E	33	A	B	C	D	E	58	A	B	C	D	E	83	A	B	C	D	E
9	A	B	C	D	E	34	A	B	C	D	E	59	A	B	C	D	E	84	A	B	C	D	E
10	A	B	C	D	E	35	A	B	C	D	E	60	A	B	C	D	E	85	A	B	C	D	E
11	A	B	C	D	E	36	A	B	C	D	E	61	A	B	C	D	E	86	A	B	C	D	E
12	A	B	C	D	E	37	A	B	C	D	E	62	A	B	C	D	E	87	A	B	C	D	E
13	A	B	C	D	E	38	A	B	C	D	E	63	A	B	C	D	E	88	A	B	C	D	E
14	A	B	C	D	E	39	A	B	C	D	E	64	A	B	C	D	E	89	A	B	C	D	E
15	A	B	C	D	E	40	A	B	C	D	E	65	A	B	C	D	E	90	A	B	C	D	E
16	A	B	C	D	E	41	A	B	C	D	E	66	A	B	C	D	E	91	A	B	C	D	E
17	A	B	C	D	E	42	A	B	C	D	E	67	A	B	C	D	E	92	A	B	C	D	E
18	A	B	C	D	E	43	A	B	C	D	E	68	A	B	C	D	E	93	A	B	C	D	E
19	A	B	C	D	E	44	A	B	C	D	E	69	A	B	C	D	E	94	A	B	C	D	E
20	A	B	C	D	E	45	A	B	C	D	E	70	A	B	C	D	E	95	A	B	C	D	E
21	A	B	C	D	E	46	A	B	C	D	E	71	A	B	C	D	E	96	A	B	C	D	E
22	A	B	C	D	E	47	A	B	C	D	E	72	A	B	C	D	E	97	A	B	C	D	E
23	A	B	C	D	E	48	A	B	C	D	E	73	A	B	C	D	E	98	A	B	C	D	E
24	A	B	C	D	E	49	A	B	C	D	E	74	A	B	C	D	E	99	A	B	C	D	E
25	A	B	C	D	E	50	A	B	C	D	E	75	A	B	C	D	E	100	A	B	C	D	E

FOR TPR USE ONLY	V1	V2	V3	V4	M1	M2	M3	M4	M5	M6	M7	M8

Expert Advice

www.review.com

Talk About It

www.review.com

Pop Surveys

Paying for it

www.review.com

THE
PRINCETON
REVIEW

www.review.com

Getting in

Word du Jour

www.review.com

Find-O-Rama School & Career Search

www.review.com

Finding it

Best Schools

Maximize Your Chance Of Playing College Athletics...
Enroll In The Student Athlete Information Link!!

The Student Athlete Information Link (SAIL) is the nation's premier athletic recruiting and information service for student athletes of all abilities. SAIL will help college coaches find you and make sure you are ready when they call!

How does SAIL help maximize your chances of being recruited? Complete the Student Athlete Profile and your credentials become available to every college coach nationwide at no cost to the college. Using the technology of the Internet, you gain national exposure for a very low cost. Your personal webpage includes your academic and athletic accomplishments along with your photo. You may also include a letter of recommendation, newspaper clippings, or other key information.

SAIL is much more than a recruiting service. It is a total information source for college-bound student athletes. The SAILMAIL newsletter provides valuable guidance to you and your parents on topics such as NCAA regulations and academic requirements, and understanding the scholarship and recruiting processes. The SAILMAIL newsletter is absolutely free with all paid SAIL enrollments.

Many college coaches maintain information on potential recruits as early as their sophomore season. Individuals may enroll in SAIL as soon as they complete their first high school season or similar time period for those athletes not playing for their high school. Not only will you increase your exposure by enrolling early, but you will have the benefit of receiving SAILMAIL for the entire time.

WHAT YOU RECEIVE
- Your own personal webpage including your photo
- Exposure to college coaches nationwide
- The SAILMAIL newsletter
- Up to 3 free updates

GET STARTED NOW

Complete the Student Athlete Profile on the back of this page or register on-line at **www.studentathletelink.com** and SAIL will build your personal webpage. You may also include a photograph with your profile at no additional cost— preferably an action photo or one of you in uniform. Finally, you may update your profile three times during the course of the year for free. Upon receiving your profile we will send you the appropriate sport statistics form.

For those interested in enhancing their profile, you may add a letter of recommendation, newspaper clipping, or other such item to your profile. A page of this type can provide coaches with many additional qualities you possess. The fee is only $15 per customized page (8 1/2 x 11).

Return your completed profile, photo, and any customized pages along with your check to SAIL: P.O. Box 2382; Columbia MD 21045. It will take approximately 3-4 weeks for your profile to be placed on the Internet. You may view it by accessing the "Athlete Interact" page of our website.

If you have any questions or would like more information about SAIL, contact us at (410) 418-5380 or visit our website at www.studentathletelink.com.

STUDENT ATHLETE INFORMATION LINK (SAIL)
STUDENT ATHLETE PROFILE

INSTRUCTIONS: Please print clearly. Complete as much information as possible. The profile does not have to be complete to be valuable to college coaches. If you have any questions please contact SAIL at (410) 418-5380 or visit our website at www.studentathletelink.com. For your information, your Social Security Number and address cannot be viewed by the college coach or Internet user. We will send a sport statistic form for you to complete upon receipt of your profile.

PERSONAL INFORMATION

_____ _____ _____ ____-____-_____
LAST NAME   FIRST NAME   MI   SOCIAL SECURITY #

_____ _____ _____ _____
ADDRESS   CITY   STATE   ZIP CODE

___/___/___   M___ F___   (____)____-_____   Do you want your home phone on the Internet? Y____ N____
BIRTH DATE   GENDER   HOME PHONE   If NO the college coaches' point of contact will be your high school.

___'___" _____LBS. R____ L____ RACE   Caucasian ____   African-Amer. ____   Asian ____
HEIGHT   WEIGHT   DOMINANT HAND (Optional) Hispanic ____   Amer. Indian ____   Other ____

PARENTS ANNUAL INCOME (Optional)   Less than 20,000____   20,000–40,000____   40,000–80,000____   Over 80,000____

E-MAIL ADDRESS _____

ACADEMIC AND ATHLETIC INFORMATION

_____ _____
HIGH SCHOOL   (PRINT FULL HIGH SCHOOL NAME)   ZIP CODE OF SCHOOL

_____ _____ _____ (based on 4.0 scale)   I have applied for NCAA Clearinghouse.(circle one) Yes or No
SAT   ACT   GPA

(____)____-_____
ATHLETIC DIRECTOR PHONE NUMBER

H. S. GRAD. YR _____   # OF YRS PLAYING VARSITY SPORTS____   # OF VAR. SPORTS PLAYED____   AAU PARTICIPANT Y___ N___

_____ _____ (____)____-_____
NAME OF CLUB TEAM OR CAMP ATTENDED   NAME OF CLUB COACH   CLUB COACH PHONE NUMBER
(OTHER THAN HIGH SCHOOL)

            VERT. JUMP_____in.   SQUAT____lbs.   BENCH____lbs.   SPEED IN 40YDS____
AWARDS: ALL-CONFERENCE/DISTRICT___   ALL-STATE___   ALL-AMERICAN____

Please list the sport(s) you would like to play in college. We will send you the appropriate form so you can provide your statistics to include with your profile. You may include up to three sports.

1._____   2._____   3._____

I understand that the information provided above may be relied on by coaches and/or athletic directors and do hereby verify and attest that the information provided above is accurate to the best of my knowledge.

STUDENT SIGNATURE _____   DATE _____
PARENT'S SIGNATURE _____   DATE _____

PAYMENT INFORMATION: CHECK ENCLOSED ___   VISA/MASTERCARD ___   DISCOVER CARD ___

NEW STUDENT ATHLETE PROFILE FORM @ $30 $____   _____
                                                         CREDIT CARD NUMBER   EXP. DATE

CUSTOMIZED PAGE(S) @ $15 PER PAGE (8_ X 11) $____   _____
                                                         CREDIT CARD NUMBER   EXP. DATE

TOTAL AMOUNT INCLUDED WITH PROFILE $____   _____
                                                    ADDRESS (If different from above)   CITY   STATE   ZIP

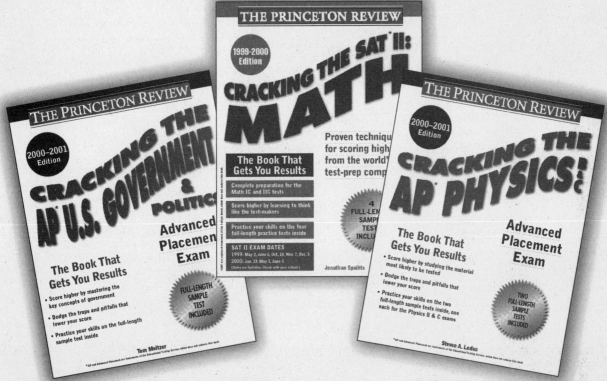

FIND US...

International

Hong Kong
4/F Sun Hung Kai Centre
30 Harbour Road, Wan Chai,
Hong Kong
Tel: (011)85-2-517-3016

Japan
Fuji Building 40, 15-14
Sakuragaokacho, Shibuya Ku,
Tokyo 150, Japan
Tel: (011)81-3-3463-1343

Korea
Tae Young Bldg, 944-24,
Daechi- Dong, Kangnam-Ku
The Princeton Review- ANC
Seoul, Korea 135-280,
South Korea
Tel: (011)82-2-554-7763

Mexico City
PR Mex S De RL De Cv
Guanajuato 228 Col. Roma
06700 Mexico D.F., Mexico
Tel: 525-564-9468

Montreal
666 Sherbrooke St.
West, Suite 202
Montreal, QC H3A 1E7 Canada
Tel: (514) 499-0870

Pakistan
1 Bawa Park - 90 Upper Mall
Lahore, Pakistan
Tel: (011)92-42-571-2315

Spain
Pza. Castilla, 3 - 5º A, 28046
Madrid, Spain
Tel: (011)341-323-4212

Taiwan
155 Chung Hsiao East Road
Section 4 - 4th Floor,
Taipei R.O.C., Taiwan
Tel: (011)886-2-751-1243

Thailand
Building One, 99 Wireless Road
Bangkok, Thailand 10330
Tel: (662) 256-7080

Toronto
1240 Bay Street, Suite 300
Toronto M5R 2A7 Canada
Tel: (800) 495-7737
Tel: (716) 839-4391

Vancouver
4212 University Way NE,
Suite 204
Seattle, WA 98105
Tel: (206) 548-1100

locations

National (U.S.)

We have over 60 offices around the U.S. and run courses in over 400 sites. For courses and locations within the U.S. call **1 (800) 2/Review** and you will be routed to the nearest office.